VOYAGER TAROT
Way of the Great Oracle

Other Works by James Wanless
published by Merrill-West Publishing

Deck
Voyager Tarot Deck, 1985

Books
New Age Tarot, 1987
Voyager Guidebook, 1987
Prophecy 1987, 1987

Home Study Courses
StarTree (step-by-step correspondence course in symbolism and Tarot),1988

The Complete Voyager (twelve-cassette program on *Voyager Tarot*), 1988

How to Read Tarot (four-cassette series from workshops), 1988

The Marriage Dance (two-cassette series on an inner shamanic journey), 1988

VOYAGER TAROT
Way of the Great Oracle

JAMES WANLESS, PhD

Symbolist

with a foreword by Lynn V. Andrews

MERRILL-WEST PUBLISHING

Carmel, California

Printed in the United States of America

10   9   8   7   6   5   4

ISBN   0-9615079-3-4

This book was produced by
Ex Libris / Julie Kranhold, Carmel Valley, California

Merrill-West Publishing
Box 1227
Carmel, California 93921

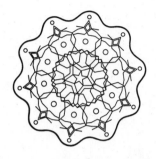

What is the most fascinating thing on Earth
My own Being
I, a microcosm of the Universe.

                    —Robert Muller

Foreword

Symbols are messengers of the spirit, and *Voyager Tarot: Way of the Great Oracle* is a modern message of symbols to seekers and healers everywhere. Symbols take us into the "sacred dream wheel" of the unconscious. Here, in the spirit or infinite void, we become whole. Healed and empowered by the experience, we transform ourselves and our planet.

It is vital that we return to the "way of the shaman." *Voyager Tarot* offers such a way through the world of symbols. Symbols are windows through which we can transcend our ego and our thinking mind, which is what my teacher, Agnes Whistling Elk, calls the "self lodge." In this state, beyond time and form, we reunite with the Great Spirit.

Remember Yourself

The ancient Tarot is a symbolic pathway back to spirit. Like the Tarot's Fool card, it is a Fool's journey for having forgotten our spirit origin and essence. Where traditional Tarot decks use medieval or Egyptian symbols to represent this journey, *Voyager Tarot* uses useful and modern symbols from our everyday world. Anyone can use *Voyager's* universal language of symbols to reunite with their higher selves. *Voyager Tarot* is an outpouring of our natural-yet-forgotten state of enlightenment. Look at its picture-symbols. Think about what they represent. Then see in your mind's eye how you have experienced them. In retracing the steps from the outer world of tangible symbol to inner spirit of origination, you rediscover yourself. Because we have forgotten our spiritual origins, we suffer and live in pain. The concept of the "remembered self" in *Way of the Great Oracle* is essential for personal and planetary healing to take place.

To "remember" ourselves means literally to put our members back together—to become whole. The ancient myths of the wounded gods Osiris, Dionysus and Tammuz healed by the great mother goddesses Isis, Demeter and Ishtar depict our present condition and hope. Go into the goddess and spirit through the womb window of tarot symbols and emerge healed. Like the Tarot's Hanged Man, surrender the ego and die the "ego death" of the Death card, and be reborn whole, as symbolized in the Art card.

Through its universe of symbols, *Voyager Tarot* heals us by helping us "remember" the universe that we are. Our "unconscious" self is the spirit essence of life, which encompasses the life of the universe. In *the Voyager's* picturebook of the universal unconscious, we remember our animal self—whether it be wolf, spider, or elephant. We remember our plant consciousness—as a rose, a cactus, or a redwood tree. We remember our mineral essence—whether as a "guardian" diamond, a "transmitter" quartz crystal, or as "reflective" obsidian. We remember our "rainbow" self—the colors and hues that compose our spirit. We remember our star—the sun, and moon that we are. We remember our past lives and places. We remember our inner child, our inner man and woman, and our old soul.

In recognizing this universality, we become one, as a universe within ourselves and with the outside universe. We heal ourselves. Remembering our different selves is medicine to restore ourselves to wholeness.

By remembering our universality, we transcend the limitations of our thinking mind and our personal ego. The voyage into the inner universe frees us from the self-imposed jail of our limited self-image. *Voyager Tarot* , as a mirror of our vastness, gives us back our power and greatness. Take the message from this modern mandala of the spirit and seize back your power.

In moving from the "island of the conscious" to the "island of the unconscious" via the symbol, you see your destiny. The *Akashic Record*, the spirit origin in which your life path is inscribed, is accessed through the unconscious. In the death of the ego as you enter the unconscious, you see your own death. In your death you will find your rebirth. By dying, you can live as a shaman—as a healer and revealer.

The Heyoka Tradition in Tarot

To reach our destiny, the limited mental way in which we see and think about ourselves must be overturned. Understanding our connection to the Great Spirit through intuition is the way. This is possible through the process of "reading" the Tarot. Selecting cards blindly at random in a reading is an act of trust in the universe. This is like the Native-American Heyoka tradition. Here things are done backward (and successfully) just

to show that the Great Spirit is always
present. Being the "Heyoka," which
is like the Tarot's "Fool," helps us
see that we are part of a greater
power beyond ourselves and our
"rational" way of thinking.

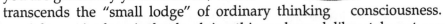

Allowing the Tarot's sym-
bols to speak to us without any
censorship from the thinking
judgmental mind is like dreaming. Interpreting symbols while
fully conscious is "lucid dreaming."
In this state of the "waking dream,"
you are guided by your intuition, which
transcends the "small lodge" of ordinary thinking   consciousness.

A key point here is that by doing this we have deliberately put ourselves in a position to access the spirit. We have begun to consciously
weave our own destiny in accordance with the higher power. A shaman,
a person of power, takes responsibility for creating his or her destiny.

A unique gift of *Voyager Tarot* is that *you, the interpreter,* are encour-
aged to read the symbols in accordance with your own intuition — your
own dreams and visions. None of the simplistic, puerile, and definitive
meanings of symbols that accompany many decks are present here. In
fact, so many possibilities are presented by each card that the individual
viewer is forced to decide what is valid in light of their own experience.
Voyager is like the Heyoka trickster — so many definitions that there are
none.

Although symbols are tangible manifestations of spirit, they do not
help us touch our spirit being unless they are endowed with evocative
power. Symbols must move us in order for us to be moved into union
with the spirit behind them. *Voyager Tarot* is an "act of power," for it
comes from the heart and soul. *Voyager* symbols are moving. They stir
the heart. Through the strength of our feelings for the symbolic imagery
we are pulled into understanding their higher meaning for us. Follow the
feelings that the cards evoke and you will find your spirit essence.

Voyager Tarot: Way of the Great Oracle presents a way for each of us to
create our own "act of power," which is necessary for our enlightenment.
The "Seven Steps of Power" involving the "Card a Day" practice gives us
a clear and simple way to discover our power through symbols. This
book takes us beyond the traditional "reading of the cards" into the most
important practice of Tarot, which is creating our own symbols and cards.

In my work with Agnes Whistling Elk, I found my power through the making of my own medicine bundle, my shields, my doll, my altar, and my books. These are no different than the making of your own Tarot cards.

The value of this practice is that you see yourself more clearly by the symbols, the colors, the style, the arrangement that you create. In connecting with these different facets of yourself, you become healed in the process. As you heal yourself, you are able to heal others. The act of physically weaving together what arouses your vision is a first and essential step in the process of "living your dream"—which is to follow your destiny.

In taking responsibility for acting out your dreams, you indeed "become your own oracle," as suggested in the *Voyager Tarot: Way of the Great Oracle*. Initiated into the path of the shaman as a seer, you become a teacher to others. Every great teacher empowers their students to find their own way in alignment with their connection to the Great Spirit. The reformulation of the ancient Tarot symbols in *Voyager* and the practice of doing the Tarot in *Way of the Great Oracle* has evolved the Tarot into a viable and invaluable pathway for spiritual seekers to find themselves. These symbolic messengers are true teachers.

Lynn V. Andrews

Preface

Oracles are misunderstood. The portal over the great ancient oracle of Delphi in Greece read, "Know Thyself." Oracles speak the truth about our human nature, but they only infer about our future.

Oracles are a time-honored way of understanding ourselves as a microcosm of the universe. Through their symbolic way of telling this truth, they give us a way for "getting it all," for realizing the universe of riches that each of us possesses.

Symbolic oracles, whether they be cards, stars, or crystals, provide a visual reminder of our natural wealth. These visual signs inspire us to realize this richness—for oracular symbols are powerful catalysts and motivators.

By constant practice of consulting an oracle, recognition of our universality is firmly implanted in our consciousness—we remember ourselves. Through repeated oracular counsel, this seed within grows into actions, and our lives unfold fuller and richer in all ways.

This book is about how to use symbolic oracles for self-knowledge and enrichment. It will teach you how to "read the signs," and how to apply them in your daily life for greater success. In the process, you will become your own "oracle maker," the creator of your own destiny.

Voyager Tarot is the medium I have used to write this book. Through its wealth of symbols, it represents more of our universal richness than other oracles. It is a master oracle that includes many traditions and symbols. *Voyager* gives us power and inspiration to "get it all," for it is symbolically and visually evocative. As this oracle is ancient yet contemporary, profound yet easy-to-use and fun for everyone, and useful for all occasions and questions, we seek to consult the *Voyager* oracle often. By frequent remembering of our infinite nature, we reclaim the universe within us.

James Wanless
March 1989

Contents

The Oracular Way

The Great Oracles

VOYAGER TAROT
Way of the Great Oracle

Part One

THE

ORACULAR WAY

The "oracular way" is a way of using oracles to know your-self fully and, in so doing, to realize the universe of wealth within you. To use oracles in this way requires that you know the purpose of your being. You were born to grow in con-sciousness, which means to know yourself. This life purpose is told in the "Four Golden Truths" in Chapter 1. Awareness of these truths is the conceptual basis for practicing the oracular way.

Realizing these "Golden Truths" by living them is achieved through "The Seven Steps of Power" in Chapter 2. By following these steps, you use an oracle as a tool for creating your own oracle within yourself. The oracular way is a way of self-empowerment. You find the power within yourself to make your own reality—to manifest your vision.

CHAPTER ONE

The Four Golden Truths

The *Way of the Great Oracle* is a way to realize all your hopes and aspirations. This "way" is built upon four "golden truths." If you know and practice these truths, your life will be golden. Like gold, your heart will be sunny and rich, your spirit will shine, your ideas will be brilliant, your body will radiate energy, and your hearth will be full of gold.

The first golden truth is that "we want it all." Ironically, the second golden truth is that "we have it all" already. The third golden truth is even more paradoxical in that even though we have it, "we must seek it all." The fourth golden truth tells us that "we have a way to get it all," to reclaim all of our inherent wealth.

First Golden Truth

"WE WANT IT ALL"

The truth is that we all want it all. All life is based on wanting. "I want to have ...," "I want to be ...," I want, I want, I want. Without want there is no growth, there is no change, there is no life.

The more we get, inevitably the more we want. Either we want more of the same, or now that we have enough of that, we want more of something else.

What does "all" mean? All is all. It is everything and nothing under the sun and beyond the sun. All is the universe. The universe is the limit. Wanting it all is to be the universe, as powerful as the sun, as rich as all the gold, as bright as a star, as beautiful as a rose, as strong as an ox, as clean as a whistle, as pure as a doe, as solid as a rock, ...

Second Golden Truth

"WE HAVE IT ALL"

In truth, we have it all. We have all the "qualities" of the universe. Every phenomenon in the universe is a symbol for a quality within us. Name any thing or event in the universe, and we can see how it represents an attribute that we possess.

How about a tree? Simple. I grow upwards like a tree to the light, to grow and unfold, to live. What about a computer? Like a computer, I store information in my brain, which I can access through a command. Space? Every moment between a thought or between a breath is nothing but empty space. A tablecloth? My ability to protect myself, my sixth sense, let alone my clothes and skin. A window? How I see, whether through the window of a word, a belief, or a vision in my mind's eye.

How about an event such as a marriage? I marry when I unite my imagination with my reason, my feminine side with my masculine, my inner world with my outer world. Landing on the moon? I go to the moon when I realize my dreams. War? War is when my expectations and realities differ and go to war causing pain and distress. Earthquake? The jolt that occurs when I have a shift in my understanding.

The trick in this game is that if you can define any phenomenon, then you know it. You cannot know anything outside of your experience. If you know it, then you have it. You cannot know anything you do not have. To know the universe is to be the universe.

Third Golden Truth

"WE MUST SEEK IT ALL"

The most fundamental want in our lives is to know ourselves. It is behind our every drive and aspiration. Wanting to know who we are is the unconscious source of motivation for everything we do. It is the life essence. If I want to get rich, I really want to see how rich I am. If I want to become enlightened, I really want to know how conscious I am. If I want to have a happy marriage, I want to find my other half.

"Know thyself" is the ultimate life force. To live is to seek the answer to the question, "Who am I?" Life does not exist without this want. Alive, we must seek ourselves.

To know ourselves is to know our allness. We are it all, the universe. We are compelled by the life force to seek it all, for we are it all.

"Getting it all" means simply to "re-cognize" or to remember who we are. Once we recognize ourselves, we know that we have it all. We can then repossess "it all," our inherent richness. Our universe of resources must only be "re-sourced" or remembered for their conversion from potential into reality.

Fourth Golden Truth

"THERE IS A WAY TO GET IT ALL"

"Getting it all" means getting back what we already have. To do this, we need a process that helps us remember that we have it all. Oracles, through their symbols and signs, remind us of our universe of wealth. *Oracles use symbols from the universe of human experience and natural phenomenon to represent our destiny.* Our destiny is always to find ourselves. We find ourselves in the symbols of the oracle.

In consulting the oracle, we are consulting ourselves. The oracle is our symbolic mirror. Through symbols, oracles point the way to a truth we have forgotten. The symbolic telling of the truth helps us "re-cognize" ourselves—for in knowing what the symbol means, we remember what we mean. No symbolic oracle can be wrong as long as we can understand its symbols.

The oracle's picture-symbol, or mirror, works for us because the picture sticks in our mind. Rendered through the magic and mystery of the oracular process of the seemingly random yet always appropriate selection of the card, hexagram, or rune, the symbolic picture has an extraordinary force that imprints itself on our consciousness. The picture-symbol keeps reappearing in our mind, continually reinforcing its message—that we possess the quality symbolized by the picture. We repossess that quality each time the symbolic image appears.

The symbolic image and its meaning in our mind is a seed that ultimately blossoms into physical reality. Every image and concept that enters our conscious awareness always manifests physically. All visions and ideas have physical form. A negative thought is dark and cavelike. An insightful vision is brilliant and diamondlike. The more intensely or frequently the idea or picture is held, the denser its physical form, which in its ultimate manifestation is the acting out of it through our physical body. In a negative state, I stay inside, alone in the dark and cold. In an insightful state, I seek the light and warmth of color and life.

Oracles come true because in taking in their seeds of counsel, we inevitably must give them some form of physical birth. *All oracles are true because we self-fulfill their prophecy.* This is the great danger of oracles, but also why they can have such extraordinary positive creative power. This is why your choice of oracle to consult is so important. Select an oracle that plants healthy seeds of growth and illumination. *How* you consult your oracle of choice is also important. Consult the oracle in a way that gives you the opportunity to make your own prophecy for your own highest good.

To "get it all," or to fulfill your highest hopes and goals, requires the frequent use of a symbolic oracle with as broad a spectrum of universe qualities as possible. In selecting an oracle as a tool for "getting it all," it must be conceptually and symbolically grand and expandable.

The oracle must be compelling and entertaining enough to inspire and hold your interest for a continuous period of long duration. It is so easy to forget ourselves. We need constant reminding or we *"lose it all."*

The more often we consult the oracle, and the greater the variety and richness of symbols and qualities depicted by it, the more swiftly and deeply we can recognize and realize our riches.

CHAPTER TWO

The Seven Steps of Power

Power by Magic

The power to get all that you want, by regaining the universe within, can be yours through magic. Magic actually means power; it is derived from the Indo-European root-word for power, *magh*. The seven steps of power get you what you want because they follow the laws of magic, which are the laws of manifestation. Power by magic to manifest your dreams is done by seeing without a doubt the truth about your universe of gifts, visualizing how you are going to live that truth, and inscribing that truth on your consciousness through action and sharing. This is the essence of the seven steps of power.

The Seven Steps

1. Consult the Oracle
2. Read the Symbols
3. Dialogue with Yourself
4. Envision Yourself Living the Truth
5. Inscribe Your Vision
6. Share the Truth
7. Stay on Track

STEP ONE: CONSULT THE ORACLE

How Often Should I Consult the Oracle?

. . . A CARD A DAY EVERY DAY

We forget the truth that we are as rich as the universe. Oracles help us remember this truth. The more often we consult the oracle the better we can recall the wealth of resources within us. If you rely on the oracle too often with too many cards, the truth is dissipated into too many truths, and they are forgotten. *Select a card a day as your truth for that day.*

What Should I Ask the Oracle?

... "WHAT IS THE TRUTH ABOUT ME?"

Ask the oracle for the truth. Consult the oracle for the answer to "who am I?" The first step in the enrichment process is enlightenment, getting a true picture of your true nature. Always ask for the "right" card that reveals the true reality of your richness.

The cards are always true. They are universal eternal truths about all humans all of the time. Each card is a facet of the big truth—that you are as rich as the universe.

Once you have selected the card(s), philosophize about the universal truth it represents. Take a moment to reflect on the eternal principle of life that the card symbolizes.

Establishing the truth is empowering, because it cannot be diminished or in any way compromised. Try as your critical mind will, it cannot put down the truth. You cannot doubt the truth, and on the enrichment path there can be no doubt. Indisputable truth is firmly planted within us when we see it as universal to all human experience.

The secret to this "way of the oracle" practice is constancy. Practicing the Seven Steps of Power with a "card a day every day" will make each day a new day that brings new riches. *To be constant means entertaining yourself with the practice.* Make the practice fun and enjoyable, otherwise you will not practice it. The practice as described here may be entertaining enough, but if not, alter the focus. Your card for the day may refer to your truth for a special event or circumstance for that day. You may be working on a particular aspect of your life, and your day card could show how to develop that quality. In short, you can ask the oracle of tarot any question. Choose your day card to answer that question for the day.

You may also want to probe more deeply into a particular issue or theme. In this case you can do a more complete reading involving more cards as described in the *Voyager Guidebook*, or in other tarot texts, or as you choose to create. Just do not forget to select your "card a day every day."

How Do I Select a Card?

... YOUR OWN WAY

Every individual selects cards their own way. The general practice is, however, to choose cards while face down. This is an intuitive process that helps you understand *synchronicity*, which is the great law that all events are related in time and space even though there may seem to be no tangible cause-and-effect relationship. The card you select, therefore, is the "right" card for you at that time in spite of the seeming randomness of your choice. There are no accidents. With this knowledge, we gain trust in the universe and in the invisible ways that it works.

How to actually mix the cards and "intuitively" select them is again an individual preference. You may like to shuffle, cut, or spread the cards out to mix them. You may focus on your day or yourself while doing so, or maybe not. To choose the card, you may decide by the color of the card, its heat, its location. You may choose with your right or left hand, eyes open or closed, quickly or slowly. You may fan the cards out and select, or take the top one, or use any other method.

It makes no difference how you select cards. You will always get the "right" card. When selecting, however, go for the right card, not the best card. What you seek is the truth.

It may be important to you to establish a routine way of choosing cards. This routine becomes your own personal ritual. A ritualistic way of selecting cards puts you in a state of balance and centeredness, which then gives you clarity and truthfulness in interpreting the card selected.

EXAMPLE: UNIVERSAL TRUTH OF MY DAY CARD

In asking the Voyager *oracle for the truth about me today, I select the Sun card. The universal truth represented by the Sun is that we are all suns. Each of us in physical fact is made of star dust or sun particles. Like the sun, we all radiate a light of consciousness, a physical heat, and an energy of activity. As suns, we create life. We make things happen. The eternal law of life symbolized by the sun is that we are radiant, creative, conscious, alive.*

STEP TWO: READ THE SYMBOLS

A Picture Is Worth a Thousand Words

The truth is always told from the oracle in an enigmatic symbolic way in order to capture our attention and imagination. Oracles present the truth in stories, allegories, riddles, parables, and myths, but always through symbols. Pictures and stories stay more permanently present in our minds than words and textbook information, for they are stronger imprints on our consciousness.

Visual Symbols: Remembering the Truth

It is important to understand how the truth about you is symbolically stated in the oracle. This way you can remember the truth because you can see these symbols throughout the everyday objects and events in your life.

In interpreting the *Voyager* cards, you will see the truths symbolized in a variety of ways. This gives you choices and multiple opportunities for seeing the truth as it could be symbolically demonstrated throughout your day. This is why each card-truth is defined by symbols from the natural world and from the human mind-made world. Select the symbol that works for you. You should even create your own symbols. You may elect to simply remember the visual of the card itself.

Many of the symbols for the truths represented by the *Voyager* cards correspond to how other oracles define the meaning of the symbols. These symbols are not definitive interpretations, however, so you may decide to examine these oracles with greater depth to acquire different understandings.

EXAMPLE: VISUAL SYMBOLIC REMINDERS OF MY SUN NATURE

I see that my Sun Day-Card's quality of consciousness is represented by open eyes; that its quality of creativity is represented by the flowers blooming, the gold coins accumulating, and the lovers walking on the beach; that its quality of energy, activity, and aliveness are seen in the movement of the butterfly, the fish, the bird, and in the sun itself.

So, during my day, whenever I see open eyes, I see my own consciousness. When I see flowers and human-made objects and events, I remember my own creativity. When I see the sun and physical movement, I recognize my own life vitality and energy.

Symbols Are the Vehicles That Move Us

Not only do symbols serve as visual reminders, they are also motivators. Visual symbols give us the fuel to get going. They inspire us. See how we are inspired by the symbol of the heart, the dollar sign, the cross, and the smile. The inspirational pictures that such great oracles as tarot, astrology, and *I Ching* give us is the reason they endure. The way of practicing an oracle is to consciously use the motivating power of their symbols to realize your full potential. Use the symbols that move you.

EXAMPLE: INSPIRING SUN SYMBOLS

My Sun-Day Card inspires me to be the sun through the color green in the card. Green makes me feel alive and creative. Every time I see green during my day, I get sun charged. The smiling radiant face of the sun dancer, inspires me to enjoy and celebrate my sun being. The sun itself gives me energy and power. The gold coins and the golden poppies move me to create in abundance.

STEP THREE: DIALOGUE WITH YOURSELF

Once you have understood what your Day-Card means, ask yourself how it applies to you. Engage in a discussion with yourself how you do or do not live out the truth of the card. *Oracle symbols like cards are vehicles for talking with yourself. The face meaning of the card is unimportant compared to your own personal reaction.* Cards are simply catalysts for self-understanding through self-dialogue. Always make the cards make sense for you. Otherwise they have no value. Making sense of the cards comes through seeing how it could possibly apply to you in your life. Out of this discussion emerges a dominant idea that resolves doubt or confusion. This principal understanding may even be quite a departure from the general meaning of the card. That's okay.

This dialogue is a *sacred* dialogue. It is like talking to your higher self, or even to God or Goddess. Oracular self-talk can have the quality of prayer. It may be considered a discussion between your many different selves—each representing a different point of view. This latter kind of dialogue is like what Carl Jung called "active imagination." In this process, you the ego, talk to the part of yourself that is represented by the card symbol. Let that "other" self talk to you.

The major point is that because this dialogue is sacred, it is a discussion of the truth. Like the judge, be impartial and uncensoring in discussing the different ways you express the truth of the card. In the end, however, realize that in some way, even in the smallest of ways, you are always a manifestation of the truth symbolized by the card. At the culmination of your sacred dialogue, affirm to yourself, aloud if possible, that you are the quality depicted by the card. Better yet, write down your dialogue and affirmation resolution.

The following is an example of a discussion with myself about how I live up to the truth of my Sun-Day card.

DIALOGUING WITH MY SUN SELF

" I realize that I am a sun, but my sun has really been like a star. I have actively radiated and created new life for myself and others through the light that I have shown in my work. But I have been unwilling to live all that truth in full view and presence of others.

The sun to me means being very present, very visible, very committed, and very, very active in the presentation and living of my truth. Because I have been more recessive and distant, like the sun star, I have not had as much impact on others as I could have nor have I realized the material rewards of my creative labor. I want to come out now.

I do want to be the sun. I am going to share my light, my knowledge, my energy, and my joy with others more actively, more powerfully, and with more purpose and commitment. I am the sun. I am going to make more money, and I am going to do that by seriously showing others how they too can become the sun and realize all the goldenness they deserve."

Make the Cards Work for You, Even the "Negative" Cards

Suppose that your Day Card is a so-called "negative" card, such as Five of Worlds—Setback. In truth, acknowledge that some time during your day you will experience a "setback." But remember the point of this exercise—it is designed to empower you. Make the cards, even the negative ones, work for you. Use the positive meaning of the negative card—every setback is in fact an opportunity. Understand that there are no negative cards, but "opportunity" cards representing your forward growth. This is why the negative cards are defined positively in *Voyager*.

To insure your power over any negativity, you may select another card, either randomly or face-up, that gives you the way to overcome any negativity or setback. Do not self-fulfill negative prophecies in a negative way. Negatives are positives. *Always affirm your power over the negativity.*

Be aware that in life, every negativity has a positive side, and that every positive has a negative aspect. The negative cards and negative aspects of positive cards in *Voyager* are described as "unevolved." To see and understand the negative is to be evolved, but to dwell in negativity is to be unevolved. To evolve beyond the negative requires that you acknowledge the negative—then you can transcend it.

STEP FOUR: ENVISION YOURSELF LIVING THE TRUTH

"Imagination is more important than knowledge."
—A. EINSTEIN

To envision, or imagine, is at the heart of power. The word, imagine, is derived from *magh*, meaning power. The power to live your truth is based upon seeing yourself living your truth in your imagination, or in your mind's eye. The key to manifesting the oracle's truth about you is your visualization of how you are going to do it. Without the vision, there is no goal and no attainment. Mind's eye magic will work for you if you give it a chance.

Try to see as clearly as you can how you are going to live the truth represented by your Day Card. See ahead the events of your day and how you will express your truth.

VISUALIZING MY SUN-DAY

My visualization of being the sun includes the following sights:
For a day of writing, I see myself putting great energy and joy into
my work; working swiftly like fire, and spontaneously like wild
poppies. Needing to eat, I see myself eating lightly so that I will be
full of light and not fatigue. Counseling a client, I see myself being
clear, radiant, uplifting, creative, and present to his needs.
Needing some physical exercise, I see myself going for a walk on
the beach, perhaps even dancing. With friends I see myself being
supportive, encouraging, and playful. As the sun, I may
overextend and burn myself out, so I see myself at times during the
day being the setting sun—easy and compassionate with myself. I
see myself constantly encouraging myself today in my work by
seeing how much my labor is of value to others.

STEP FIVE: INSCRIBE THE VISION

To inscribe is to imprint our visualization on our consciousness by a physical act. Inscription can be done by writing down our vision in a journal. The simplest and most powerful inscription, however, is to draw a simple symbol that represents the vision. This picture is easy to recall in our mind's eye and it sets in motion within us all that we have envisioned. If it is a well-done symbolic picture, it is even inspiring and gives us extra motivation.

Inscribing is giving our vision a finalizing stamp. Like a letter, a vision goes nowhere unless it is stamped. The stamp gives the letter power to reach its destination, because it has been paid for. Inscribing our vision is a kind of payment, for we have put physical and mental labor into the inscription process. The labor will pay off. In performing a symbolic act around our vision we give the vision energy and a commitment. We establish a physical vibration around the vision that influences our consciousness and behavior. The sooner we inscribe or record our vision the greater its power to guide our actions.

Inscribing a vision through symbolic pictures is an ancient practice. It is what mandalas, Tibetan tankas, Indian sand paintings, and tarot cards are all about. In the process of inscribing you are actually creating your own symbology, your own tarot cards. In making your own symbols you discover yourself and what gives you power. The symbolic art process draws you out through your drawing. Keep these personal symbols, for they can be used again and again—just as a deck of tarot cards.

The ultimate inscription is actually physically living out your vision with the full consciousness that you are doing so. By doing this, you establish a pattern of behavior that becomes easier and easier to repeat.

SUN VISION INSCRIPTION

The symbolic picture of my Sun vision is a simple picture of my body with a sun emanating from my center, or solar plexus. My sun rays touch others and make suns out of them. This picture gives me the power and the purpose of the sun.

STEP SIX: SHARE THE TRUTH

Sharing your truth for the day with others is vital to your success. Sharing the truth means to see the truth about you in others and to communicate that to them. In so doing, you create allies—others around you who will also live that truth and see it in you. This creates a synergistic process where the whole is greater than the sum of its parts. In sharing the synergy of the group, you naturally become more expressive of your truth. In giving your truth to others, you receive it back many times over. The way to preserve the truth is to multiply it, not to hide it, or hoard it, or keep it to yourself.

In sharing the truth, we transform and heal others by bringing them back to their original state of goodness and genius. We create a medicine wheel where the community is restored to its natural state of health. In healing the community, we heal ourselves. The universe, the world, the community, and the individual are mirror extensions of each other.

Reading the cards for another is a sharing of the truth. In sharing the truth with another you also discover your own truth. We are mirrors of each other. A reading for another is a reading for yourself. We teach and say to others what we need to learn and hear ourselves. So, a Day-Card reading for yourself is really a reading for anyone else you come into contact with during that day. It is perfectly appropriate and good for you to share your truth with them, for it is their mirror as well.

SHARING THE SUN

In sharing my sun energy today, I told my business associates that their work really shined. I told my girlfriend that she was radiant and creative. I told my parents that they looked healthy and youthful. I gave my smile to as many as possible. In bringing out their smiles, I helped bring out their sun. I told a client that she had the power to create abundance and joyousness in her life. And I meant what I said, for it is the truth. We are all suns.

STEP SEVEN: STAY ON TRACK

To make sure that we are fulfilling our truth, we follow our tracks or retrace our steps. Tracking is the process of reviewing. Reviewing keeps us on track because it tells us where we have been, where we are, and it implies where we are going. Tracking gets us ready for the next time— for what we might expect and how we can improve.

To track or review how we have lived our Day Card, is done by a mental assessment and by a reading of the cards. Reading the cards is essentially a process of tracking. To track our progress by a reading, simply select a card from the deck face-down that represents how you have lived your truth for that day. You may then want to select cards that represent how you are living that truth at the present and possibly in the future. Remember, you want the cards to make sense to you. Let them confirm in some way what you have felt and seen.

Tracking is important because it is a completion. It completes your work for the day of living up to your truth. Completing makes you feel whole. It restores energy for the next day. Completion is a closure. Without a finalizing act, our power is dissipated.

TRACKING MY SUN TRUTH

The card that I selected for how I lived my sun today was the Child of Worlds—the Player. This indicated to me that living my sun truth was playful. My work was playful. In playing at my work, it was effortless and it went quickly and smoothly. Although today was a work day, it was really a play day. My work restored my youthful vitality. I was fresh and clever. The sun I lived today was the morning sun, young, alive, and full of energy. The sun represents a playful experience for me. This suggests that in wanting to be the sun or when the Sun Card arises for me again, that I be youthful and playful. Let the rising sun be my guide. Any time I want to recapture the fountain of youth, I can evoke the Sun Card and my Sun-Day Card experience.

BECOME YOUR OWN ORACLE

The Seven Steps of Power take you through the complete practice of doing tarot. Simply "reading" the cards is not enough. *Consulting the oracle is practicing the oracular process, which means to create your own oracle. To "get it all" means to become your own oracle.* This is the natural outcome of seeing that oracles are based upon the truths found in all the various phenomena of the universe. In realizing that for you to understand the oracles' universal symbolism you must possess all those qualities of the universe, you recognize that you are truly the universe. *As the universe, you have the oracle within you. You are the oracle. We use oracles outside of ourselves to recall the great oracle within.*   This "seven-step way" takes you into being your own oracle. *Anyone and everyone can do this easily with constant practice.*

As reflections of the universe, each and every aspect of the universe is a reminder of our own wealth. This is symbolized by the Universe Card from the *Voyager Tarot*. The aborigine in the upper right corner of the card sees his own reflection in the springs and flowers. As the spring and flower, he is fulfilled by the sweet waters and nectars of his life.

We are like Michaelangelo's "emerging giant" coming out of the stone. *We go to the oracle, the stone, which holds our universe of possibilities.* By looking into the stone, we see a *vision* , a reflection of ourself. We *dialogue* with that vision as we chip away what obstructs it from being reality. Discovering ourselves is like death, a letting go of limiting dense and dull self-images that hide our true nature. Becoming our highest self-aspiration is not making anything new. It is just a releasing or liberating of what is already there. *We have it all.*

We *inscribe the vision* by physically making it or sculpting it. The product is our *symbol.* That symbol constantly reminds us and inspires us to live out our vision. In living our vision, we *share* it with others. They can see themselves in us. We are in turn re-inspired by them.

The "way of the great oracle" is the way of the artist. We are all artists, here to sculpt ourself into anyone or anything. Like the artist, we have to see the possibilities. Oracles, like stones, are pregnant with all possibilities. Oracles are stone mirrors through which we see. Like the artist, we have to do the seeing, and we have to do the work. We have to become our own oracle.

Art is recreational in the greatest sense of the word. We are recreated through our recreation. By *constantly* chipping away at our vision, we become our vision. The process of creation is the work and play of the gods and goddesses. In recreating ourself, we play god and goddess. We become the deity, which is in truth our destiny.

THE "SEVEN STEPS" IS A DISCIPLINE FOR CREATING YOUR FUTURE

Practicing the Seven Steps of Power is a discipline that helps you manifest your vision. The process assists you in determining what you want for yourself through the dialogue and envisionment steps. The Seven Steps give you experience in making tangible your vision and desires through the inscribing action. You learn how to create your future or how to make what you want. You fulfill your own prophecy. The continued practice of the steps gets you in the habit of materializing your visions and dreams. You become your own oracle.

Be Your Own Oracle from Moment to Moment

At any particular time in any given place or circumstance, you have enough symbolic information around you to tell you who you are and where you are going. As you read this now, stop and look around you. Everything you see is a symbol of who you are at the moment.

As I look around me, I see written words, which represent my thinking self. I see myself in an enclosed room, symbolizing my introspectiveness and focus. I see an altar of shamanic tools and fetishes, all representative of my many different dimensions. I see a telephone, representing me as communicator. I see a watercolor painting of the moon, which depicts my feeling, feminine nature. I see brown wood walls, my earthiness. I see a window, my visionary quality. I see the sun, indicating my own sun traits. I see myself sitting, thinking, and typing, symbolizing my creativity. Everything that I see is, in effect, like all the symbols in an oracle. What you see at any given moment is like the oracle's symbol you have selected for that time and place.

To infer from that symbol at that moment what my destiny or next moment will be like is to take an intuitive leap. That leap may be very logical. Thus, my intuition says that it is very probable that I will soon get up from my chair, stretch, walk, look outside, and get a drink of water. That action and what I see around me as a result constitutes my next set of oracular symbols, such as my next Tarot Card. What will I do after drinking the water? Taking in water suggests to me taking in some new information that will change my course of thoughts and action. Like water and the glass, I will be open and receptive to the new incoming stimulus. (Indeed, upon drinking the water, the phone rang and off I went into the realm of business and book sales).

By looking at the world around us through the oracle, we get intimations of happenings, such as a simple phone call. By looking at the big symbolic picture of our general place and life patterns, more momentous directions of destiny are suggested. While it is helpful to look ahead, it is most important to look at the *here and now*. By truly understanding and appreciating who we are at the moment, we naturally take care of our future in the very best way. Living the moment is the best guarantee of the future. Knowing ourselves in the present creates the energies and situations that take us on to our next lesson and opportunity. In being open to the next moment and the next moment and the next moment, we grow and grow and grow. Like a tree, our life unfolds with its own organic logic and beauty.

The oracle of the symbolic world around us is meant to give us self-understanding and self-acceptance. With this consciousness and love, we have naturally directed ourselves toward our inherent destiny to the realization of the goddess and god within us.

Part Two

THE

GREAT ORACLES

Voyager: The Universal Oracle

Great oracles are those that empower us to manifest the richness and vastness of our human potential. The truly rich individual is a "whole universe" person, not limited by time, place, culture, race, or philosophy. That is why we use the Voyager *Oracle. It pictures our universality to a greater extent than other oracles. Its symbolism is multicultural and transracial; ancient, modern, and futuristic; down-to-earth and galactic; humanistic and transpersonal.*

As a truly universal expression of our universal nature, Voyager *necessarily encompasses other oracles and their wisdom, which is symbolized by the various aspects of the universe they specialize in.* Voyager *is, in a sense, a master oracle. You can know yourself from its many points of view represented by time-honored oracles of self-understanding.*

The Voyager *Oracle is for "voyagers," seekers of the truth. The truth is that we are multifaceted. Oracles give us a window for looking at ourselves. A window, however, is limited—circumscribed by its frame of reference. The true "voyager seeker" wants to see it all, to get it all. This means looking through a crystal, a multifaceted set of windows, and eventually even stepping outside such lenses of perception to understand ourselves through a moment-to-moment observation of the entire world before us as a mirror of our being.*

Oracles are of two types. One kind is derived from the events of nature (e.g., Astrology) and are presented in Chapter 3. The second is derived from the human mind and its capacity to create symbols (e.g.,Tarot) and are given in Chapter 4. The descriptions of these oracles are brief and are not definitive presentations.

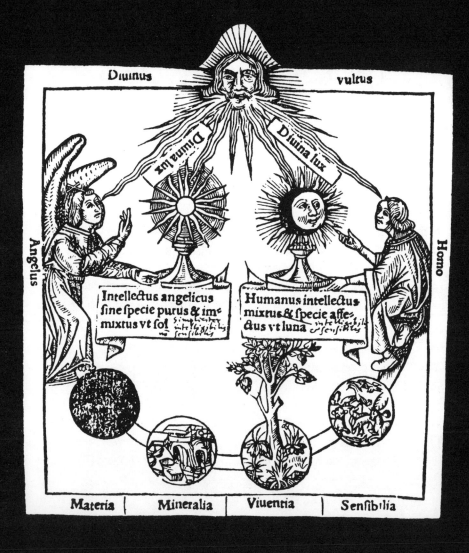

CHAPTER THREE

Nature
Oracles

Nature Oracles see natural happenings as symbolic signs of our character—for example, the alignment of our stars at birth or the lines in our palms. Sometimes, natural events such as an "ill wind" or solar eclipse, portend events in our destiny.

Through *Voyager's* "Nature Oracles," we see ourselves represented by the stars and planets of the Astrological oracle; by the natural elements of the Alchemy oracle; by the events of nature of the I Ching oracle; by the places and locations of the Geomancy oracle; by the animals, minerals, and plants of the Shamanic oracle; by the many facets, clarity, and brillance of the Crystal oracle, by the colors of the Auric oracle; and by the hands of the Palmistry oracle.

Astrology
STAR ORACLE

What's Your Star?

Astrology uses the galactic universe of planets and stars to represent us. What wonderful metaphors they are. How often do we hear of being "starry eyed," or of being a "star." Sometimes I feel "sunny," and other times a "lunatic" (moonish), generally "spacey," and occasionally "down to earth." Talk about the power of symbols to indicate our nature—nine out of ten Americans know their Sun Sign and only one in ten knows their blood type! To speak of ourselves in terms of Taurus bulls, Leo lions, and Pisces fish is commonplace.

In *Voyager*, many of the planets, stars, and galaxies are actually pictured. One of the *Voyager* suits of cards is called *Worlds*. Each Worlds card pictures planets as symbols of our condition and circumstance in the material world. For example, the Aries quality of "getting things going" is pictured in the Four of Worlds (Commencement) not only by the Ram but by Mars, its ruling planet. Each card is corresponded with a celestial phenomenon. These astral symbols give us a sense of who we are from the cosmic perspective, and show the galactic influence on our lives.

Voyager, like its namesake, the Voyager spacecraft, pictures the worlds of outer space to symbolize our own inner self spaces. *Voyager* is a child of the space age. It recognizes the cosmos as an indicator of our own cosmos. In following the signs on the Voyager galactic roadmap, we develop a truly *universal* consciousness.

Alchemy

ORACLE OF ELEMENTS

What's Your Element?

Alchemy uses the elements and characteristics of air, water, fire, and earth to symbolize our nature. From alchemy we get such expressions as a "fiery" personality, "hot to trot," "fired up," "cool," and "steady as a rock." To be "even-tempered" is a mixture of fire and water, hot and cold.

The oracle of alchemy foretells our balance and creativity according to how we temper or mix the elements within us. "From lead into gold" is the metaphor alchemists use to describe our self-enrichment or enlightenment through this process of elemental synthesis.

Voyager is like a cauldron where each card represents an element of our nature. The deck is actually a blending of opposites, such as the suit of Crystals (mind and air) in contrast to the Cups suit (heart and water); and the Worlds suit (body and earth) in juxtaposition to the suit of Wands (spirit and fire). Among the Family cards, the Sages are direct embodiments of the various elements.

By recognizing ourselves as this alchemical mix of elements, we can recreate ourselves into a "whole" state of being. Just as this "whole earth" is a synthesis of the elements, we become whole by harmonizing our own elemental being.

27

I Ching

ORACLE OF HEAVEN AND EARTH

What's Your Hexagram?

*The I Ching,** or *Book of Changes*, is an ancient Chinese oracle that counsels us on the art of living. The hexagram that symbolizes the 'throw' of the yarrow sticks or coins represents one of nature's phenomena. By following the laws of nature which indicate our own nature, we live wisely and fruitfully.

Often we describe our own state of affairs through nature metaphors: our meeting was "stormy"; I am in a "fog"; our finances have "dried up"; they are in the "sunset" of their lives; please don't "rain" on my parade. My heart is "overflowing"; the "winter" of my discontent; the "twilight" zone.

The *Voyager* oracle observes the great laws of nature. We are seen as moving through the growth cycle of the four seasons (Two of Worlds—Winter Reflection; Four of Worlds—Spring Commencement; Three of Worlds—Summer Nurturing; and Nine of Worlds—Fall Harvest). One card may picture a "volcanic" breakthrough (Seven of Worlds—Breakthrough), another a "drought" setback (Five of Worlds—Setback), another the death liberation of an "emptying river" (Death), and another the fear of "crashing waves" (Seven of Cups—Fear).

We learn through nature the *law of change*—that nothing is static; it is forever changing. Through the change of cards each time we consult them, we get in synch with our own changes. Our ability to cope and even direct our changes is supported by the card imagery which richly pictures these changes through nature's events.

*The meanings of the I Ching Hexagrams used in this book are derived from the classic translation, *The I Ching* or *Book of Changes, Third Edition*, translated by Richard Wilhelm and rendered into English by Cary F. Baynes. Copyright 1950 by the Bollingen Foundation; published by Princeton University Press, Princeton, New Jersey. All quotes about the Hexagrams come from this work.

Geomancy

ORACLE OF PLACEMENT

Where's Your Place of Power?

Divination through geography, location, or placement is an oracular art that has been obscured by the obvious. Where we live is a direct sign of our personality. We are drawn to a particular topography and environment because it matches our own energies.

We are characterized by where we live. Witness the stereoypes: "city slicker," "small town boy," "lounge lizard," "couch potato," "beach bum," "valley girl," and "mountain man." We describe our lot in life by metaphors of geography such as "reached a plateau," "on top of the mountain," "on the edge," "in no-man's land." Sometimes we are "in the doghouse," or perhaps we have come "out of the closet." Some of us are pretty "far out" while others have just "crawled out from under a rock."

The *Voyager* oracle can tell us where we have come from and where we belong for the optimum tapping of our inner wealth. *Voyager* cards take us to caves, mountains, valleys, canyons, oceans, lakes, meadows, forests, jungles, deserts, swamps, north, south, east, and west, offices, homes, churches, in cars, on surfboards, on roller coasters, in jail, in coliseums, and on all the continents and worlds and galaxies beyond.

Voyager is a "geography of the psyche." Every place on and off the earth is associated with a particular human quality. By traveling through the guided imagery of *Voyager's* "roadmap of consciousness," you journey through the structure of your own body geography and its corresponding states of consciousness and energy. You find your *power place*, a reflection of your own inner strength. A heart person discovers his or her emotional radiance amidst a garland of flowers in Hawaii (Ace of Cups—Ecstasy). A hermit type finds his or her self-sufficiency in the desert and the cave (Hermit Card). A nurturer discovers his or her ability to grow in an orchard of fruit trees (Three of Worlds—Nurturing). A person who seeks greater creativity can find it by dancing on the edge (Devil's Play). A mental person can find their genius up in the air, high above on a hilltop or in a room with a view (Sage of Crystals—Knower).

29

Shamanism
ORACLE OF NATURE

What's Your Animal and Plant Medicine?

Early oracles used the animal and plant kingdoms as our mirror. Shamans, medicine women and men who are seers into our true nature, characterized individuals by the plant or animal trait they exhibited. That's why Native Americans have such names as Sitting Bull, Whistling Elk, or Two Trees.

We often describe ourselves in such terms as "prickly as a cactus," "strong as an ox," "courageous as a lion," "timid as a mouse," and "sweet as a rose." We use metaphors from these kingdoms to describe our own growth. Like the tree, we "take root," "branch out," "unfold," and "bear fruit." We "nest," we "shed," and we "fly."

Voyager cards are profuse with animal and plant signs. Each Major Arcana card contains a bird as a symbol of a guardian angel represented by the particular quality of the card. The suit of cards called *Cups*, which represents the heart cup of emotions, is represented by flowers. Flowers, by their type, condition, and color describe our feelings. The pink rose, for example, represents a state of love and the sunflower, a magnanimous sunny disposition. The cards that symbolize signs of the zodiac also contain the corresponding animals.

Identifying yourself with an animal or plant gives you great power and sensitivity. Carrying a part of it, such as a feather, an herb, a bone, a leaf, etc., are talismans that make up your "medicine bundle," which gives you the energy of their source. *Voyager* becomes a "medicine basket" through the symbolic picturing of our animal and plant sisters and brothers.

Crystals

GEMSTONE ORACLE

What's Your Stone?

Gemstones, particularly crystals, have always been popular oracles. The crystal ball gives the seer a window to envision qualities and events. The multifaceted crystal presents different points of view and a new angle. Other stones such as obsidian, marble, jade, and lapis reflect our image essences.

The qualities of gemstones mirror our own gemstone nature. We say that a person is a "gem," a "jewel," a "diamond in the rough." We use descriptions of our crystal nature such as "clear," "brilliant," "multifaceted," "sharp," "dense," "dull," and "bright."

Voyager Tarot is a philosopher's stone. It is filled with gemstones that give us clarity about the richness of our lives. One of the suits is called *Crystals*. The Crystals cards symbolize our mind and our mental states. Like the crystal, the mind is a tool for bringing light into the matter of life. *Voyager* cards have gemstones placed in the eyes of primary figures to represent their visionary qualities. In some cards, hands offer crystals, the symbol of sharing genius.

Voyager is a crystal. Each of its 78 cards represent a different point of view. This encompassing perspective creates a crystal ball. In consulting the *Voyager* "crystal of tarot," you become a crystal. You take on the enlightening properties of the crystal. You see the light, the beauty, and the symmetry in yourself.

Aura

ORACLE OF COLORS

Anima Mercury

What's Your Color?

The auric way of self-knowledge is symbolized through our colors. Literally made of stardust, we are light beings. We give off light from our physical bodies. This is called our aura. The aura, like the halo of angels, is colorful, for light is color. Auric readers can see our colors, which are then seen as symbols of our nature.

Colors are very descriptive of our state of being. I'm "in the pink," I'm "feeling rosy," I've "got the blues," "Life is golden," I'm "green with envy," or how about, I'm "seeing red."

All the colors in *Voyager* have symbolic meaning. In fact, there are various families of cards with related qualities that are organized by color. The Priestess family, composed of the Priestess and her personality attributes (represented by all the Number Two cards), and the Woman of Crystals are all cool blue. This color represents the Priestess' emotional detachment, her coolness, and thus her clarity. The Empress family is full of pinks, symbolizing her loving heart. There is even a "rainbow" family. Each card with a rainbow symbolizes reward through some kind of creative interweaving of colors, meaning our talents and qualities. Dark cards represent our dark moods and the shadow side of our nature.

To get in touch with our colors is to become conscious or fully alive, for consciousness is light, and light is life. The *Voyager* suit of cards called *Wands* is represented by light, which symbolizes the spirit. Through "wands of light" we see into the luminosity of the universal spirit force—our life essence.

Chirognomy
ORACLE OF PALMS

What Do Your Hands Say?

Chiromancy, the oracle of palmistry, divines our nature through the lines and signs on the palm. Chirognomy, which is the oracular art used in *Voyager*, looks at the size, shape, and outward appearance of the palm. The shape of the hand, the fingers, and the joints are indicators of character and potential. Palmistry follows the principle that our inner spirit is reflected in matter, in our material world, and in our physiology. The hand is perhaps the part of our body that most mirrors our inner spirit, for it is through our hands that we carry out our spirit.

We use the traits of hands to describe ourselves: I am "all thumbs"; She's a "handy" person; I've got a "handle" on it; He's been "fingered"; It's in the "palm of my hands"; He's so "two fisted"; A "glad hander"; A "hands-off" attitude; What a "knuckle-head."

Voyager is full of hands—old hands and young, giving hands and receiving hands, open hands and closed fists, aspiring hands and protective hands, nurturing hands and touching hands, working hands and magic hands, guiding hands and healing hands. The Wands cards of the spirit are identified by the presence of a hand, for the hand is the spirit in action.

Hands move with the spirit. Through awareness of the features and postures of our hands, we have a direct insight into our state of being. The extraordinary dexterity, beauty, complexity, and utility of our hands reflects these qualities in our own spirit. Through a system of remembering our hands, we can recognize and enhance the wondrous multiplicity of our being.

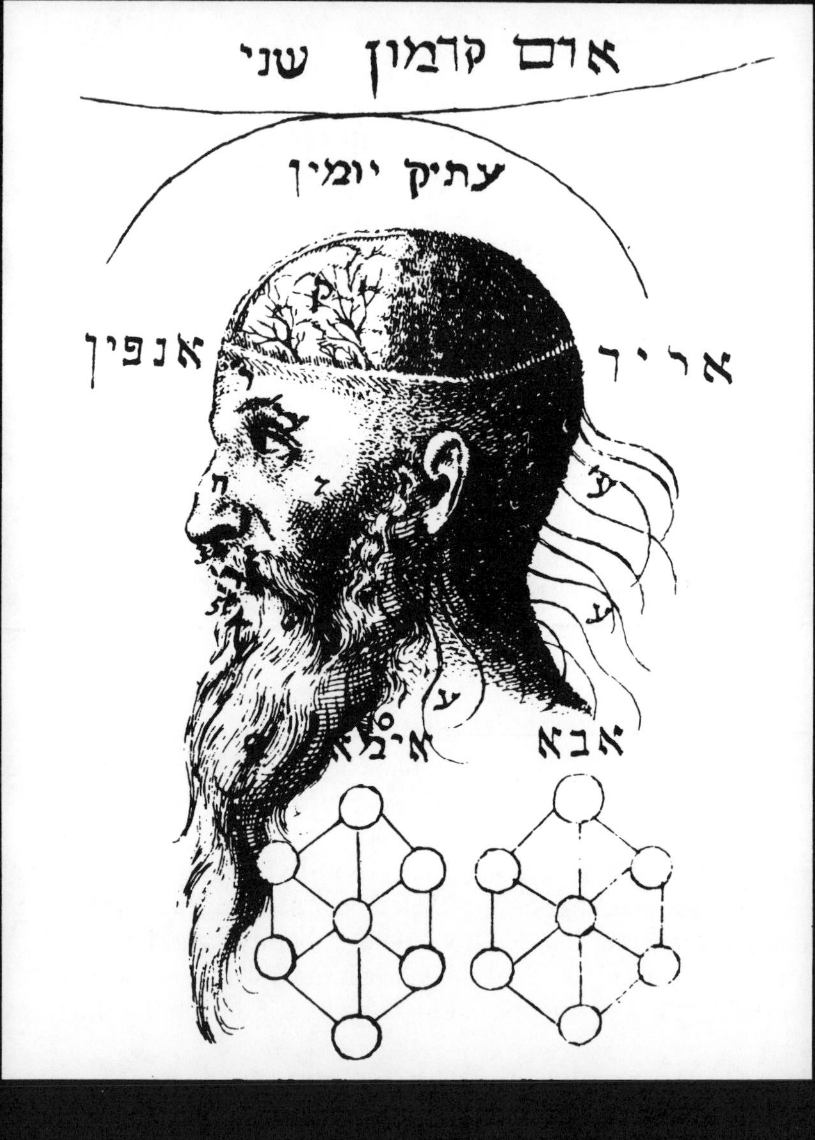
אדם קדמון שני
עתיק יומין
אריך
אנפין
אבא
אימא

CHAPTER FOUR

Mind-Made Oracles

Mind-Made Oracles are symbols invented by the human mind to characterize us. Examples of such oracles are numbers and letters that symbolize us through the number of our birth date and the letters in our name. We are symbolized by such oracles in *Voyager* through the cards of the Tarot oracle, the letters and words of the Kabbalah oracle, the hieroglyphs of the Runes oracle, the numbers and times of the Numerological oracle, the tools and artifacts of the Psychometry oracle, and the gods and goddesses of the oracle of Mythology.

Tarot

ORACLE OF CARDS

What's Your Card?

One of the great oracles for "getting it all" is the Tarot. Originated in ancient Egypt as a wisdom book and expanded into a card deck in the middle ages, the Tarot has stood the test of time as a wondrous tool for self-knowledge.

The strengths of the Tarot are many. Its visual symbolic imagery is empowering. The holistic organization of Tarot with its four suits of Minor Arcana cards, representing our mind, heart, body, and spirit, gives our inner universe a psychological structure that is practical as well as memorable. The twenty-two Major Arcana cards are mythological figures or archetypal blueprints of universal personality styles and roles. Representing our own subpersonalities, these archetypes reinforce the veritable wealth of talents that we each have.

Tarot cards represent our personality traits, such as a "Fool," a "Magician," a "Priestess," a "King" or a "Queen," a "Devil," a "Hermit," or a "Lover."

Voyager is a Tarot deck. It is structured like a traditional deck of Tarot cards. *Voyager* represents the personality qualities of the Major Arcana Archetypes in the Minor Arcana suit cards of Crystals, Cups, Worlds, and Wands. As well, *Voyager* show how these Archetypes behave in the real world by the Family or Royalty cards. Each suit in the *Voyager* has its Family cards of Sage, Child, Man, and Woman. Unlike any other Tarot deck, *Voyager Tarot* offers a truly holistic picture of our psyche. This encompassing and integrated structure of the *Voyager* "Map of Consciousness" (see page 49) brings together and helps us understand our many diverse human facets.

Kabbalah

ORACLE OF LETTERS

What's Your Letter?

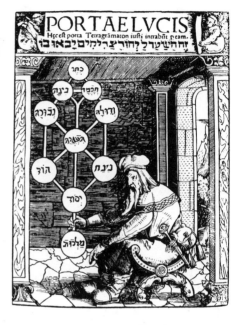

The ancient Eastern Mediterranean oracle, the Kabbalah "Tree of Life," is based on the twenty-two letters in the Hebrew alphabet. Early communication was a sound that symbolized something. A letter or symbol was then created to symbolize the sound. Out of letters, a word and sentence were developed to refine the communication.

All communication is symbolic. A sound is a symbol, a word is a symbol. Letters of the Hebrew alphabet symbolized the essential ingredients of life. For example, A (*Aleph*) is air, B (*Beth*) is house, and G (*Gimel*) is camel. Each of these features of life, in turn, represents our own "airyness," "houseness," and "camelness." These twenty-two letters were then symbolized by Kabbalists (ancient seers) into a "tree of life" composed of twenty-two branches. Our own growth and development is reflected in this tree metaphor.

How we describe ourselves is, of course, through words that are derived from letters and sounds. The Tarot's twenty-two Major Arcana cards are corresponded with these twenty-two letters. Every Major card has a letter associated with it.

By understanding through the oracle which letters apply to us, we can see the part of our universe we are constructing by the kind of qualities we are using. For example, if the Emperor card were selected, it represents the letter *Heh*, meaning window. This represents our Emperor's vision and overseeing in the creation of an outside world, such as business. By knowing all of our twenty-two letters we have a key to becoming a "tree of life," that grows into fruition, and creates new life for others.

37

Runes

ORACLE OF GLYPHS

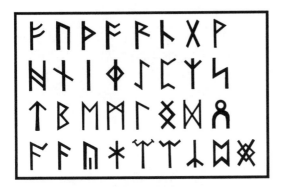

What's Your Rune Sign?

The ancient oracle of Runes is a Nordic system of sacred symbols of carved glyphs. These twenty-four glyphs were simple symbolic pictures of the eternal truths of life. They represented the stages of life from procreation to death through such symbols as man, woman, marriage, sun, cow, fire, and movement. These symbols became stylized and abstract as they eventually were associated with phonetic sounds and various European alphabets. By casting the Runes, which are carved on wood, stone, metal, or bone, we select out a Rune that gives us a profound insight into the growth stages of our life.

We often describe ourselves by the words associated with the Runes. A person in the "twilight" of their career is represented by the Rune *Dagaz*. Someone who is a real "source" corresponds with the *Uruz* Rune. A person who is a "thorn" in my side is described by the *Thurisaz* Rune. One who is called a "gift" is symbolized by the Rune *Gebo*.

These holy signs are not directly represented in the tarot but correspond very closely with the tarot's twenty-two Major Arcana symbols. Correlations are made in the *Voyager Tarot* between the Runes and the Major Arcana cards.

Numerology

ORACLE OF NUMBERS

What's Your Number?

As part of inventing a symbolic language of letters, we also created numbers for a way of counting. Knowing the count is an indispensable aspect of human culture. Thus, the oracle of numbers developed.

Numbers represent qualities that we are all aware of. We all know who "number one" is. "Dressed to the nines" is all the way. "At odds" means things aren't quite even or "four-squared." "She's a ten, while I'm nothing, just a zero."

Tarot cards are all numbered, except for the Royalty or Family cards. The four suits of cards are Ace through Ten, and the Major Arcanas are numbered Zero through Twenty-One. Each of these numbers represents an inner-self quality or worldly situation. A Number Two card like the Priestess represents our two-legged balance and our ability to reflect another. A Number Four card like the Emperor symbolizes our stability and the four cornerstone foundation of our "empire." A Number Ten card like Fortune is tops—a reward for sure.

Cards One through Ten take us all the way through the life journey from the beginning to the highest achievement. "Midlife crisis" is reflected at Number Five; all the five cards represent our lessons. Whether we go on to reach our destiny, represented by Number Ten, Fortune's number, depends on how well we learn our lessons. Ten, when added together (One plus Zero) equals One. As soon as we culminate we go back to the beginning as One.

The numbers of our cards indicate where we are on the never-ending spiral of completions and beginnings. They indicate what stage of the life journey is available to us for optimum use so that we can go on higher to the next stage.

Time

ORACLE OF TIMING

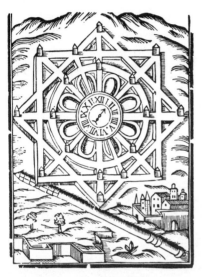

What's Your Time?

Numbers are the basis for time. Both numbers and time are products of the human mind's sequential linear thinking ability. They represent our capacity to be aware of past, present, and future. The oracle of timing is the skill of seeing when one leads to two and two leads to three. This is the most difficult of all phenomena to know because life is organic, mysterious, and complex. We do not necessarily grow in linear fashion, as the mind would have it. We move in fits and starts, with different paces, and different timetables.

We use time all the time to describe ourselves. Some of us are "morning persons" and others "night persons." We "keep time," and we "make time." We can be either an "early bird," or a "late bloomer," or simply "timely." Some are "nine-to-fivers," others "up tempo," and others in "slow motion." We all know when it's "showtime."

Voyager Tarot cards signify times through their number. A number Seven card could signify seven days, seven weeks, seven years, seven lifetimes. Times are indicated by the subject matter of the card. A work card could indicate weekdays, nine to five. A pregnancy card, nine months. A moon card, in the night. A change card, sunrise or sunset. A play card, after school. Times are indicated by the season pictured in the card or by the zodiac month represented by the card. Child cards represent early times, and Sages late in the day. Earth Worlds cards move slower and have longer time frames than Wands cards of Fire, for fire moves more quickly than earth. Much of the time the card will not give a specific number time but rather suggest that *when* the quality represented by the card is fulfilled, it will be the right time.

Voyager encourages us to experience the consciousness associated with all times. By experiencing all times, you find your right time (a universal person is "on time" at any time).

Psychometry

ORACLE OF POSSESSIONS

What's Your Tool?

Physical objects carry our vibrations, our history, and our probable future. Objects we wear close to our person are great indicators of who we are. The oracle of psychometry uses any of our possessions to see us. Most telling are objects that we have handcrafted ourselves. A painting, our handwriting, the arrangement of our furniture, and how we dress are all symbolic of our personality. All of these items are tools for self-expression. Over time some of these tools are termed *artifacts*, and give us an understanding of an entire culture. In fact, we are a walking time capsule, capable of being dated and known by all our material possessions.

LE · BATELEUR

We use our tools or possessions in identifying personal traits. "Razor sharp," "steel-trap" mind, "old bag," "garbage" mouth, a "jock," "polyester" personality, "kittenish," "bookworm," "well heeled," "moneybags," "Ivy league," a "doormat," "homebody," "swinger," "basket case," "battle axe," "horsetrader," "wheeler-dealer."

Voyager cards are full of stuff—the stuff of life. They are busy with all the trappings of our busy life. *Voyager* suggests that life is a living collage, a mix of objects and tools. All of our possessions put together make a mandala of personal artifacts that represents the universe we have created. That universe of things reflects the universe of the spirit within.

You are what you have. Take a look at what you have accumulated and ask yourself if you like what it represents about you. The cards may suggest getting rid of some things and accumulating other things. A cluttered household of stuff may indicate you are carrying a lot of old baggage, memories, and history that keep you weighed down. A spare

41

existence might show a poverty of spirit and a lack of generosity. Mechanical objects reflect a mechanical mind. A garden, fecundity. Chairs,
a sedentary being. Windows, a visionary.

In reflecting on your possessions as mirrors of yourself, you may
discover what objects or tools give you power, or peace, or love, or
creativity. As the Tarot deck is a paper altar of power objects, you may
be inspired to create your own altar or your own medicine bag of your
own tools that work for you.

Mythology

ORACLE OF DEITIES

What Goddess and God Are You?

"Archetypal psychology" developed by Carl Jung views human nature as composed of universal, eternal, cross-cultural personality types. These types are aptly described as gods and goddesses, for they appear in all cultures past and present, as mythological figures. For example, every culture has its wizard, whether it is portrayed as a shaman, witch, sorceror, magician, or medicine woman. The seed energy responsible for all these universal manifestations of the wizard is the goddess/god or deity of magic. Archetypal psychology can look at your dreams, your aspirations, your talents, your art, and determine your goddess/god energy.

We often refer to others as an angel or saint. A beautiful woman is Aphrodite, a strong man Hercules. We refer to a maternal woman as the Mother Earth goddess. Many of our gods and goddesses are stars, people who have appeared bigger than life and like a star are distant and mysterious. Modern communications media has created a new pantheon of deities. A great artist is a Picasso. A great humanitarian is a Mother Teresa. A great thinker is an Einstein. A great lover is a Don Juan. A great beauty is a Garbo.

The mythological deities in the *Voyager* oracle are portrayed in the Major Arcana by works of art that express archetypal energy. For example, the Emperor card is represented by a sculpture of Alexander the Great, the Chariot card by the ancient Greek sculpture *Charioteer*, the Lovers card by the Brancusi sculpture *Embrace*, the Hierophant (spiritual teacher) Card by a giant sculpture of the Buddha, the Hermit by a bust of a Mayan sage, and Death by a New Guinea death mask. Each of these Major Arcana cards has a bird in it to signify an angel—that the archetype is a quality brought to us from the heavens.

In recognizing our archetypal nature, we see the goddess or god that we are. We get in touch with our divinity. We have only to remember our heavenly origins to create our own heaven.

Part Three

THE
ORACLE SPEAKS

The Voyager oracle is composed of seventy-eight cards, each containing numerous symbols that represent the wisdom of the "great oracles." These oracular symbols speak to you about your state of mind, heart, body, spirit, and actions.

The seventy-eight cards are arranged in three groups. The first, the "Major Arcana," is presented in Chapter 5. These cards represent archetypal personality types. The second, the "Minor Arcana" in Chapter 6, are cards that symbolize specific personality attributes of the "Major Arcana" personality archetypes. Chapter 7, "The Inner Family," is the third group of cards. These represent the family within each of us.

Regardless of what the oracle cards tell you in this book or any other book, they must be interpreted by your psyche. The oracular advice given by each symbol are suggestions that may or may not be taken literally. They are, in any event, a catalyst for your intuition. Each of us has the capacity to oracularize. Through the intuitive accessing of our psyche, we determine how to "read" the signs. Symbols, whether a palm line or number, can be defined differently for different people for different circumstances and different issues. Our intuitive faculty determines the nuance or the slant that the interpretation will take. This is why emphasis is placed on the individual as the source of understanding and on the "Seven Steps of Power" as a technique for developing your own intuitive knowing and for becoming your own oracle.

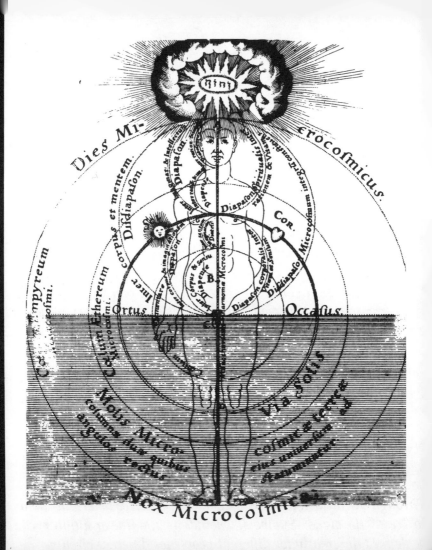

CHAPTER FIVE

Major Arcana Archetypes

The most important card-symbols in the *Voyager* oracle are the Major Arcana cards. These represent the major secrets to life, the universal principles of life. These twenty-two cards or principles are found represented in the wisdom books of ancient Egypt. They correspond to the *twenty-two letters of the Hebrew alphabet*, which are symbols on the Kabbalah "Tree of Life," an ancient oracle. The Major Arcana cards also correspond to the *twelve zodiac signs* and the *ten planets* in our solar system.

The Major Arcana are called *Archetypes* in *Voyager*, for they represent universal personality types. Each of us, in fact, is a composite of subpersonalities symbolized by these Archetypes. We are all Archetypal Magicians, Fools, Hermits, etc., in our own way.

As Archetypal personalities, the Major Arcanas have mental, emotional, physical, spiritual, and worldly qualities. Each Major Archetype card is interpreted according to these aspects. If your "card for the day" is the Magician, for example, the *Voyager* oracle will tell you how to think, feel, sense, perceive, and act like a Magician. To be a Magician, or any Archetype, means living it out fully on all dimensions.

These various attributes or qualities of the Major Archetype cards are represented by the Minor Arcana suit cards and their corresponding number. For example, the number one Archetype, Magician, has the mind of the number one Crystals suit card, the Ace of Crystals—Brilliance. The Magican's emotional state is represented by the number one Cups suit card, the Ace of Cups—Ecstasy. The physical and worldly quality of the Magician is symbolized by the number one Worlds suit card, the Ace of Worlds—Success. The Magician's spirituality is represented by the number one Wands suit card, the Ace of Wands—Illumination. (The Minor Arcana Crystals are mental card-symbols, Cups are emotional, Worlds are physical and worldly, and Wands are spiritual).

As there are only ten numbered Minor Arcana cards for each of the four suits, only the Major Arcana Archetypes One through Ten are specifically related to Minor Arcana suit cards. (If you wish to know the qualities of a One-through-Ten Major Archetype card, see Chapter 6, which groups and defines the Minor Arcana cards according to their number.) For example, all the Magician's Number One qualities are represented by the number One Minor Arcana Aces which are lumped together as a group. Number Two, the Priestess Archetype, is represented by the number Two grouping of Minor Arcana cards.

The Major Arcanas are archetypal blueprints of human personality and, as such, represent primal energies inherent within each of us. The personification or living out of these natural strains of being in the world is represented by the Family cards in the *Voyager Deck*. Symbolized by pictures of real human beings, in contrast to the Major Arcana Archetypal sculpture pieces, each of the Family cards represent a particular Major Arcana Archetype. You may look at the beginning of the Family cards (Chapter 6) to see the correspondences. These linkages help you to further understand and live out your primordial archetypal drives and potentials.

Voyager presents, in effect, a complete and holistic profile of your psyche. By the various correspondences between Major, Minor, and Family cards, constellations of personality types and their qualities are created. These different subpersonality communities help you integrate the diverse dimensions of your being. You become healed and whole—a complete person fulfilling all of your potential.

Holistic Map of Consciousness

Archetypes (Major Arcana)	Attributes (Minor Arcana)				Family (Royalty)
	Crystals (Mental)	Cups (Emotional)	Worlds (Physical)	Wands (Spiritual)	
0—Fool Child	0	0	0	0	Child of Crystals, Cups, Worlds, and Wands
I—Magician	Ace Brilliance	Ace Ecstasy	Ace Success	Ace Illumination	Man of Wands (Actor)
II—Priestess	2 Equanimity	2 Equilibrium	2 Reflection	2 Purity	Woman of Wands (Sensor)
III—Empress	3 Creativity	3 Love	3 Nurturing	3 Compassion	Woman of Worlds (Preserver)
IV—Emperor	4 Logic	4 Anger	4 Commencement	4 Aspiration	Man of Worlds (Achiever)
V—Hierophant	5 Negativity	5 Disappointment	5 Setback	5 Oppression	Sage of Crystals (Knower) Sage of Wands (Seer)
VI—Lovers	6 Confusion	6 Sorrow	6 Synergy	6 Trust	Woman of Cups (Rejoicer)
VII—Chariot	7 Dullness	7 Fear	7 Breakthrough	7 Courage	Man of Cups (Surfer)
VIII—Balance	8 Synthesis	8 Stagnation	8 Change	8 Harmony	Woman of Crystals (Guardian)
IX—Hermit	9 Narrowness	9 Fulfillment	9 Harvest	9 Integrity	Sage of Cups (Regenerator) Sage of Worlds (Master)
X—Fortune	10 Delusion	10 Passion	10 Reward	10 Growth	Man of Crystals (Inventor)

0

FOOL-CHILD

Traditionally in the tarot, the Fool-Child is called simply the Fool. The Fool-Child is the closest and most natural expression of the universe, hence its association with the child. *Like the Fool-Child, be innocent and spontaneous, curious and playful.* The Fool lacks worldly wisdom, as does the Child. Both Child and Fool live in a dreamland—the breeding ground for intuitive inspiration and ingenious innovation. They are the breath of fresh air—the life force of the "great spirit"—that brings joy and new life. The Fool-Child returns to the magic and mystery of our origins and to the limitless potentials of the life spirit.

The Fool represents the Child within us. The Child cards in the *Voyager* oracle symbolize different aspects of our Fool nature. *Be inquisitive like the Learner—Child of Crystals. Like the Feeler—Child of Cups, express all your feelings without reservation. Have fun with life like the Player—Child of Worlds. As the Seeker—Child of Wands, search for truth and seek to grow.*

The Fool-Child illustrates the law in the universe. *As a child of its perfect order, place your trust in the hands of the universe.* Like a fool, dependent and with limited understanding of your purpose, have faith that the universe will take care of you. *In accepting and following the higher order of the universe, relax and be yourself, playfully experience its wonders, and begin the learning journey to the realization of the universe within.*

The innocence of a fool is further developed through its association with the child, for the child possesses the virtues of the beginner's mind—originality, receptivity, presentness, directness, and natural genius. *Be a beginner.*

The *I Ching* Hexagram for the Fool-Child is #4 *Meng*/Youthful Folly.

> *Fool and folly mean the immaturity of youth . . . rather than* mere *stupidity. Youthful folly has success. It is not I who seek the young fool, the young fool seeks me.* (I Ching, p. 20)

Kabbalists associate the Hebrew letter, *Aleph,* meaning "air or breath," with the Fool. The origin of the word, *fool,* is the Proto-Indo-European *bhel,* which means "to blow or swell." In Latin it is *follis,* meaning "bellows, windbag." The Fool is the life-breath, spiritus, prana, as well as the old fool full of hot air. *Breathe in new air, new life, and new beginnings.*

The Fool-Child is symbolized by the number Zero, which like the spirit is untouchable and limitless. Zero symbolizes the Fool-Child's mystical spirit, for it represents the beginningless beginning, sourceless source, endless ending, all things, and no-things. *Go back to zero and begin again, and again, and again.*

The Rune for the Fool-Child is *Fehu,* which is the "all-encompassing and omnipresent" life force. *Fehu* represents the Fool-Child's primal energy of "movement and expansion" that creates the eternal process of life-death-rebirth.

Jesus Christ is a figure often identified with the Fool, for he was "of the spirit." He was the life-breath—omnipresent and infinite. His innocence and faith in the universe led him to be fooled by man, but not by God. *Trust your creator.* Other mythological/historical representations of the Food-Child are Aditi (Hindu), Kneph (Egyptian), Parsifal (Germanic), Jester (Medieval), Clown (Modern), and "Nowhere Man" (Beatles).

Your "Fool-Child" Qualities

MENTAL

CHILD'S FACE: Be open minded; Have a fresh point of view; Be hopeful and optimistic.
Unevolved: CHILD: Naivete; Fooled again.

EMOTIONAL

LEAPING CHILD: Be exhilarated and excited; Be fearful and fearless.
Unevolved: SKINNED FACE OF CHILD: Disappointment because of
emotional attachment to your expectations, hopes, and dreams.

PHYSICAL

CHILD: Be active; Leap, fall, fly, tumble, climb, twirl, crawl; Be aerobic.
Unevolved: CHILD FALLING: Injury due to foolishness (lack of balance
and overextending).

ACTION IN THE WORLD

LEAPING CHILD: Seek new ways; Be adventurous; Risk; Experiment.
Unevolved: FETUS: Dependency; Security bound.

SPIRITUAL WISDOM

FETUS AND CHILD FOLLOWING BIRDS AND FALLING INTO WAITING HANDS: Follow
your spirit guides (birds), and take a leap of faith and trust into a
new state of being; Expect a miracle.

Your "Fool-Child" Oracular Universe

ASTROLOGY

URANUS: Dare to be unconventional and unusual; Expect the unexpected; Be unpredictable.

ALCHEMY

AIR: You are up in the air and unsure of the outcome.

TIME

ZERO: Your time is anytime; Now; In the present.

GEOMANCY

LEAPING INTO THE AIR: Your place is between here and there; Transition
zones: No man's land; Far out.
CLIFFS: You live on the edge.

SHAMANISM

OWL: You can see in the dark (subconscious knowing of probability
amidst uncertainty).
ORCHID: You can live off the air (spiritual forces); Little need for material security and success.

AURA

WHITE LIGHT: The energy of your spirit is pure; Innocence; Purity of following your own light.

PSYCHOMETRY

DOLL: Your genius is found in your childhood passions.

CHIROGNOMY

MANY VARIETIES OF HANDS: Be adaptable; Changeable; Interested in all of life.

Consulting the Oracle:

"Fool-Child" Way

BE SPONTANEOUS, OPEN, TRUSTING, PLAYFUL

Be spontaneous. Let out what comes to mind when you see the card symbols and signs. Do not be afraid to be foolish. Do not censure your thoughts. Be open-minded. Play with your ideas. Trust your intuitions and thoughts.

QUESTION-AND-ANSWER READING

The Fool is symbolic of the child you are. Oracles are for the childlike, the inquisitive, for those who want to know and learn about themselves and life.

What do you want to know? Ask the oracle of tarot for an answer. Play with the cards face-down while focusing on your question. Then select a card, and you will have an answer. If the answer is not clear, choose another card-symbol that will clarify it. These answers may provoke other questions you can ask the cards. Tarot is an endless question-and-answer process, as is life.

You consult the oracle to receive answers for your uncertainties. But your questions are often vague and unformed. You are unsure of exactly what you want to know. The tarot helps you formulate your questions. It is as though you are experiencing the Fool-Child, the embryo, symbolizing the formless spirit coming into form.

The clearer the question, the more effective the answer. In forming your questions, you are actually engaged in clarifying the answer. If you are consulting the tarot for others, part of your role is to help define their inquiries.

For example, all of us want to know about our lovelife. But what about it? What do we want to know? Who to love? How to love? Where to find love? We need to be specific with our questions, and ask many questions.

You may be unsure what can be asked of the tarot oracle. It will answer questions pertaining to any general or specific aspect of your inner personal life or external world. You can ask, How? Why? When? Where? Who? and What? It will give you answers about the past, present, and future. You can ask about certainties, probabilities, and possibilities. The tarot will respond to questions about shoulds and should nots, needs, requirements, and abilities. You can ask about means and ends, realities and potentials. Cosmic questions are allowed as are mundane ones. The tarot is an open forum for self-inquiry and discussion.

I

MAGICIAN

The Magician has all the tools of transformation and materialization. These tools are symbolized by the four Aces of the Minor Arcana. Your Magician's Crystal tool is the Ace-like mind—brilliant, sharp, and creative. Your Magician's Ace of Cups emotional nature is represented by the rainbow garland of flowers that is healing and beautifying. As the Magician, you hold the Ace of Worlds in hand—health, wealth, and success. Your Magician's Ace Wand is the staff of light which illuminates and energizes.

The Magician uses these tools to transform. Like the Actor (Man of Wands), the archetypal Magician's personification, you can perform this transformative magic in any arena and in any role. The Magician is the bolt of lightning that can strike swiftly anywhere and anytime.

The word *magician* is derived from the Proto-Indo-European word *magh*, which means "to be able, to have power." The I Ching Hexagram for the Magician is #1 *Ch'ien* / The Creative, which means "primal power."

The essence of power is the ability to "make it happen," which is symbolized by the Magician's number, One. The number One is the zero-spirit transformed into physical form. The Magician is able to materialize. The universal law symbolized by the Magician is talent—your ability to create by transforming and materializing. *Make your Fool-Child hopes and dreams come true.*

The Magician's power is explained by the Kabbalist's association of the Magician with the Hebrew letter, *Beth*, which means "house." A house is built by the application of scientific knowledge (science in ancient times was known as magic). The source of the Magician's ability is in the understanding of the laws of nature, or as the *I Ching* would say, "in apprehending and giving actuality to the way of the universe (tao)." *Build your house (fortunes) with all the tools and resources at your command.*

The Magician is associated with various mythological characters who carry a "magic" wand, such as the Egyptian Thoth and ankh, Hermes and caduceus staff, Aaron and rod, or Merlin and crystal. With their wands, symbols of wisdom and power, they are able to enlighten, awaken, and resurrect. *Use your gifts of insight to help others find their own talent.*

The Magician's Rune is *Ansuz*, which symbolizes the use of word and song to make magic. *Express your intellect through your medium of communication to manifest your goals.*

Magicians who are sorcerers, alchemists, shamans, wizards, and medicine men include mythological figures such as Nebo (Babylonia), Hanuman (Hindu), Huitzilopochtli (Aztec), and the Tibetan-Buddhist Mahasiddhas and Dakinis. With their ability to transmute, Magicians can be tricksterish (symbolized by the Native-American Indian Coyote) and malevolent (black witches).

Your "Magician" Qualities

MENTAL

PLANET EARTH IN THE EYE: Be imaginative; See a world of possibilities; Visualize.

Unevolved: SWIFT COMMUNICATOR: Contradictory; Verbose.

EMOTIONAL

RAINBOW IN THE OFFERING HAND: Communicate your visions and feelings with passion and inspiration to weave your rainbow dreams into reality.

Unevolved: WINE GLASS: Abuse of intoxicants to get "high."

PHYSICAL
FLYING MAN: Be swift; Move; Be light; Dance.
Unevolved: INTOXICANT AND MOTION: "Speed freak." Run down from overexcitation and addictions.

ACTION IN THE WORLD
TALENTS IN HAND: Act; Do a lot; Produce; Influence; Help others.
Unevolved: MAGICIAN: Manipulation; Trickery; Deceit.

SPIRITUAL WISDOM
UNIVERSE ABOVE THE HEAD: You are a medium, a channel, a vehicle for the energies of the universe to express themselves and manifest in the material world.
Unevolved: MAGICIAN: Black Magic; Egotism; Vanity.

Your "Magician" Oracular Universe

ASTROLOGY
MERCURY: Conceptualize; Think quickly and act; Make adjustments swiftly.

ALCHEMY
FIRE, AIR, WATER, EARTH, and GOLD: Use all the elements in your life to manifest your highest aspirations.

TIME
LASER-LIGHT WAND: Use timing purposively.
RISING SUN, EPHEMERAL RAINBOW, BUTTERFLY METAMORPHOSIS: Follow your own time and you will know the right time, the appropriate moment, the natural time.
MOON: Night (dreams and visions).
SUN: Day (action).

GEOMANCY
MAGICIAN'S VERSATILITY: You have magic anyplace, anywhere.

SHAMANISM
MONKEY: Be versatile; Be able to "ape" any role.
TULIP FLOWER: Be androgynous (Tulip's trumpet maleness and cup-like femaleness).

AURA

RAINBOW: Express all your feelings; Use the energy of different colors to create and communicate your mood.

PSYCHOMETRY

MASK: Play out your many different subpersonalities or personas.
TABLET: Develop your own personal symbols; Try different mediums of communication to express yourself.

CHIROGNOMY

SPATULATE SHAPED HAND: Use your restlessness to be inventive.
OPEN LEFT HAND: Express in the world the creative genius within you.

Consulting the Oracle:

"Magician" Way

BE EMPOWERING

As the oracle for others, you take on the persona of the Magician. As the Magician, you are able to transform another, turn their situation around, and bring out their potential.

The Magician represents your ability to conceptualize through *logos* or word, and externalize this through some medium of communication. Every idea in your head and every utterance from your mouth is an emanation that can explode with the power to inspire and enlighten.

In consulting the oracle for others, remember that you have the power of the Magician. Your counsel has the ability to heal, catalyze, and devastate. An oracle is a powerful technology or tool that can be used for good or bad. Use the power of your position with responsibility and care.

Your Magician power is in your perception. Looking with clear and open eyes through the Magician's prismatic wand, you are able to perceive a world of many possibilities. Use your power of perception to clarify options and open new doors. Let the oracle's symbols suggest new alternatives.

It is the Magician's gold crown, symbolizing your positive mental attitude, that enables you to help others physically manifest visions and ideas. All things are possible with self-confidence and positiveness. As a Magician, you are a morale booster, a supporter, and a cheerleader.

With infectious optimism and clear vision, you can change people's lives. Always offer hope, a way, and a solution. Show how the "impossible" can become a "do-able" opportunity.

Consulting the oracle is your chance to exercise your power, which is to empower others. The Minor Arcana Ace cards are your tools of empowerment. Your power is derived from your vision (Ace of Wands—Illumination), the articulation of the vision (Ace of Crystals—Brilliance), your emotional vitality (Ace of Cups—Ecstasy), and your physical energy (Ace of Worlds—Success).

II

PRIESTESS

The Priestess symbolizes the law of inherent wisdom. As the Priestess, *intuit the truth*, which comes from within the depths of the universal collective unconscious and from your own personal genetic inheritance.

Like the Priestess, *probe what lies below the surface reality*. Your dreams and meditations bring to surface the hidden, the subconscious, the past, and the future.

Like the calm mountain lake, *be still and reflect*. As the Priestess you can see to the depths and get to the bottom of things (Two of Worlds— Reflection).

The Priestess in you conserves your understanding of life's meaning and its laws. You are a temple, like the temple of Delphi, wherein you receive the immutable truths of life. Like the deep-seeking Dolphin, *listen and sound out the truth*, which is echoed back to you through your own inner temple.

Priestess comes from the Greek word *presbuteros*, which means "elder, one who is knowing and wise." The wisdom of the Priestess is derived from her equilibrium and equanimity, symbolized by her number Two—which represents balance derived out of the harmony between the tension and conflict of opposites. Because she is equilibrious, the Priestess has the the inner stillness to see clearly. The Priestess' equilibrium is symbolized by the duck on a river, for the Priestess flows through the ups and downs and changes and bends on the river of life with balance (Two of Cups—Equilibrium). *Stay in balance and have clarity.*

As suggested by her planet, the reflective moon; by her number, Two; by her element, water; and by her animal, the sonar dolphin, the Priestess is the perfect echo or mirror. Through her, others can see their true nature. She sees clearly and counsels wisely, because like the sky-blue sapphire, the Priestess is objective. She is objective because she is detached from the confusing hubbub of life (Two of Crystals—Equanimity). *Be objective.*

The Priestess is clear of vision because of her honesty. She is as pure as the crystal-white snowflake (Two of Wands—Purity). *Be honest.* The Priestess' Rune is *Hagalaz*, the cosmic ice egg that contains the mystery of the framework of the world. In harmony with the hailstone and the snowflake, the Priestess knows the cosmic harmony of life. *Be true to yourself and you will be in harmony with the cosmos.*

Cool blue as the cold hard crystal diamond, the Priestess keeps her cool and her clarity. Detached from the heat and passion of life, she guards the purity of her crystal-clear vision, her greatest inner resource (Woman of Crystals—Guardian). *Do not compromise your vision.*

Kabbalists relate the Hebrew letter *Gimel*, meaning "camel," to the Priestess. The camel, which contains its own waters, symbolizes the material and emotional self-sufficiency of the Priestess. The Priestess is free of emotional and worldly entanglements that could prejudice and cloud her purity of vision. *Be self-sufficient.*

The *I Ching* Hexagram ascribed to the Priestess is #2 *K'un*/The Receptive. This means that she is the epitome of the yin—a perfect receiver. The Priestess' receptivity, which is the result of equilibrium and independence, enables her to know the pure truth, unadulterated by time and space. Like Cassandra, the great prophetess, the Priestess is a seer. *In your own way, you are a seer.*

As the camel who journeys on the sands of time, the Priestess carries and conserves wisdom. Other such Priestesses in history or herstory include Artemis (Greek), Isis (Egyptian), Miriam (Hebrew), Nix (Teutonic), Ashi (Hindu), and Bona Dea (Roman).

Your "Priestess" Qualities

MENTAL

DIAMOND EYE: Have a multifaceted awareness; Be clear; Be sharp; Reflect; Concentrate.
Unevolved: CLOSED MOUTH: Inarticulate.

EMOTIONAL

MOUNTAIN LAKE: Be emotionally self-sufficient—you are the spring and source of your own emotional fulfillment; Guard your deepest feelings; Be calm.
Unevolved: WINTER: Cold; Lacking warmth and passion.

PHYSICAL

WATERS: Purifiy; Heal; Take fluids for cleansing; Be flexible.
Unevolved: COLD: Frigid; Rigid.

ACTION IN THE WORLD

QUEEN NEFERTITI AS PRIESTESS: Combine the metaphysical realms with the material world; Use the psychospiritual arts in your worldly life; Be independent.
Unevolved: DARK DEPTHS: Secretive; Fear of emotional commitments and relationships.

SPIRITUAL WISDOM

MOON ON HEAD: Know yourself; Let your subconscious be revealed to your conscious mind through dreams, meditation, intuition, visions; You are psychic.
Unevolved: CLOUDS: Dishonesty clouds the truth.

Your "Priestess" Oracular Universe

ASTROLOGY

MOON: You receive illumination through being passive and receptive.

ALCHEMY

WATER: Purify—Accept and dissolve the problems and negativities of others.
SNOW (FROZEN WATER): You have emotional reserves; Preserve your innermost feelings.

TIME

NIGHT: Your time of reflection is during physical inactivity and silence.

GEOMANCY

MOUNTAIN LAKES: Seek a place of calm and quiet; Retreats; Springs.
WINTER COLDNESS: Contract into inner spaces and inner sanctums.

SHAMANISM

OWL: See in the night—Know the dark, shadowy, hidden regions.
DOLPHIN: You have sonar perception—pick up and listen to vibrations.

AURA

WHITE: You are virtuous.
INDIGO: Feel and see through your third eye for psychic vision.

PSYCHOMETRY

TEMPLE: Your inner self is the sanctuary for the consultation of the truth.
BOAT: Journey to the other side, from illusion to reality, superficial to absolute, physical to metaphysical.

Consulting The Oracle:

"Priestess" Way

The Priestess symbolizes that aspect of yourself that intuitively knows the truth. You are a repository of knowledge accumulated over eons of time and experience. Like stone from which the Priestess' face is carved, this knowledge is enduring. As a sensitive biocomputer, like the dolphin, you are capable of quickly sounding out the truth of a situation. You are intuitive by nature.

USE CARDS AS MIRRORS

When you read the tarot, the card-symbols will tell you what you intuitively already know. The cards, like the reflecting pool in which the Priestess dwells, mirror yourself. The tarot clarifies what you have already perceived, but which you have not fully recognized in your conscious thinking mind.

BE WATER

In reading the cards, be open and receptive, like water. You are like a dolphin with a sonar intelligence capable of swiftly detecting the most minute and distant vibrations. Flow with what the card-symbol tells you. To be water, you cannot be defensive, judgmental, up-tight. Insecurity, which comes from a lack of self-confidence in your perceptions, makes you like rock. It is difficult to perceive anything in this state of hardness.

HEAR THE TRUTH

After a card is selected in a reading, sit passively and wait. Wait until you hear a voice that tells you what it means. Notice in the Priestess Card how the Dolphin is next to the Priestess' ear. Listen for the message. Be patient. Wait until all the static has dissipated. Communicate that message once it has come through, "The oracle says . . . ."

FORGET THE LITERAL MEANING OF THE CARDS

Symbols trigger intuition. Intuition is Queen and King in the tarot. If the cards selected are "terrible" for example, your personal intuition about the person or situation may be vastly different. In this case you may want to ignore the literal meaning of the cards and go with your own sense. The cards are only points of departure for intuition. They can be read in any way, even in a totally reverse way. Cards do not have to appear upside down to be read in a reverse manner.

BE TRUTHFUL

Always read the cards as truthfully as possible. Respect for yourself as a person and as a reader of tarot comes from your truthfulness. Even if the cards are bleak and your intuition can only see darkness, in truth there is always a way out. Truthfully explore the path to light. That path may not be easy. Truthfully state that it will not be easy. Only in truth can you be of service to others and to yourself.

BE PURE

The Priestess is as pure as snow and clean as the mountain spring. She is as detached and distant from worldly life as the mountain snows. Never use the reading for your own personal gain, in the sense of trying to gain personal power over another or to get something from another outside of the reading.

A reading is a powerful tool for manipulation of others. It can corrupt your integrity. Like the Priestess, be detached and truthful. Give the reading and then let the person go. Never compromise your integrity to make a dollar or to gain approval.

III

EMPRESS

The Empress, symbolizing the *law of preservation*, is the guardian of life. Standing before the earth, she represents your charge to protect it and all that lives.

Life is a golden miracle. The Empress honors and respects all of life for its inherent richness and beauty. No fruit is too small, no being is too weak, no idea is too foolish, and no emotion is too immature. The Empress is one with all. The earth and all of its animals, minerals, vegetables, and human beings are of her seed. Everyone and everything are her children.

The Empress represents the pink blush of love. In her love for life, she is the *creatress* and *protectress*. In your "heart cup" of love (Three of Cups-Love), which is symbolized by the earth, nest, womb, and egg, you preserve the essence and quality of life (Woman of Worlds-Preserver).

As the Earth Mother or Mother Nature, *conserve* life by giving birth to its seed, which you carry within. Empress is derived from the Latin word, *parere*, "to beget, give birth." Three, the Empress' number, symbolizes the synthesis of opposites (One and Two), which gives birth to a third. The Empress represents creative union. Birthing is first conceived in the mind. The Empress gives birth to new ideas (Three of Crystals-Creativity), which flower into fields of fruitfulness.

Like the Empress, *nurse* and *nurture* your life creations into full flower (Three of Worlds-Nurturing) with a protective, *healing*, and *compassionate* hand (Three of Wands-Compassion). Kabbalists associate the Hebrew letter-word *Daleth*, meaning "leaf of a door," with the Empress. *Daleth* is like the mother's womb, a nurturing entry and exit that admits life, protects it, and preserves it.

Upon the physical death of your "life creations," the Empress (represented by the Priestess Selkut in the card) assists the journey of the spirit into rebirth. *Recreate new life by honoring what needs to die.*

The Empress, symbolizing *responsibility for maintaining life,* is associated with the *I Ching* Hexagram #8 *Pi*/Holding Together (Union).

> *Such holding together calls for a central*
> *figure around whom other persons may unite.*
> *To become a center of influence is a grave*
> *matter and fraught with great responsibility.*
> *It requires greatness of spirit, consistency,*
> *and strength. (I Ching, p. 36)*

These qualities of character correspond with the Latin wordbase for the Empress, *imperare*, which means "to command."

The Empress is the mythological Mother Goddess. Other Mother figures include Cybele of the Mediterranean region, the Roman Venus, the Sumerian Innini, the Babylonian Ishtar, the Greek Gaea and Demeter, the Hindu Dyava-matar.

The Empress is *Uruz*, the U-Rune, the mother of manifestation. Mythologically, this is represented by the cow, Audhumla, symbol of fertility and nurturing. This is similar to the Egyptian Empress, Hathor, the cow goddess.

Your "Empress" Qualities

MENTAL

FLOWER ATOP THE HEAD: Be imaginative; Dream; Be poetic; Be open-minded and nonjudgmental; Create.

Unevolved: Lacking in precision thinking and analysis.

EMOTIONAL

OPEN ARMS, DOVE: Give unconditional love; Show your feelings.
Unevolved: Smothering mother; Possessive; Jealous.

PHYSICAL

FEMALE BODY: Take care of your female organs; Reproductive centers; Femininity; Fertility; Sensuality.
PREGNANCY: You are in a time of fertility; Fecundity.
Unevolved: Sedentary; Heavy.

ACTION IN THE WORLD

MOTHER: Take responsibility; Have endurance and patience; Mother; Provide; Nurture; Nurse; Heal; Manifest; Produce; Be practical and down-to-earth; Take care of the home.
Unevolved: Homebound; Conservative and protective to the point of stagnation and death.

SPIRITUAL WISDOM

PRIESTESS SELKUT (PROTECTOR OF TUTANKHAMUN'S SPIRIT): Honor the spirit of the dead; Be connected with the "other side." Revere the spirit essence of life.
EARTH TEEMING WITH LIFE: Treat the earth as a living conscious being, as your own body.
Unevolved: Stuck in the material world, the physical plane.

Your "Empress" Oracular Universe

ASTROLOGY

EARTH: Be of this earth; Perform your earthly responsibilities.
MOON: Keep strong emotional attachment to your loved ones.

ALCHEMY

FIRE, AIR, WATER, EARTH: Creative synthesis.
MAGMA (MOLTEN MATTER THAT CREATES STONE): Your creativity provides a new grounding and foundation.

TIME

FLOWERING: Your time is when you express yourself and your feelings; Prime-time; Summer.
FULL MOON: Your time is when you are full and strong.

GEOMANCY

EARTH , EGG, WOMB: Be in community; Your friendship circle; Your comfort zones.

SHAMANISM

DOVE: Be gentle; Be pure of intention; Be amorous.
POPPIES: Preserve by multiplying.

AURA

PINK: Strive for perfection in love.
BLUE: Love with wisdom.
GOLD: Seek the heights of perfection.

PSYCHOMETRY

NEST: Be a homebuilder.

CHIROGNOMY

OPEN HANDS: You are open; Receptive; Loving; Compassionate.

Consulting the Oracle:

"Empress" Way

BE NURTURING

The seed of greatness is within us all. For that seed to flower we must see this potential and understand the principles for its growth. See the counsel of the oracle in terms of your creative expression. Life is a creative unfoldment. We are all Mother-Empresses giving birth to new ideas, new emotions, new projects, and new beings. We must manifest and produce or we are not alive. Only in the creative life is the deepest essence of our human being fulfilled.

Using the universal principles of creative growth into personal wholeness represented by the tarot cards, your reading can never be wrong. It can only contribute to growth and evolution. A reading is your act of service to the universe—for saving and transforming it like the Mother Protectress.

BE SUPPORTIVE

As the cards mirror our consciousness, they seldom tell us anything really new. A card reading therefore offers the opportunity to be supportive—

to support and give confidence to another. Read the tarot to reassure yourself and others that who you are and what you are doing is okay. The tarot gives us permission to be ourselves and share our own beautiful being.

BE LOVING

Reading the tarot is an offering. Give your loving heart, your creative mind, your physical energy, and your spiritual understanding to help yourself or another unfold. Your offerings are the foodstuffs that nurture and nourish growth.

To give everything you have into a reading is an act of love. In the expression of love, the "life source" is revitalized. You are deeply transformed through the creative mix of this most fundamental alchemy of life—the sharing of love.

What particular technique you use to read the tarot is unimportant. How you read the cards makes no difference as long as you come from your heart—the path and technique that allows you to be most loving, supportive, and nurturing.

BE COMPASSIONATE

Reading the tarot combines love and wisdom—the essence of compassion. We all grow through open-hearted encouragement and understanding. Be kind and be gentle, be firm and be clear. Treat the reading in the way a mother treats her child—with compassion.

IV

EMPEROR

The Emperor, symbolized by King Philip and his son Alexander the Great, represents the law of construction. The Emperor constructs the material world. This is symbolized by his number, Four, which denotes the four cornerstones of any building. Four also represents the four sides that comprise a square, which means the material world with its boundaries of four seasons, four directions, and four elements.

Like the Emperor, *build your empire*. Use the Emperor's qualities to bring you success. Like the Emperor, *aspire to the top*.

See and strive for high goals (Four of Wands—Aspiration). Build according to *a logical and practical set of plans* (Four of Crystals—Logic). Act upon your goals and plans. The Emperor is a doer, a real go-getter (Four of Worlds—Commencement). When and if your plans go awry, like the Emperor who becomes angry, very angry (Four of Cups—Anger), *use this anger to motivate you* ever more strongly. Like the Emperor, do not be denied. In the end, you will achieve your vision (Man of Worlds—Achiever).

The Emperor symbolizes the inner fire of Aries and Mars that compels him to build and to achieve professional recognition and monetary reward. *Do not shirk from your drives and desires, your passion and fire.*

The Latin etymological source for Emperor is *parere*, meaning "to beget, give birth." Through worldly ambition, the Emperor fathers a new world and changes civilization. *Be a father.* Contribute to his worldly evolution through your construction efforts. Build a better world for yourself and others.

The Emperor *I Ching* Hexagram is #35, *Chin*/Progress:

> *Sun rising over the earth;*
> *Ever widening expansion and clarity. (I Ching, p. 136)*

Derived from the Latin word *imperare*, "to command," the Emperor is a leader. The Emperor is associated with all mythological leaders, whether they be called King, President, Commander, Captain, Chief, Director, or Chairman. *Lead the way.*

As a leader, the Emperor possesses *vision* and is responsible, attributes associated with the Kabbalah letter-word *Heh*, meaning "window." *Heh* represents the ability to see and oversee. *Oversee your work to insure that it is solid.*

Your "Emperor" Qualities

MENTAL

BUILDINGS: Put your ideas and goals into practice; Use your logical and analytical organization; Be a planner and strategic thinker.
Unevolved: Headstrong; Will not take "no" for an answer.

EMOTIONAL

RAM'S HORNS, EAGLE'S BEAK, WHALE'S SNOUT: Determined; Resolute.
Unevolved: Anger when things do not go according to one's will, plans, and/or timetable; Negative manifestation of ego.

PHYSICAL

YOUNG TREE, YOUNG ALEXANDER: Youthful; Vital; Energetic.
ARIES: You are susceptible to head problems; Sight; Headaches.
Unevolved: Pushing the body to extremes; High blood pressure; Heart attack.

ACTION IN THE WORLD

BUILDINGS, CANAL: Be a developer; Pioneer.

MONEY, GEMS: Make money; Be entrepreneurial.

ALEXANDER THE GREAT: Explore; Pathfind; Be political; Keep your territory.

Unevolved: Overly competitive; Ruthless; Power hungry; Insecure; Treats others as objects, pawns, tools; Overextended; Burned out; Does not finish what is started; Obsessed with fame and fortune.

SPIRITUAL WISDOM

CROWN: Maintain dominion over your mind (EAGLE), your emotions (WHALE), and your body (RAM).

Unevolved: Egocentric.

Your "Emperor" Oracular Universe

ASTROLOGY

ARIES (RAM): Strive for primacy; Be number one.

SUN: Use your power responsibly.

ALCHEMY

FIRE: Expand; Extend outwards; Consume.

TIME

ARIES: Act in the spring; Beginnings.

PROFESSIONAL LIFE: You feel best during the work week; Working hours.

GEOMANCY

OFFICES: Your strength is at work sites.

MOUNTAIN PEAKS: Go to challenging places; Heights.

SHAMANISM

EAGLE: Be daring; Heroic; Courageous.

WHALE: Think big; Act big.

RAM: Be unyielding and impatient.

PINE TREE: Be bold; Express your male sexuality.

AURA

RED-ORANGE: Get aroused; Pumped up; Heated.

PSYCHOMETRY

MONUMENTS: Manifest through your ego; Leave a legacy.

CHIROGNOMY

CUPPED HAND: Nurture.

Consulting the Oracle:

"Emperor" Way

HAVE A GOAL

Being goal oriented, the Emperor symbolizes the principle of establishing your aims and objectives. Before consulting the oracle, ask what you want to achieve from the reading. Make the reading specific to your needs and interests.

It is surprising how often we do not really know what we want, or are afraid to admit our desires. A reading should clarify intent or purpose.

MAKE A PLAN

Once your goals are established, use the oracle to help you determine how to achieve your objectives. Make this a step-by-step plan. This is the way the Emperor builds his empire.

Rather than to predict the future, it is far more important for the oracle to provide the path for a successful future. Let the oracle give you the tools that will enable you to determine and create your own future.

DECIDE

Every person is a government unto herself or himself. Self-government, like any government, requires some order established through law. The Emperor symbolizes the laws and principles that govern.

The tarot helps establish a self-order through the principles of the Major Archetypes, which compose a philosophical structure for living. These principles create a personal constitution—a set of life laws based upon beliefs about the nature of humankind. This constitution provides stability in your life.

These laws or principles provide the superstructure upon which the decisions that guide us through the course of life are formed. Decision making is a legislative process that must consider all the interests within the body politic, of the self, or the state. The Emperor, as he gazes over his domain, looks out for the rights and goals of all his constituents.

The constitution of the tarot establishes that the imperatives of the physical body (Worlds), the aspirations of the mind (Crystals), the passions of the heart (Cups), the limitations and opportunities of the world external to the self (Worlds), and the pull of the spirit (Wands) must be represented and consulted in the decision-making process.

The art of self-government is the ability to bring these interests together and fashion decisions with which all of these constituents can live and benefit. The Emperor symbolizes this skill as he is the builder and the number Four—both traits representing his ability to fit together opposing and cross-cutting aims and demands into a structure that supports and houses all interests.

If you have decisions to make and are confused, consult these various aspects of yourself and your world. Use the tarot as a consultant in the decision-making process. Ask the oracle what it has to say about the mental, emotional, physical, worldly, and spiritual consequences of any decision.

$\mathcal{V}$

$\mathcal{HIEROPHANT}$

The Hierophant symbolizes the law of life-mastery. Through a Buddha-like meditative awareness and philosophy that views every experience as a lesson-learning opportunity for growth, the Hierophant passes the steps or tests of life. *Life is your teacher.*

The Hierophant represents the philosophical bedrock of the human being. As you are created out of the earth like the Buddha-Hierophant statue, you suffer its cracks and fissures (Five of Crystals and Five of Cups—Negativity and Disappointment), its droughts and devastations (Five of Worlds—Setback), and its entrapping density and heaviness (Five of Wands—Oppression). As the Buddha-Hierophant, *transmute your earth faults (San Andreas faultline) into the philisopher's stone—a solid understanding that rifts and conflicts are openings for new life to take seed (poppy flower).* Like wrinkled skin, the scorched earth of human experience reveals our age-old wisdom. *Use this earthly life as a stepping stone to the top of the temple (Machu Pichu and Tibet) and to the light .*

The Hierophant is represented by the number five, which stands for Humankind (the head, two arms and two legs being the five points). Five symbolizes the human state of consciousness that is higher than the animal realms but lower and less perfect than the gods. *Your opportunity is to use the human situation of evolved qualities in order to transcend your unevolved aspects.*

Life experience makes the Buddha and other great teachers (masters, sages, professors, gurus, rabbis, priests, and preachers) a guide to others in their quest for wisdom. Hierophant is a combination of two Greek words, *hiero* meaning "sacred" and *phainein* meaning "to bring to light." As a seeker of the light and truth, the Hierophant reveals the sacred laws of the universe to others. *Share your life-learned wisdom with others. You are a teacher.*

The Rune for the Hierophant is *Raidho*. This R-rune means "keeping the right order of the universe through organized religion." The Hierophant preserves the cosmic law by rituals that have become institutionalized. *Practice sacred rituals.*

By understanding these laws, the Hierophant inevitably assumes a humility that is suggested by the *I Ching* Hexagram #15, *Ch'ien*/Modesty:

> *When a man holds a high position but is nevertheless*
> *modest, he shines with the light of wisdom. (I Ching, p. 64)*

The Kabbalah letter-word associated with the Hierophant is *Vav*, meaning "nail or hook." Like the nail, which holds things together, the Hierophant keeps things together when all appears to be falling apart. This is symbolized by the "setback" and "disappointments" exemplified in the Hierophant's attributes (number Five of the Minor Arcana card-symbols). *As a supporting nail, be a support for others during the trials and tribulations of their life journey.*

Your "Hierophant" Qualities

MENTAL

BARE FEET ON EARTH: Be a realist; Practical; Stable; Down-to-earth.
Unevolved: Fixed beliefs; Archaic beliefs.

EMOTIONAL

SPARROW IN THE HEART and VENUS CROWN OVER THE BUDDHA: Love; Have
    compassion and tenderness; Seek purity of heart.
Unevolved: Unexpressive of feelings—emotions of stone.

PHYSICAL

TAURUS BULL BEING BOUND (On gold cup): Harness your physical energies; Tame physical/sexual urges.

TAURUS: Neck; Throat; Voice.

Unevolved: Lethargic.

ACTION IN THE WORLD

CHILD ON STEPS: Learn continually; Grow from life experience; Experience is your best teacher; Follow a teacher or a philosophy of life; Go to school; Teach yourself.

Unevolved: Tradition bound; Meaningless ritual.

SPIRITUAL WISDOM

BUDDHA AND CRESCENT CROWN OF LIGHT: Seek a path of enlightenment to free yourself from unhappiness and conflict; Listen to your own "inner Priestess."

Unevolved: Spiritual materialism—Using spirituality to feed ego.

Your "Hierophant" Oracular Universe

ASTROLOGY

TAURUS (BULL): Sacrifice and give of yourself so that others may grow and evolve.

VENUS: Bright planet—Enlighten others as a teacher.

ALCHEMY

EARTH: Be spiritually grounded—walk the spiritual path with your feet on the ground; Use the worldly life as a forum for personal growth.

TIME

BUDDHA AWARENESS: Be in the present; Now; No clinging to the past; No craving for the future.

TAURUS: You feel strong in the month of Taurus (March-April).

GEOMANCY

CAVE: Find your place of refuge; Your temple; Your meditation spot.

MACHU PICHU, ANCIENT EGYPTIAN TEMPLE: Explore the religions and philosophies of the ancient world; Discover your past life; Respect old traditions.

SHAMANISM

BULL ELEPHANT: Work at clearing away the stagnant, dense, and oppressive in order to have clarity, liberation, and enlightenment; Be of service.

POPPY FLOWER: Out of the compost, the mud and refuse of life, you grow, flower, and disseminate seeds of experienced wisdom.

AURA

BROWNS: Be humble; Simple; Modest.

PSYCHOMETRY

PAINTS (TIBETAN PAINTING ON STONE) : Inscribe your hopes, fears, and growth.

CHIROGNOMY

BUDDHA'S HAND POSITION: Buddhist mudra that means "perfection." Realize that everything is always perfect in spite of what your negative mind might say; Trust that you are in good hands as a child of the universe.

Consulting the Oracle:

"Hierophant" Way

FOLLOW A RITUAL

The Hierophant represents your respect for ancient knowledge and its ritualization. The ancients thought in symbolic terms and lived a symbolic life. Actions were symbolic of "higher" intention.

The tarot, being a symbolic tool and action, is given to ritualization. Tarot books explain how to shuffle and select cards. These ways become rituals that tarot practitioners believe they must follow. Not so.

It is best to establish your own ritualistic way of practicing tarot. A ritual is a habitual and symbolic way of doing tarot that feels comfortable. It is a vital centering process that gives you Priestess equanimity and clarity.

One of the unevolved aspects of the Hierophant consciousness is rigid and empty adherence to ancient traditions. Nothing wrong with traditions, but to *have* to follow them is not the way to your own enlightenment. The Buddha-Hierophant declared that everyone has their own path. Establish your path in the particular way that you practice the tarot.

ESTABLISH A PHILOSOPHY OF LIFE

Tarot is a philosophy of life. The card meanings convey implicit values and normative prescriptions for living. To practice the tarot is to follow a philosophy. The cards represent the structure or "bones" of that way of belief.

Tarot is, however, an open-belief system. Many philosophies can be created through it because symbols are open to such a variety of meanings.

If the explanation books for the cards do not contain a message you believe in, feel free to alter their meaning. This can be done by determining other meanings for the symbols in the cards, which can be derived from either your own mind or from a dictionary of symbols.

The underlying tarot belief systems are critical. As the Buddha-Hierophant said, it all starts in the mind. A healthy *growth philosophy* supported by visual symbols is a powerful tool for self-unfoldment. A philosophy of life is the stone from which you can leap into higher consciousness.

EMPHASIZE THE PRIMACY OF THE MIND (CRYSTALS)

"It's all in the mind," stated the Buddha. Place particular importance on the Crystal cards, for they describe your states of mind. The most critical of the Crystals is the number Five—Negativity. Here is where all your problems begin. The "negative" mind is the inherent nature of the mind not to accept the present reality, regardless of what it is. Nothing is good enough for the mind. Either the mind wants more or wants to hold onto what is—either way it is unsatisfied. The mind is like a monkey, always moving, always grabbing, always fooling.

This "craving-for-more" monkey mind creates adverse developments that run throughout your entire inner being and work into your worldly life. The negative mind creates emotional disappointment (Five of Cups) which then enters into the physical body (Five of Worlds—Setback). When the mind, heart, and body are in negative states, your spirit is oppressed (Five of Wands). The outcome is negative manifestations in your external world of relationships, professional life, and so forth.

Any so-called "negative" card can be traced back to the Five of Crystals as the source. You can actually explain this negative syndrome in a reading if you deem it important enough.

USE "NEGATIVE" CARDS AS OPPORTUNITIES

The Hierophant teaches us that life is a continual learning process. The number Five cards in the tarot are associated with the Number Five Hierophant and are all problematic, indicating that not only do we learn from our successes but from our mistakes. When so-called "negative" symbols, such as setback or disappointment, appear in a reading they are in fact "opportunity" cards, affording the opportunity to prevent and/or manage these problems in the future.

It is assumed that we will always have difficulties throughout life. A negative card does not necessarily depict greater problems than before, but in fact, symbolizes an area for personal growth and breakthrough. Negative or, more accurately, opportunity cards are to be welcomed. They indicate you are ready to learn a lesson and move up a grade, another stair on life's voyage. With this understanding, it becomes easier to handle the shocks and quakes of life and heal the rifts.

VI

LOVERS

The Lovers symbolized by Brancusi's *Embrace* sculpture, the union of male and female, is the law of union. Oneness, through the marriage of opposites, is represented by the mythological bride and bridegroom, Solomon and Shulamite. The Lovers represent communion with others, and the integration of inner self-polarities. This outer and inner union creates an androgynous or whole being, exemplified by the Buddhist *Yab-Yum*. *Find your inner lover, your inner "soul mate," and you will find yourself and your "earth mate."*

The word "lovers," comes from the Indo-European, *leubh*, which means "to care for, desire, love." The Lovers Card represents the irresistible attraction to another, creating a sense of wholeness. The Rune for the Lovers is *Wunjo*, the W-rune. This rune means the force of attraction that we have toward others. It is this force that binds us together as lovers, partners, family, and community. *Do not resist those to whom you are attracted.*

Like the duck, which sees its duality reflected in nature's mirror, the lake, we are the embrace of opposites: sun male and moon female, airy mind and jungle emotion, black negativity and white positiveness. *Let these contradictions be.*

In our duality we are whole. To trust and embrace the opposite, the other, the different, the foreign (Six of Wands—Trust) is to synergize (Six of Worlds—Synergy), to bring together and weave one world, one self, one family, one basket. *Seek out the different and you will become more whole.*

Oneness is composed of twoness. Like the two-headed snake, the reality of the one mind is dualistic—it is yes and no, this way or that way (Six of Crystals—Confusion). As easily as things come together they come apart (Six of Cups—Sorrow). *Know that for every negative there is a positive and for every positive there is a negative.*

The Lovers card contains the disunion between opposites. Its *I Ching* Hexagram is #6, *Sung*/Conflict, which means ". . . the two halves move away from each other" *(I Ching, p. 28).*

Disintegration is explained by the Kabbalistic association of the letter-word *Zain*, with the Lovers. *Zain* means "sword or weapon." An instrument that separates and divides, it symbolizes the discriminating mind—the mental ability to see differences and similarities, and to cut down and slay with critical judgment. This discriminating intelligence is a Gemini trait, the astrological sign of the Lovers. *Use your discriminating judgment to make decisions.*

The Lovers number is Six, the product of Three (synthesis) times Two (antithesis). Six represents "together but not together," "unity but disunity." *Live with ambiguity, contradiction, and paradox. Embrace the opposites and maintain the center.*

Wholeness is love, which is the nonjudgmental acceptance and embrace of the dualities. To be the rose, torn in two, and to transcend into one lotus is the law of life, the sweet and sour essence of love.

The Lovers Card is associated with the Gemini twins, which represent sameness and difference, oneness and twoness. Twins are famous throughout mythological history. They include Apollo and Artemis (Greek), Theseus and Perithous (Hebrew), Rama and Luxman (Hindu), Grettir and Illuga (Icelandic), Ioskehi and Tawiscara (Huron), Cupid and Psyche (Roman), Castor and Pollux (Greek), Tristan and Isolde (Brythanic), Ch'ien Niu and Chih Nu (Chinese).

Your "Lovers" Qualities

MENTAL

UNION AND POLARITY OF MALE AND FEMALE (LOVERS *EMBRACE* SCULPTURE): See another point of view; Analyze (break down) and synthesize ideas; Use reason and imagination.

Unevolved: Indecisive; Overly analytical and judgmental; Schizophrenic.

EMOTIONAL

UNION OF TWO LOVERS: Love; Empathize (feel what others feel); Engage in emotional intimacy; Share.

Unevolved: Emotional insecurity—need approval from others for emotional fulfillment; Addicted to romance.

PHYSICAL

LOVERS: Express your sexuality; Heal through touch; Smell.
Unevolved: Sex addict.

ACTION IN THE WORLD

LOVERS EMBRACE: Use your relationship skills (sociability, creativity, communicativeness, teamwork, conflict resolver, leader/follower) in all kinds of partnerships (love, family, friends, business, team, community) to build bonds and to synergize.

Unevolved: Dependence on others; Possessive; Meddlesome; Cannot live with uncertainty and ambiguity.

SPIRITUAL WISDOM

ONE-EYE AWARENESS (THE EYES OF THE LOVERS IS A SINGLE DIAMOND): See the unity and interdependence of life. Understand the *Law of Duality.* Opposites are two sides of the same phenomenon; "You cannot have one without the other." Maintain a philosophy of oneness: "We are all carved out of the same block." Transcend thought, word, and logic by the ability to hold the opposites—to see the opposite as equally valid. Know that you have extrasensory perception (you are naturally tuned into another).

Unevolved: Egotistical narcissism.

Your "Lovers" Oracular Universe

ASTROLOGY

GEMINI TWINS: Know that you have a soul mate; Bond with others who are your twins.

ALCHEMY

AIR: Your mind blows this way and that way.

TIME

MOON ABOVE AND SUN BELOW: Change; Be unpredictable.
GEMINI: Consider new ideas in the period of May-June.

GEOMANCY

LOVERS: Seek appropriate places for different kinds of relationships.

SHAMANISM

DUCK: Fly and swim (be involved but above it).
SNAKE: Be flexible.
LION: You are a beauty and the beast (refined yet primitive).
TORN ROSE: Be able to handle disappointment and sorrow when things come apart and die.
LOTUS: Know that everything is always perfect for the spirit to grow.

AURA

RAINBOW: Harmonize with variety; Express all your colors.

PSYCHOMETRY

FLUTE: Integrate your active male principle (breath) with your passive female principle (flute) to create (sound).

Consulting the Oracle for Others:

"Lovers" Way

TRUST YOUR "TWIN INTUITION"

As we are all twins, we are naturally connected to each other. Trust that you are "in sync" with the person you are reading for. You do not have to try to be intuitive. Be yourself. Say what comes to mind and it will be appropriate. If a person does not agree with your assessment, it is simply a difference in perception that does not, however, invalidate your own.

In keeping with the ambiguity and duality of the Lovers, realize that although your intuitions are inevitably accurate, they will manifest in another person in another way. We are not the same. Your counsel is right but wrong. If your counsel is found to be inaccurate, it is inaccurate only in the sense that what you have perceived has been seen differently by the other person.

READ FOR ANOTHER AND READ FOR YOURSELF

Again, assuming we are all twins, what you pick up from another person is something that also exists within you. Every reading for another is a reading for yourself. The cards of another person's situation mirrors in some way your own situation. Thank the other person for giving you the opportunity to know yourself better through the reading.

MUTUAL SHARING

A reading does not have to be a one-way communication. Like the sharing of the Lovers, reading the tarot is a way of mutually figuring things out between reader and readee. It is perfectly appropriate to solicit the readee's perceptions and opinions about the cards and about your counsel. Undoubtedly, two minds are better than one. The interplay between yourself and another leads to creative new insights that are mutually beneficial.

VII

CHARIOT

The Chariot, symbolized by the Greek "Charioteer," represents the law of motion. The Indo-European root for chariot is *kers*, meaning "to run." The Chariot is always in motion. The mind, heart, body, and spirit are constantly running. *Move.* Movement brings change, and change brings new experience, learning, and growth—it leads to the achievement of your evolutionary destiny.

This sanskrit mantra extols the virtue of Chariot-like movement:

GATE GATE *(Going Going)*
PARAGATE PARASAM GATE (Going Beyond the Beyond)
BODHI SVHA *(Hail the Goer)*

To be moving is to be alive. The Charioteer, the goer, conquers inertia and entropy—the twin forces of death. Pulled by the horse, his primal soulmate, the Charioteer breaks through (Seven of Worlds—Breakthrough) the stonewalls of ignorance (Seven of Crystals—Dullness).

With the heart, will, and courage of the warrior (Seven of Wands—Courage), the Charioteer exorcises the inner demon of fear (Seven of Cups—Fear), the greatest obstacle to life and growth. Piloting the solar wheel of the great spirit over impassable mountains and uncrossable seas, the Charioteer affirms the victory of life over death. *Challenge yourself.*

The Charioteer searches for self-realization. Like the great mythological explorers, Odysseus, Icarus, and the Argonauts, the Charioteer seeks the highest point of personal attainment. *Go for it!*

The Chariot is the vehicle or road to this realization. It could be like Hussain's magic carpet, the golden fleece, Icarus' wings, Noah's ark, Muso-Byoye's kite, Surya's solar chariot, or Odin's steed. The Chariot Rune is *Ehwaz*, which means "horse," symbol of a powerful means to reach your highest aspirations. *Find a vehicle that will take you to victory. Trust and work in harmony with your "way," and you will reach your goal.*

The Chariot's number, Seven, symbolizes temporary perfection and success. It is as perfect as the seven planets, seven colors in the rainbow, seven musical notes on the diatonic scale, and seven days of the week. It is only temporary perfection because true wholeness is attained with the return to the One. Seven is both the stasis and stillness of attainment, but as the final ascent to the perfect (ten or one), it also represents movement and beginning. *Honor what you have achieved and dedicate yourself to even higher successes.*

Paradoxically, Seven as the stasis of attainment, is part of overall movement and higher ascension. Things are moving in spite of appearing to be still. The Charioteer is still amidst movement. This is reflected in the *I Ching* Hexagram #52, *Ken*/Keeping Still:

> *Keeping still means*
> *When it is time to stop, then stop.*
> *When it is time to advance, then advance.*
> *Thus movement and rest do not miss the right time.*
> *And their course becomes bright and clear. (I Ching, p. 653)*

Follow your own timing.

The Kabbalah letter-word associated with the Chariot is *Cheth*, meaning "fence." A fence symbolizes the ability of the Charioteer to focus on the goal by keeping out distractions. *Shut out what is keeping you from reaching your goals.*

Fences are movable, suggesting the ability to have boundaries (one's sense of self-identity and purpose) while moving about. As Cancer, the Charioteer carries the shell or home (self-security) on his/her back and is at home wherever. *Travel and test your sense of inner security.*

Your "Chariot" Qualities

MENTAL

CHARIOTEER: Have a purpose, a plan, an ideal; Set goals and objectives, and the routes and means for their achievement.

Unevolved: Movement; Addicted to movement without completions and achievements.

EMOTIONAL

SURFER: Be balanced amidst your emotional ups and downs; Be bold; Be courageous.

Unevolved: Lacks emotional self-control.

PHYSICAL

RUNNER, SURFER, FLYER, RIDER, DRIVER, CYCLIST: Be athletic; Stay in shape; Be at home in the water, the air, and on the earth.

CANCER: Pay attention to your stomach; Digestive system.

Unevolved: Overexertion; Burned out.

ACTION IN THE WORLD

VICTORY WREATH: Commit to victory and success.

Unevolved:

EGYPTIAN WARRIOR: Runs over others to achieve goals

HUNTER: Uses others for sport.

SPIRITUAL WISDOM

TRANCE STARE OF CHARIOTEER: You have meditative awareness at all times, and thus are: Centered amidst change; At home wherever ("home" is awareness); Detached, resulting in effortless action; Inner stillness amidst movement and action;

Unevolved: VICTORY WREATH: Ego vanity.

Your "Chariot" Oracular Universe

ASTROLOGY

CANCER: You are an enigma to others because you hide your true feelings; Be a homebody yet traveler, protective yet sensitive, earthy yet watery.

MOON: Self-reflect; Move with your emotions.

JUPITER: Express yourself; Expand outward.

ALCHEMY

FIRE AND WATER: Be elusive yet steady; Move outward and inward.
BRONZE: Hold to old values and traditions.
SILVER: Revelations come through your dreamworld.
GOLD: Create your future.

TIME

HORSE: You are good in the stretch run.
BALLOON: Ascend.
SURFER, ROCKET: Take off.
HIGHWAY: Do not turn back.
CANCER: Your time for moving is June-July.

GEOMANCY

CHARIOT: Hit the road; Be here and there; In vehicles; Explore; Adventure; Seek.

SHAMANISM

TORTOISE: You have past life recall.
FALCON: Maneuver swiftly.
HORSE: You are clairvoyant.
CRAB: Your insecurity leads to defensiveness or offensiveness.
FLOWER: You are ephemeral—here today, gone tomorrow.

AURA

RED AND BLUE: You blow hot and cold; Fickle; Keep your options open.

PSYCHOMETRY

VEHICLES: Be efficient; Act quickly.

Consulting the Oracle:

"Chariot" Way

KEEP YOUR INTUITION MOVING

Like the movement of the Charioteer, travel in a reading to different places in your life and personality. Cover ground. Keep the reading moving. Like the tortoise, go through the the outer persona and into your depths. Like the Lunar Rover, explore the subconscious. Like the surfer, venture into the emotional waters. Move laterally like the crab into your physical nature. Like the hunter, hunt down the answers to their questions. Go back in time and go ahead. Like the visionary Charioteer, look at the future possibilities. As the pilot, drive the intuition through a complete journey into the self. Like the spaceship, go swiftly through some subjects, and like the balloon, slowly through others. Soar with falcon-like inspiration but occasionally land on the runway of mundane practicality. The more you move, the more you trigger the interest of the intuition, and the more you know yourself and your richness.

Do "Readings-on-the Go"

Readings are centering when you are traveling. When traveling, you are performing the archetypal role of Charioteer. Like the great Chariot traveler, you do not want to lose your sense of self when on the road. To be a good traveler means, like the crab, you carry your home on your back. To be at home wherever you are is knowing yourself—being centered. Consultation of the tarot keeps you in touch with yourself. The cards bring out familiar aspects of yourself even in the strangest of places. The cards, like your car, are your home away from home. Like the crab shell, tarot offers a sense of self-security.

VIII

BALANCE

Balance is the law of action and reaction. For every action there is an equal reaction. The *I Ching* Hexagram for Balance is #63, *Chi Chi*/After Completion.

> *When perfect equilibrium has been reached, any movement may*
> *cause order to revert to disorder. (I Ching, p. 244)*

The number for Balance is Eight, its equal spheres suggesting balance. Eight turned sideways is the symbol for infinity. Things are infinite only because they are constantly changing. Eight represents balance amidst ever-present change. As every change creates a new balance/imbalance, Balance is a dance, a continuum of Libra-like mental adjustments to keep your equilibrium.

Balance is dancing in harmony with life (Eight of Wands—Harmony), moving to changes of our inner and outer seasons (Eight of Worlds—Change), and rotating between the right and left hemispheres of the mind

(Eight of Crystals—Synthesis). The "dance of balance" is to move lightly with the wind like the flute, to blend in with the leaves like the chameleon, and to change perspectives like the crystal. The balance of the dancer is a state of mind, an awareness of the "now" and a mental flexibility to act in appropriate response. Balance is treading the edge, able to go this way or that way. Stagnation—Eight of Cups, meaning frozen, dried-up, still, hard, is the death of the dance of life. There is no life without revolution and rhythm. *Keep the mind moving, the body fluid, and the spirit soaring.*

Balance is called "Justice" in the traditional tarot deck. Balance is maintained by the fairness or justice you extend to each aspect of yourself. *Be fair to your mind (bird), heart (cup), body (sphere), and spirit (dancer).*

Like Themis, the Greek goddess of Justice, *you are your own best judge.* We hold the scale of balance in our hand. Balance is composed of two Latin words: *bi* meaning "dual," and *lanx* meaning "scale." The balance between opposites suggests its Rune symbol, *Tiwaz. Tiwaz* represents the Norse god of law and justice, Tyr, who ruled in favor of the right and honorable action. *Follow the "high" road.*

The Kabbalah letter-word for Balance is *Lamed,* meaning "to teach." *Teach yourself (learn) through your continuously changing incoming stimuli—learn through adjusting.* Balance is your teacher.

Your "Balance" Qualities

MENTAL

BIPARTITE MIND (FACE SPLIT DOWN THE MIDDLE): Balance your left and right brain—be analytical and creative, intellectual and dreamy, decisive and reflective; Objectively judge by seeing both sides, pros and cons.

Unevolved: Either overly structured, idealistic, and principled, or too soft headed, blows with the wind, agrees with the last person.

EMOTIONAL

SOFT FACE: Empathize; Have compassion.

Unevolved: Emotional moderation—don't fully express feelings.

PHYSICAL

DANCER: Strive for health, balance, lightness, flexibility, rhythm, discipline, expression.

LIBRA: Watch out for your spinal chord; Posture.

Unevolved: Rigidity.

ACTION IN THE WORLD

THOUGHTFUL REPOSE: Think before acting; Add up pros and cons; Be cautious; Make decisions by weighing and evaluating.

Unevolved: Unable to make adjustments; Cannot act because always in the mind evaluating.

SPIRITUAL WISDOM

VIEW FROM ABOVE: Pay attention to karma; Make sure that your thoughts, speech, and actions are pure; Be above pettiness and jealousy; See from the highest and noblest point of view.

Unevolved: Haughty; Above it all.

Your "Balance" Oracular Universe

ASTROLOGY

LIBRA: You know how to structure; Organize.

VENUS: Follow your aesthetic tastes; Honor your sense of beauty, form, proportion, composition, design.

ALCHEMY

AIR: Be able to constantly make subtle adjustments; Fine tune .

DIAMOND: Stay "adamant" on your high standards.

TIME

BALANCING SCALE: Moments of equipoise.

LIBRA: Your time to make decisions is September-October.

GEOMANCY

CROSS (REPRESENTED BY THE HORIZONTAL POINTS OF THE SWORD AND THE VERTICAL POINTS OF HEAD AND DIAMOND): Find your balance at the midpoint; Centerpoint.

HEIGHTS: Go to vantage points to see the big picture; Total view.

SHAMANISM

HUMMINGBIRD: Maintain position.

AURA

BLUE AND WHITE: Be pure and clear before acting.

PSYCHOMETRY

SAMURAI SWORD: Use your sharp, insightful, piercing intelligence; Be
  honorable and virtuous.
BALANCING SCALE: Be precise, orderly, even-tempered, scrupulous, tidy;
  Maintain equality.

Consulting the Oracle:

"Balance" Way

CONSIDER THE ALTERNATIVES

The principle of the Balance/Justice card is to give all points of view a fair
hearing. Look for alternatives and their pros and cons. An oracle does not
make decisions for you, but points out the various possibilities. This
throws the decision back to you—who are in fact the best judge of what
is right for you. The oracle may offer its advice on a decision, particularly
when the cards and your intuition are very clear and strong. On occasion,
the cards and intuition are ambiguous and uncertain. The responsible
position to assume is to carefully and objectively weigh the pros and cons
for the alternatives.

LOOK FOR IMBALANCES

An oracle is intended to balance a person. It may be appropriate at some
point in a reading to ask the cards what is unbalancing or what can help
create a new balance in a person's life. It is useful to select out a particular
card from the reading or from the deck that you feel is a good balancing
focal point.

Imbalances are revealed in a variety of ways: a particular suit of cards
may be missing from the reading; particular types of cards may dominate,
such as male/dynamic/red cards, or female/passive/blue cards, or the
Child cards.

To evaluate Balance requires seeing many cards so that a balanced
judgment can be rendered. It is best to consider the balance/imbalance
issue near the end of a reading or segment of a reading.

IX

HERMIT

The Mayan *Inward Turning Sage* sculpture is symbolic of the Hermit who shuts out distractions to complete the spiritual pilgrimage and temporal work. The Hermit symbolizes the law of wholeness—to become complete by uniting the highest state of attainment in the material and spiritual realms. The Hermit's number Nine, three Threes, symbolizes this unity of mind, body, and spirit. Nine is the number of completion and wholeness. *Use your work in the world as a spiritual path to achieve your higher destiny.*

The Rune for the Hermit is *Jera*. As the marriage of heaven and earth, *Jera* represents the harvest that comes to us if we work in harmony with nature's laws and with right and honorable intention. *Take your time and do your work right with correct planning, proper sowing, constant nurturing, and timely harvesti*ng.

The Hermit achieves the pinnacle of perfection by following his or her own path with warrior-like steadfastness and courage (Nine of Wands—

Integrity). Through focus and discipline, the Hermit finds the light of illumination at the end of the dark cave of life's trials and tribulations (Nine of Crystals—Narrowness). In touch with the light of the inner self, the Hermit converts personal qualities and potentials into a wheatfield of material harvest and abundance (Nine of Worlds—Harvest). Through the manifestation of these inner gifts, the Hermit enjoys the fruits and fulfillments of the harvest (Nine of Cups—Fulfillment). *Use your inner resources fully.*

Materially secure, the Hermit seeks solitude in order to go inwards. The Greek word root of hermit is *eremites,* meaning "desert and solitude." Through solitary introspection, the Hermit journeys into the inner temple to live in union with the divine. *Meditate.*

The Hermit's *I Ching* Hexagram is # 20, *Kuan* /Contemplation (View):

> *To apprehend the mysterious and divine laws of life,*
> *and by means of the profoundest inner concentration*
> *to give expression to these laws in their own person. (I Ching, p. 83)*

As the inner voyager, the Hermit is mythologically associated with the Pilgrim, Monk, Sage, Sadhu, Yogi, and Ascetic.

The Hermit's Kabbalah letter-name is *Yod,* which means the "open hand." In touch with the "higher self," the Hermit touches others. The Hermit brings the higher powers through the hands to heal and guide. Complete and whole, the Hermit is a way-shower and guide to others— truly the wise old owl. *Use your own way of healing to touch others, to reveal and heal.*

Your "Hermit" Qualities

MENTAL

CLOSED EYES OF HERMIT: Contemplate; Be thoughtful; Study and research in depth; Keep focused; Concentrate.

Unevolved: CLOSED EYES: Narrow minded; Closed; Fixed.

EMOTIONAL

CONTEMPLATIVE HERMIT: Be serious and sober; Keep steady and even; Emotionally self-sufficient.

Unevolved: CLOSED EYES: Unexpressive; Fearful.

PHYSICAL

CLOSED EYES OF HERMIT: Relax; Rest; Sleep; Regenerate and heal the body.
VIRGO: Pay attention to your stomach, intestines, and digestion.
Unevolved: Physically hard on yourself; Lacking physical play.

ACTION IN THE WORLD

HERMIT: Focus on your work; Say "no" to passing diversions; Enjoy
   solitude; Be self-sufficient, even self-employed.
Unevolved: Perfectionist to a fault; Secretive.

SPIRITUAL WISDOM

CLOSED EYES OF HERMIT: Seek the truth (Who am I?); Gain knowledge
   through the laboratory of the self; Know that self-knowledge is
   knowledge of the world outside; Seek your inner riches; Defend
   your inner self and your integrity; Shut out the undesirable.
Unevolved: Running away from the world.

Your "Hermit" Oracular Universe

ASTROLOGY

VIRGO: Complete; Be patient; Be prudent.
MOON: Remember your dreams; Dive into the subconscious, the past.

ALCHEMY

EARTH: You are fertile; Grow; Be down to earth and practical.
GOLD: Seek perfection; Know that you are golden.

TIME

VIRGO: Harvest in August-September and at completion times; Fall;
   Full moon; Nines.

GEOMANCY

CLOSED EYES: Explore your inner spaces.
CAVES: Seek isolated spots like deserts and deep spots like caves.
INDIAN PUEBLO, MAYAN SCULPTURE, EGYPTIAN FRESCO: Investigate ancient
   civilizations and their practices; Archaeology.

SHAMANISM

SQUIRREL: Be insured; Take care of security; Be prepared.

SNAKE AND REPTILES: Revitalize through hibernation (rest) and
    completions (shedding of skin); Learn to heal yourself; Confront
    demons.

WHEAT: Live simply; Attend to the essentials, the basics; Eat
    nutritiously; Get on the land; Follow the principles of nature.

AURA

GOLDISH BROWN (FALL COLORS): Harvest what is ripe.

PSYCHOMETRY

HIEROGLYPH: Inscribe your insights, your successes and failures. Make
    the past serve the future, be a scribe, historian, preserver of the
    past.

CHIROGNOMY

KNOTTY HANDS: Philosophize.

Consulting the Oracle:

"Hermit" Way

READ FOR YOURSELF

Integral to your Hermit-like self-sufficiency is the ability to perceive
where you are in life, and to make critical life-direction decisions by
yourself. The oracle of tarot helps you do this. Reading the card-symbols
for yourself is difficult, however. Because of your emotional closeness to
yourself and your emotional investment in your life situations, it is
difficult to tell whether you are interpreting the oracle accurately, or
whether you are being unduly generous or unfair to yourself. This
problem dissolves when the following principle is understood:

> *In reading for yourself, it is not important what particular*
> *cards you select. What is important is your reactions to the*
> *cards. The card-symbols are simply catalysts to your true feelings.*
> *Allow your feelings to be the answer for you, and not the cards per se.*

To be prudent and complete like the Hermit, you may want to read
whatever card appears both positively and negatively, for all the meanings it could possibly have. You will know in your heart of hearts which
interpretation is true for you. Reading for yourself is invaluable for
developing self-sensitivity and integrity--for seeing what is right for you.

X

FORTUNE

Fortune represents abundance on all levels of being. *Fortune comes from following your passions* (Ten of Cups—Passion). Your strongest feeling is where your talent lies. *Fortune is the manifestation of your talents so that you are rewarded in return* (Ten of Worlds—Reward).

To follow your passions and strive for the "Big Apple" is risky business. Fortune is like the roulette wheel—it is a gamble on which we place our hopes and dreams. We never know whether our dreams are just that—pipedreams or delusions (Ten of Crystals—Delusion). Like the thirsty person in the desert, we are compelled to search for water, whether it turns out to be a mirage or not. Only by risking such misfortune do we grow. To seek our fortune is to grow (Ten of Wands—Growth). *Like the giant redwood that stretches itself to find the light, extend yourself to reach your own destiny.*

Fortune is the realization of your destiny or fate, which is what the Latin origin of the word "fortune" (*fortuna*) means. Good luck, meaning the realization of your destiny, comes with *working hard* to realize your passions and visions, and with the *courage* to reach for the stars.

The Rune for Fortune is *Naudhiz*. This N-rune represents fate—good luck and bad. the principal lesson of the Rune is *go with fate and do not strive against it*. Like the Fortune wheel, be able to turn with the unexpected.

The blackamoor in the Fortune card who carries the "Treasures of Dresden" symbolizes the law of prosperity. Good fortune is the outcome of being receptive to the wealth of opportunities provided by the universe, and to be able to turn these gifts into realities. Treat everything as an opportunity. By doing so with an optimistic mind, fearless heart, and sense of egoless service to the planet, this good karma brings success and reward on all levels of life.

Fortune's number is Ten, which means "perfection." The number Ten reduces to the number One, which implies "perfect unity." This sense of wholeness comes with the completion of one's work, which is symbolized by the number Nine (Hermit). Perfection is the sum of being number Four, the Emperor's perfection of the worldly life; number Three, the Empress' perfection of emotional life; number Two, the Priestess' perfection of spiritual life; and number One, the Magician's perfection of mental life. The sum of these numbers is Ten—perfect. Add this total to the Hermit's number (Nine) and the total Nineteen is derived, the number of the Sun Card, which reduces to Ten (One plus Nine) and to One (One plus Zero), perfect again.

The Kabbalah letter for Fortune, *Kaph*, means "curved" and suggests a "grasping hand." It is symbolized by the gold hand on the wheel in the Fortune Card. The hand grasps the gold ring of Fortune. It says, "I've got it!" Indeed, we do have it. Perfection and fortune are yours; all you have to do is grab it and claim it.

Self-recognition of your goldenness requires clarity within. The *I Ching* Hexagram for Fortune is #55, *Feng*/Abundance:

> *Clarity within, movement without—*
> *this produces greatness and abundance. (I Ching, p. 213)*

Inner stillness is like the hub of the wheel. It is the quiescent center of your being which is perfect. To find that inner core is to tap your inner resources from which you create your external worldly fortune.

Fortune's planet is Jupiter, which is seen directly behind the blackamoor on the card. The largest planet in our solar system, Jupiter symbolizes abundance. *Fortune comes with Jupiter-like action of expansion—* of becoming bigger and better. Fortune is often associated with the mythological Roman god, Jupiter, the bringer of prosperity, and with such contemporary archetypes as the "high roller," and the "big wheel."

Your "Fortune" Qualities

MENTAL

DIAMONDS: Use your creative imagination; Consider many ideas and viewpoints; Keep a bright outlook.

Unevolved: Delusions of grandeur.

EMOTIONAL

ROLLER COASTER RIDER: Thrill seek; Fun love; Passion live.

Unevolved: Unable to accept periods of boredom, dullness, routine.

PHYSICAL

DANCER ON WHEEL AND MATADOR: Be active and move; Be flexible; Be balanced; Breathe; Spin.

Unevolved:

WHEEL AS STOMACH: Consumptive, as in overeating.

SPINNING WHEELS: Use of stimulants to speed up and heighten experience.

ACTION IN THE WORLD

GOLD HAND SPINNING WHEEL OF FORTUNE: Revolutionize and transform; Take gambles; Be a risk taker; Be opportunistic; Recycle; Be entrepreneurial.

Unevolved: SHOW DANCER: Ostentatious; Conspicuous consumtion; Showy.

SPIRITUAL WISDOM

HAND ON FORTUNE WHEEL: Get a handle on your destiny (You may not be able to absolutely control the external world and its events but have a handle on your inner self-fortunes); Recognize what thoughts and actions create success; Know the law of karma—cause and effect; Move with changes; Follow the circular flow of life, of receiving and giving, of creating and letting go.

Unevolved: MATERIAL ABUNDANCE: Materialistic to the point where success and, in fact, all of life is measured in terms of material possessions and worldly achievements.

Your "Fortune" Oracular Universe

ASTROLOGY

JUPITER: Use all available resources and energies to create; Synergize.

ALCHEMY

AIR AND EARTH: Manifest your ideas; Earth your visions.
GOLD: Seek your highest; Desire only your best.

TIME

GOOD LUCK: Feel the right time.

GEOMANCY

GOOD LUCK: Feel the right place.

SHAMANISM

PEACOCK: Do not be afraid to be colorful, flamboyant, and expansive; Strut your stuff.
BUTTERFLY: Be light and fly; Be agile; Give and take.
GRAPES: Harvest.

AURA

GOLDEN: Be sunny, optimistic, positive, confident; Believe in yourself; Trust.

PSYCHOMETRY

WHEEL: Convert inputs into outputs; Wheel and deal; Spin things around; Convert; Turn it over.
TRAY: Offer your riches to the world; Philanthropy.

CHIROGNOMY

"MIXED" TYPE OF GOLD HAND: Anticipate and adapt to whatever trend arises in your field.

Consulting the Oracle:

"Fortune" Way

FORTUNE TELLING

Foretelling the future is never certain. Future projections are only that—projections. Reading the future is assessing odds and probabilities. Once the probable future has been foreseen through the cards, it has already begun to change. The consciousness of the viewer of the future naturally alters the future. In physics this is called the "Heisenberg Principle"—to get close to and see an object is to change it through our own energy.

A deterministic reading that supposedly foretells the future with absolute certainty is the "old tarot." It is akin to the "old physics"—before Einstein. We now know that reality is relative to the point of view of the viewer. It is our choice as to how we view it. There is choice. Deterministic readings deny choice. Without choice we might as well return to feudal times, which is exactly where the old tarot originated.

The only phenomena that can be foretold with certainty are the universal principles of life that are represented in the cards. A reading can never be wrong if it is couched in these principles, such as growth, change, creativity, love, learning, etc. Readers go wrong in predicting material, worldly events and their time frames. That a "tall, dark stranger will enter your life on X date" is taking a real chance with the odds of probability.

Just as we cannot predict the future with certainty, we cannot control our worldly life with absolute predictability. Our worldly life is a spinning wheel of fortune that brings its successes and failures, some of which are out of our hands. We can control our attitude toward the material events of our life. We can insure that we have a "wheel-of-fortune mentality," which is a prosperous and opportunistic perspective.

BE OPPORTUNISTIC

Tarot readings teach us to see every event in our lives as an "opportunity." Every card selected in a reading is an opportunity card, as is everything in our life. Emphasize this in your readings. Be explicit and ask the cards what is the opportunity for this situation or that circumstance. The Fortune mentality sees everything as opportunity; there is a wealth of opportunity that exists every moment. It is this attitude that helps us create our wheel of fortune on the material, physical plane of existence. Our consciousness creates our reality.

EMPHASIZE THE INNER SELF

In readings it is vital to emphasize your inner richness or poverty. A dark mind creates a dark reality. A golden attitude creates a golden life. It is far more important to dwell on the inner self rather than predict a worldly event. By doing so, you give yourself the tools and principles to work with to forge the future. This principle of reading goes back to the Hierophant—every reading is a teaching rather than a prediction.

XI

STRENGTH

As Leo and the Lion, Strength represents rulership and control, which translates into the law of self-dominion. This means the full and free but controlled expression of mind, heart, body, and spirit in yin and yang forms. Strength is total living. *Live in full accord with the undiluted multiplicity of your being.*

Strength's number Eleven, as double One's , symbolizes your *confident and self-assured expression of the Magician abilities* (number One). Following Fortune (number Ten), *act upon Fortune's attainments and resources.*

The digits of number Eleven added together create Two—symbolizing dualistic expression, yin and yang. This dualistic versatility is what gives "Strength" its strength. This is in accord with the Kabbalah letter-name for Strength, *Teth*, which means "snake." Like the snake, Strength represents the fiery yang quality of the snake-like kundalini energy source, and also the watery yin flexibility of the supple snake. The Strength archetype has the capacity to destroy (poisonous quality of the snake) and the the power to regenerate and heal (snake's ability to shed old skin), again dual qualities of the snake.

The origin of the word, "strength," is from the Old English, *strengthu*. The mythological "strong men" Hercules and Samson are raw physical yang representations of the Strength archetype. More refined yin mythological figures associated with this archetype are the Egyptian cat-goddesses Bast and Sekhet. The feline qualities of Strength were related in Egyptian mythology to Isis the priestess and moon goddess. Interestingly, the number Eleven is associated with the Priestess (number Two) in the Tarot. Strength, like the Priestess, possesses cat-like sensitivity, patience, and ability to see in the dark (symbolic of revealing insight). *Be like a cat.* The "lion-tamer" is an appropriate popular mythological aspect of Strength, for it represents the ability to harness our cat-like qualities. In the traditional tarot, Strength is depicted by a woman holding the jaws of the lion, symbolic of taming your leonine powers and drives.

The Rune for Strength is *Elhaz*. This Z-rune represents protection and victory—attributes of Strength. It is through a mystical communication with animals that the power of the human spirit is preserved. *Find your power or medicine animal that gives you strength.*

The "taming" of our nature represented by Strength corresponds with the *I Ching* Hexagram # 26, *Ta Ch'u* / The Taming Power of the Great.

This hexagram is composed of the two trigrams, *Ken* and *Ch'ien*. *Ken* means "keeping still" (patience), which produces great power. *Ch'ien* points to strong creative power. There is restraint (taming) here of power, and yet the time of obstruction is past. The energy long dammed up by inhibition forces its way out and achieves great success.

Like its ruling planet, Leo the sun, Strength represents a coming out, a breaking through. Strength in its sun-like essence is the creative source. It must be strong to force through denser and duller energies. Strength stands out and is felt by others in its drive to give new life.

Your "Strength" Qualities

MENTAL

LION : State your ideas vigorously; Hold your ideas strongly; Think
   boldly.
Unevolved: TERRITORIAL LION: Headstrong to the point of
   inflexibility; Rigid; Dogmatic.

EMOTIONAL

FLYING BIRD'S EXPRESSION: Feel intensely; Pronounce your feelings.
Unevolved: UNEXPRESSIVE FACE: Emotionally insensitive.

PHYSICAL

LION: Be strong—muscular but supple; Fulfill your animal appetites
and drives; Follow your instincts; Sense; Taste.
Unevolved: KING LION: Physical show-off; Vain.

ACTION IN THE WORLD

PARTHENON: Build; Construct with your creative energy; Use your ego
to build in your name; Establish your territory; Act majestically;
Build for longevity.
Unevolved: LION: Exploitive; Selfish; Domineering; Oppressive;
Intimidating.

SPIRITUAL WISDOM

HAND SUPPORTING FACE: Give yourself self-consent; Be yourself; Accept
yourself and control yourself.
Unevolved: CAT: Succumbs to passing physical pleasures to the
point of overindulgence; Not in control of lower chakra drives;
Pride of ego.

Your "Strength" Oracular Universe

ASTROLOGY

LEO: Be courageous; Be creative; Be dignified and outrageous.
SUN: Exercise your power and influence; You can make others feel
great or small.

ALCHEMY

FIRE AND WATER: You are volatile; Changeable; Explosive; Enigmatic.

TIME

LEO: July and August are your times of great courage.
BREAKING OUT OF EGG: It is time to destroy/break through and create/form.

GEOMANCY

STONE LIONS: Go to your place of strength—your power spot.

MONUMENTAL STRUCTURES: Find the place where you can make a state-
    ment; Get your point across; Have impact; Make a mark; Leave a
    legacy and a lasting impression.

SHAMANISM

LION: Be natural yet kingly; Hunt; Provide; Organize the social order.

BUTTERFLY: Do not be afraid to change; Be strong regardless of size and
    form; In spite of your fragility you are strong.

PINK FLOWER: Be unafraid to stand out; Be colorful; Be noticed; Be
    sexual; Act erotically.

AURA

REDS: Show your fire; Be upbeat; Act now.

PSYCHOMETRY

MASK: Be versatile; Act; Be able to play different roles; The world's a
    stage for you.

EGYPTIAN GOD "SHU" HEADREST: Bring order into your life and structure to
    your dreams.

CHIROGNOMY

CONIC HAND SHAPE: You are an artist in some way; Use your imagina-
    tion; Act creatively on your impulses.

Consulting the Oracle:

"Strength" Way

AFFIRM YOUR INDIVIDUALITY

A tarot reading is meant to confer strength by affirming all of your
individual qualities. Tarot gives you strength by helping you see your
many qualities through its rich and diverse symbolism. Each card and
symbol is an affirmation that declares, like the calling of the smallest bird,
that "I am!"—that I do possess all the virtues of the universe.

Keep the Strength Card in mind during your consultation of the oracle, and your individualities will be constantly affirmed. Strength means being yourself, being authentic, which is to follow and express your own desires, your own feelings, your own passions, your own beliefs, and your own instincts. To be yourself means to have cat-like self-perceptivity—to be sensitive to what you are feeling at every moment. This is uncensored self-observation. The neutral observer is your "higher self" which naturally adjusts your behavior. Nonjudgmental self-awareness is the light but controlling hand that you have on yourself. This is symbolized by the hand on the lion in the Strength Card.

Being yourself means knowing yourself. To know yourself, be like an animal, do what comes naturally to you without engaging in self-doubt. Being yourself is self-aware, uncensored, spontaneous behavior.

XII

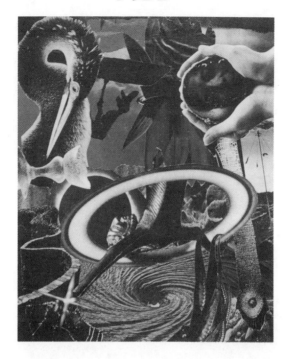

HANGED MAN

The upside down hanging man, the Hanged Man, represents the universal law of reversal. *Do the opposite of what is ordinarily expected to achieve victory and you will victor.* Turn the Hanged Man card around and it becomes a symbol of victory and liberation. *Salvation is attained by passive surrender rather than by assertiveness and forceful resistance.*

Surrender is represented by your complete *letting go of self-aspiration and personal ego.* This is symbolized by the Hanged Man's identification with the sea and water, which is the Hanged Man's Kabbalah letter-name, *Mem.* In the ocean, we can let go. In plunging to the depths, a metaphorical death is experienced. However, death by drowning in the oceanic collective unconscious brings new life.

Rising back to the top, rebirth comes in its own time and cannot be rushed by your own timetable of egotistic desire. The Hanged Man lives in accord with the I Ching Hexagram #5, *Hsu*/Waiting:

> *The gift of food comes in its own time, and for this one must wait. . .*
> *We should not worry and seek to shape the future by interfering in things*
> *before the time is ripe. . . . Only a strong man can stand up to his fate. . .*
> *This strength shows itself in uncompromising truthfulness with himself.*
> *It is only when we have the courage to face things exactly as they are,*
> *without any sort of self-deception or illusion, that a light will develop out*
> *of events, by which the path to succcess may be recognized.*
> (I Ching, pp. 24-25)

So, be patient, accept yourself, and know that by understanding your human limitations success will come. Face your self-deceptions. Look at your "shadow side," at what you have hidden.

By diving into the "dark night of the soul," you turn the shadow into light. You gain dominion over the unseen forces that were controlling your life.

The Hanged Man represents karmic burdens. *Give in to the cross you must bear,and your karmic challenge is completed and transmuted into strength and victory.* The Hanged Man is symbolic of the mythological Odin and his later manifestation as Christ. Their wisdom and power was attained through giving in by self-sacrifice. Through ego surrender and acceptance of our fate, we are redeemed and resurrected. By hanging upside down from the "tree of life" or by immersing ourselves in the purifying waters, conversion and rebirth are possible.

As number Twelve, the Hanged Man symbolizes the circular order of things (12 months) and the sense of going around and around on the wheel of life. This gives you a feeling of stasis, of going nowhere on a treadmill. *In understanding and accepting the circular nature of life, however, you are ultimately taken off the wheel. Saved, at last!*

Your "Hanged Man" Qualities

MENTAL

HANGING UPSIDE DOWN: Take an opposite point of view; Turn your
thoughts around; Keep your beliefs on hold, in suspension; Sacrifice
your ego identification with your ideas.

Unevolved:

HANGING: Clinging to beliefs as security blankets; Fixed.

SUN IN ECLIPSE: Self-oppression by only looking at the negative.

EMOTIONAL

HANGING CHRIST: Sacrifice your own desires; Give in to your feelings.
Unevolved:
> HEAD HUNG DOWN: Despondent; Despairing.
> SUN IN ECLIPSE: Feeling dark.
> WHIRLPOOL: Emotionally suffocated and drowned out.
> BROKEN DRINKING GLASS: Debauch and indulgence to the point of emotional stagnation; Numbness of feeling.
> MARTYRDOM: "Poor me"; Self-pity; Drowned in one's own sorrow.

PHYSICAL

HANGING: Stretching; Yoga; Relaxing.
Unevolved:
> ECLIPSED SUN AND PITIFUL DOG: Lack of energy; Fatigue; "Dogging it."
> EXPOSED RIBS OF CHRIST AND DOG: Weak; Ill-health; Lack of proper nutrition.
> BROKEN DRINKING GLASS: Alcoholism; Drug abuse; Chemical dependency.

ACTION IN THE WORLD

UPSIDE DOWN: Be unconventional; Opposite to the standard way.
HANGING CHRIST: Personally sacrifice in order to help others; Give; Let it be; Hang it up; Accept suspensions.
Unevolved: WHIRLPOOL: Let things slide and go downhill; Feel suicidal and a failure.

SPIRITUAL WISDOM

CRUCIFIXION: Self-sacrifice; Self-abnegate; Be compassionate; Forgive; Transcend; Look to the higher powers; Out of body soul flight.
Unevolved: Escape responsibility.

Your "Hanged Man" Oracular Universe

ASTROLOGY

NEPTUNE: Do not be deluded and deceived by appearances, for there is calm under the turbulent surface of life.
SUN IN ECLIPSE: Explore your inner self; Nonaction in the world.

ALCHEMY

WATER: Go with the flow, and there is an easy and smooth transition to regeneration.

OBSIDIAN: There is light in the dark; Things only appear dark.

TIME

HANGING SUSPENDED: This is a time of limbo, which presages reversal and change.

GEOMANCY

WATER: Hang out near oceans, springs, lakes, rivers, ponds, puddles, swamps.

ENCIRCLEMENTS (COBWEB, WALL, SATURN RING): Seek confined, enclosed, constricted, dark spaces for your inward search into the light of your soul.

SHAMANISM

WATER BIRD: Dive into the abyss, into the unknown, into the universal unconscious, and into the personal subconscious to be nourished and reborn.

OCTOPUS: You feel caught by forces beyond your control.

LOTUS: Like the lotus which grows out of the dark mud, unfold from the "seeming" darkness of your own life.

AURA

BLUE: When you have the blues, feel the blues.

PSYCHOMETRY

OBSIDIAN MIRROR: Look at yourself.

Consulting the Oracle:

"Hanged Man" Way

WHEN IN DOUBT HANG OUT, TIME WILL TELL

The purpose of tarot is to help you see the truth about yourself—in effect, to surrender like the Hanged Man to your true nature. Sometimes it is difficult to see the truth through the cards, for you are somehow not prepared to understand their message. Whenever this occurs, follow the advice and behavioral style of the Hanged Man: Let it be. Don't try to force your way into understanding. Patiently hang out with the cards. Time will reveal their meaning. Suspend your interpretation until it crystallizes. In the letting go, a space is cleared in your consciousness that allows the seed of understanding to germinate and eventually break through.

SEEING THE "SHADOW" SIDE

"Evolved" and "Unevolved" Interpretations

Every card, like every phenomenon in life, has an evolved and unevolved side. How do you interpret cards to reflect this reality? As an example of how to do this, let us suppose the Hanged Man appears in a reading. How to interpret? Consider the evolved side of this personality Archetype— a person who looks for the truth of the situation (the facts) and then accepts them. The implicit warning of this card, however, is indicated by the unevolved side of the Hanged Man personality type—a person who feels the situation is bad, but does not really look at it, and then becomes mentally, emotionally, physically, and spiritually dragged down by the seeming terribleness of it all. An accurate "reading" of the person and situation would include both of these possible scenarios. Emphasize how the positive Hanged Man is the possibility to keep in the mind's eye and to work toward. Emphasize the negative Hanged Man as a warning that needs to be heeded.

Reversed Cards

In the traditional tarot, negatives or reverse aspects of cards are indicated by a card chosen upside down, which would indicate the opposite meaning of the card. There is nothing wrong with this method. It does limit, however, the flexibility and possibility of seeing any and every card from both an evolved and an unevolved point of view—which is the way life really works.

Block Cards

Another way of dealing with the negative aspects of life through the tarot is to deliberately build into a reading a position or question that asks, "What is the negative(s) of a situation?" The tendency in a reading is to get carried away with a spate of fabulous cards. In the interest of true-to-life accuracy, for life is generally not always such a bed of roses, be the Hanged Man: Ask, "What are the hang-ups or blocks that might be confronted in the situation?" Having done your "realism" work, then put on the hat of the Magician. Show a way through the block. Maybe the way will be through the way of the Hanged Man—simply to see the block as accurately as possible. In this kind of Hanged Man assessment, a way out or a solution naturally presents itself over time. More often than not, surrendering to the reality opens the doorway to a new and "better" reality, which once again inherently carries the possibility of negative outcomes.

XIII

DEATH

Death symbolizes the law of impermanence . All things must come to an end. Death's number, Thirteen, signals the ending of the stasis associated with Twelve. It represents the death of the old order. As Scorpio, this death is a life-giving transformation. Like the snake, a Scorpio symbol, Death means a shedding of the old (skin) to be reborn. *Shed what is dead in your life.*

Death is a liberating metamorphosis. It is represented by the *I Ching* Hexagram #59, *Huan*/Dispersion (Dissolution):

> *Wind blowing over water disperses it, dissolving it into foam and mist.*
> (*I Ching, p. 227*)

Death is the dissolution of obstruction, a freeing up, the breakup of blockage and constriction which is represented in the tarot by the Hanged Man. *Free yourself from what is holding you back and hanging you up.*

Death is a renewal, a rebirth on all levels of being. In this way, it is like the rising Phoenix, the mythological Scorpio bird symbol of regeneration. Death is the new life associated with its Kabbalah letter-name, *Nun*, meaning "fish." The fish is symbolic of prolific generative power that spawns new life in the darkness (death) of the seas (unconscious). The Hanged Man represents the submergence into the sea, and Death the rising out of the sea to new life.

The Rune for Death is *Berkano*. This B-rune stands for the birch goddess who represents the "rites of passage" in life. To move from birth to youth to adulthood to death and to rebirth is always a death and liberation. *Do not be afraid to die, for it means moving on , which signals maturation and growth.*

Death in the tarot, and in general, has received an unfortunate connotation. It is frequently associated with the skeletal "Grim Reaper," (also known as Cronus, Father Time, Saturn). Another horrific representation of Death is the Hindu Kali with her necklace of skulls, protruding tongue of blood, and belt of bloody hands. These concepts of death make it out to be a painful cutting away of life. What it really means is the deliberate and *conscious cutting out of things* which have become dead, heavy, and stagnant. This process is symbolized in the *Voyager* by the Heron eating the crayfish and by the sharp, knife-like beak of the New Guinea death mask. *Cut away excesses, simplify, get to the core essence.*

Another concept of death is a *gentle letting go or passive shedding.* This natural, evolutionary process is represented by the snake shedding its skin, the changing color of the leaves, the river (the Snake River, in fact) letting out into the cosmos, and the turn of day and sun into night and moon (as seen at the Dead Sea, in fact).

Your "Death" Qualities

MENTAL

SNAKE SHEDDING OLD SKIN: Let go of restrictive, oppressive, limiting attitudes and beliefs; Let go of dead, outdated ideas; Let go of excessive theorization and thinking; Rid yourself of mental clutter and complexity.

Unevolved: BLACK AND WHITE: Fixed belief that things are black and white; Intolerance of ambiguity and gray areas.

EMOTIONAL

FALLING LEAVES AND SNAKE SHEDDING SKIN: Let go of outlived emotional
   attachments, of feelings from the past that have kept you confined;
   Release your feelings through expressing them; Let your emotions
   out; Purify yourself.
Unevolved: COLD BLOODED: Heartless; Cruel; Cold; Vicious.

PHYSICAL

SNAKE RIVER: Shed impurities out of the body; Liquid fast; Release
   tensions; Relax; Let go.
SCORPIO: Organs of elimination, reproduction, and sexuality.
Unevolved: DEATH-LIKE: Stiff; Rigid.

ACTION IN THE WORLD

SNAKE SHEDDING SKIN AND LEAVES FALLING: End; Quit; Leave and create a
   space for new opportunities to come in.
Unevolved: Security-bound through possessions, place, familiarity;
   Fear of change.

SPIRITUAL WISDOM

DEATH MASK SPECTER: Accept the ever-present specter of death and
   impermanence; Live fully in the moment, knowing that every
   moment may be the last, knowing that you are being devoured
   daily by forces greater than yourself.
Unevolved: Fear of death; Self-destructive.

Your "Death" Oracular Universe

ASTROLOGY

SCORPIO: You have power to transform and regenerate through change.

ALCHEMY

WATER: Adapt; Change form but retain your essence.
DEAD SEA: Salt—Dissolves and kills; Dries up.
          —Purifies (preservative)
          —Revives (smelling salts)
          —Heals (Epsom salts)
          —Cleans out (mineral salts, catharsis)
          —Death gives zest to life, for without the continual specter
           of death, we languish (seasoning salt)

TIME

SCORPIO: Finish in October-November; Fall; Sunset; Endings.

GEOMANCY

EXPANSES: Seek out vast expanses, such as oceans; High skies; Desert.

SHAMANISM

SNAKE: Periodically hibernate (quiet rest period that brings renewal).
LEAF: Create new life by transforming (light into food by photosynthesis and carbon monoxide into oxygen).

AURA

BLACK: Void; Empty.
WHITE: Void; Lighten.

PSYCHOMETRY

BOAT: Change by moving from one place to another; Cross over; Go with the flow; Follow the path of least resistance.

Consulting the Oracle:

"Death" Way

CUT THROUGH MIND CLUTTER

An aspect of Death is the process of cutting through the ponderous conceptual baggage of notions and beliefs about yourself that you have accumulated over your lifetime. These concepts are often in conflict and keep you in a state of conflict. The mind endlessly invents theories and explanations that are fun to play with but are often confusing and dead ends.

Tarot, like the sharpness of the Death Mask's nose beak, cuts through this confusion created by the intellect. The pictorial symbols of the tarot very simply and directly penetrate into the heart of your life situation. The messages in the tarot are not clouded by a specialized vocabulary or an elaborate system of psychological theory. The tarot lays bare what you know about yourself in your heart and soul. You get the picture. Like liberating death, the tarot frees you from the self-confusion created by the thinking mind. Mind-stuff keeps you trapped in the mind, where you spin forever in circles but never get anywhere. Tarot helps you get out of the mind maze.

READ WITH YOUR "GUT"

The next time you select a card, do not ponder it. Let it speak to you immediately and directly. Do not look up what it says in the guidebook or in your own mental file of meanings. Simply look and feel. Carry the image with you but not all the words. Let the picture be the talk. You will find that such an approach has great power. The image will strike you at deeper levels than will the mental meaning. It will be absorbed into your visceral and subconscious levels of awareness. You will be moved from the gut level up.

You cannot select many cards at a single sitting using this process. Let a single card work its magic. Too many cards give too much information and too much dissipation of the energy. Experiment and see how a one-card, one-second reading works for you.

XIV

ART

Art, represented by Athena, the Greek patron goddess of the arts, symbolizes the law of creativity—being a creative artist in all aspect of being and in all endeavors of worldly life. *Consider yourself an artist in all phases of life.*

Creativity is an alchemical art that first requires the dissolution or death of old forms. The separated new elements can then recombine into a higher synthesis. Reintegration is the keyword in the Art Archetype. The Indo-European root word for art is *ar* which means "to fit together." Art's number, Fourteen, represents fusion, putting together a new order after the number Thirteen dissolution of the old number Twelve order.

Fourteen is really a Four number (Ten plus Four), which stands for foundation represented by the four cornerstones. The Kabbalah letter-name for Art is *Samekh*, meaning "tent peg or prop," which is the equivalent to the foundation of a house. In this case, the foundation of the self is represented by the union of the four element/attributes of fire-spirit, air-mind, water-emotions, and earth-body. *Combine, put together, integrate, synthesize.*

121

The mythological correspondences with Art are the Sagittarius centaur and archer, which again emphasize the integrative aspect of the Archetype. Composed of half-man and half-horse (synthesis of opposites), the centaur shoots his three-headed arrow (synthesis again). The flight of the arrow from the bow replicates the curvature of the rainbow, another symbol of Sagittarius. The rainbow is a weaving (synthesis) of different colors. Hence, also, Art's association with the Mayan goddess, Ixchel the "weaver," and with the spider.

It is by *weaving together the opposites* that Art becomes the creative and integrative process it is. The *I Ching* Hexagram for Art is #38, *K'uei/* Opposition.

> *As the flame which burns upward and the lake which seeps downward,*
> *the oppositions when reconciled bring about*
> *the creation and reproduction of life. (I Ching, p. 148)*

The Rune for Art is *Dagaz*, which literally means "day." This D-rune is the first and last light of day, sunrise and twilight, and thus represents the union of day and night into a creative synthesis. *Go into the night, your subconscious and dream world, and integrate these visions into your day world through action.*

Creativity, like the revolutionary Sagittarian, is revolutionary. It is revolutionary because it weaves new elements together into a new dynamic wholeness. Art is a transformative Archetype. By being creative like the Art Archetype, you are re-created in the process. To be creative requires using all your inner resources. In that act, all the elements of your inner self are woven together. *Create and become naturally whole and healed.*

Your "Art" Qualities

MENTAL

LIGHTNING BOLTS IN THE MIND OF ATHENA: Imagine; Envision; Dream.
Unevolved: Caught up in the separate elements so that you cannot see how it all fits together; Small vision; Myopia; Narrow-minded.

EMOTIONAL

OPEN HANDS POURING OUT MERCURY: Communicate your feelings; Pour out your emotions; Express the range of feelings: Fire—Passion and Anger; Cool Blue—Stoicism and Peace; Rainbow—Love and Joy; Rain—Tears and Sorrow.
Unevolved: Emotionally fragmented; Not whole.

PHYSICAL

HANDS: Use your natural physical aptitudes to manifest ideas and inspirations; Act on your dreams.

SAGITTARIUS: Thighs.

Unevolved: Physically disjointed.

ACTION IN THE WORLD

ATHENA (PATRON GODDESS OF THE ARTS): You possess a talent, a genius, an art. Strive to be a creative artist in all domains—work, home, relationships, finances; Create through recreation.

Unevolved: Ignorant of your art or genius.

SPIRITUAL WISDOM

BASKET WEAVING: Become whole like the spirit by the creative process—the integration of all faculties: fire-vision creating airy ideas about which there are watery feelings and finally manifestation through physical hands.

Unevolved: Being reactive instead of creative.

Your "Art" Oracular Universe

ASTROLOGY

SAGITTARIUS: Explore; Search out; Seek the cutting edge.

ALCHEMY

FIRE: Expand dynamically; Go with your drives; Be a catalyst, firebrand, revolutionary.

MERCURY (QUICKSILVER): Combine unlikely partners and elements; Swiftly communicate your vision—that is where your intuition and genius is.

TIME

SAGITTARIUS: November-December is your time of creativity.

MIX OF DIFFERENT ELEMENTS: In the dawn and twilight you are creative.

GEOMANCY

BOUNDLESS: The world is your studio.

SHAMANISM

SPIDER: Weave and consume; Do not be afraid to gather strength
    through a creative "act of power."

HERON: Take flights of imagination; Soar.

ORCHID: Your art is naturally exotic, sophisticated, and aesthetic.

AURA

RAINBOW: See, think, and dream in color; Inspire others; Heal; Resolve
    conflict; Harmonize; Synergize.

PSYCHOMETRY

BASKET WEAVING: Make a symbol for yourself and you create yourself.

CALDRON: Purify by burning down the old structures to create anew.

CHIROGNOMY

FIRM, BROAD LIFELINE: Your zest for life comes by being creative and
    recreative; Create, create, and create.

Consulting the Oracle:

"Art" Way

SELF-CREATE

Like art, tarot is an alchemical process. Certain elements are distilled
from a symbol and mixed together with other symbolic elements (or other
cards) to create a synthesis of view. This synthesis is a weaving together
not only of symbols but of your various faculties. The portrait is a product
of your intuitive sense (the caldron of inner light and fire) that moves up
like lightning to strike the mind with an idea or vision that has power
because it is loaded with feeling and value (water in the sky). This
inspiration is physically expressed by hand and voice to form a rainbow
weaving that has life, texture, and color.

   The process of tarot, being a creative act, is naturally self-integrating.
All the inner elements of mind, body, heart, and spirit are united.
Through every reading you are created anew. That is why consulting the
oracle of tarot is such a refreshing and healing experience. To be
reinvigorated is fun. Tarot is recreation or re-creation through this
creative healing quality.

If you feel the need to renew yourself, pull out your cards. You don't even have to try. You will naturally be regenerated and reborn.

RECOMBINE

Upon completion of a reading, an effective process for yourself is to rearrange and recombine the symbols or cards into a different symbolic pattern. This follows the style of the Art Archetypal personality, which is to break down the old and recombine into a new order. The new synthesis will reveal a whole new set of patterns and dynamics. It presents another face, a new window that adds light to your original portrait.

XV

DEVIL'S PLAY

See good and evil as the same; both are merely God's play.

—VIVEKANANDA

Devil spelled backwards is "lived." Devil's Play means to live fully and joyously, and to work and play to the point where play and work are the same. Celebrate the expression of your creative energy.

Devil's Play symbolizes a Dionysian exaltation of life, albeit on occasion in drunken exuberance. The pre-Christian concept of the devil is Pan, the Capricorn half-man half-goat that led all with his pan pipes to dance and sing and rejoice for the harvest and the fruitful life. These Bacchanalian festivals depicted by satyrs and fauns were later turned by the Christians into the "evil" work of the Devil.

The *I Ching* Hexagram for Devil's Play is #16, *Yu*/Enthusiasm:

Thunder comes resounding out of the earth
The image of Enthusiasm
Thus the ancient kings made music
In order to honor merit
And offered it with splendor
To the Supreme Deity. (I Ching, p. 68)

The goat/Capricorn/Pan aspect of Devil's Play brings to life an irrepressible sense of humor and pranksterism, yet originality and vitality. The original word in Greek for devil, *diaballein*, means to "set at variance"—in other words, to disrupt the order. The goat has always been noted for destroying the vineyards, and getting drunk in the process. This conforms with Devil's Play number, number Fifteen, which represents feeling the power, vitality, and wholeness following the new life of number Fourteen and by being associated with number Five. Five is the Heirophant's number, which also represents cracks, fissures, and fractures. The Devil's iconoclastic compulsion for disrupting the order and foundation of number Four is always in evidence.

The Rune for Devil's Play is *Thurisaz*. This TH-rune represents a forward thrusting of destructive power that breaks down the established order. As cosmic phallic energy, it is an instinctual will without consciousness. *Act spontaneously, realizing that your actions will disrupt yet bring about a new awakening.*

It is when this disruptive force gets carried away in a drunken-like frenzy that the devil within works its evil—evil in the sense of ignorance. When you have too much to drink (meaning to become "carried away" with enthusiasm), you become blind and step off your conscious boundaries represented by Saturn, the ruling planet of Capricorn.

The Kabbalah letter name for Devil's Play is *Ayin*, which means "eye." When your eyes are closed, you ignore your step and step into trouble. *Watch your step.*

When the eye is closed or drunken, a different reality is presented. Devil's Play symbolizes *altering your state of consciousness*. Hence, the "devil's advocate" represents seeing the other side, the side not wedded to convention and traditional belief. Seeing stoned blind is the "way of the Devil" to bring out your true original genius.

Your "Devil's Play" Qualities

MENTAL

DEVIL: Be a devil's advocate; Present unconventional ideas and a different, perhaps irreverent, point of view; Do not fall prey to superstitious beliefs.

Unevolved: STONE DODO BIRD AND INTOXICATED REVELERS: Stoned; Unaware; Ignorant.

EMOTIONAL

LAUGHTER: Have a high time; Amuse yourself; Laugh; Show your enthusiasm, exuberance, and fullness of life.

Unevolved: Panic; Fear; Paranoia.

PHYSICAL

EROS AND PHALLIC MUSHROOM: Express your sexuality and sensuality; Skip and go naked.

CAPRICORN: Keep your knees flexible.

Unevolved: INTOXICATION AND MUSHROOMS: Abuse of body; Toxins; Hangovers.

ACTION IN THE WORLD

BROKEN STATUARY: Revolutionize; Break tradition; Act uninhibited; Do not fear social censure.

Unevolved: STEPPING OFF THE EDGE OF SATURN: Undisciplined; Expanding beyond your means; Going overboard; Stepping too far; Self-destruction.

SPIRITUAL WISDOM

DEVIL EXORCISM DANCERS (MASKED FACES): Exorcise superstitions, bedevilments, and fears.

Unevolved: SEDUCED BY BACCHUS' WINE AND SONG: Weakness of will.

Your "Devil's Play" Oracular Universe

ASTROLOGY

CAPRICORN: Aspire to the heights of success; Take risks; Work.
SATURN: Celebrate your successes; Reward yourself; Harvest and then party.

ALCHEMY

EARTH: Be earthy; Play on the earth; Lie on the earth; Sit on the earth; Dance on the earth; Celebrate nature.

TIME

CAPRICORN: Play in December-January; Frolic in nature; Weekends; After work; Happy hour; Halloween; Harvest; Spring.

GEOMANCY

NATURE: Exhalt in unrestricted free spaces; Fresh air; Mountaintops; Edges.

SHAMANISM

GOAT: Be agile and keep your balance; Do not be afraid to tread a fine line between success and failure; Take on a challenge; Enjoy being on the edge; Be friendly, sociable.
MUSHROOM: You have the power to arouse, influence, and even poison.

AURA

RED: Have the courage to be personally visible and provocative.

PSYCHOMETRY

FLUTE AND DRINKING FLAGON: Carry yourself away with music and wine into nonordinary, right-brain, dream realities; Dance.

Consulting the Oracle:

"Devil's Play" Way

PLAY AT YOUR "WORK"

The tarot is an alchemical blend of fun and work. It is fun to play with the cards. Tarot is in the form of a game, a card game, and games are fun to play. What makes this play even more fun is that it is playing with your own self-creation, your highest form of "work." Find the most fun way to play the game of tarot. Remember that one of the great reasons why tarot is such an effective tool for self-growth is that the more you enjoy your "work" the greater are your successes.

SOBER UP WITH TAROT

Life is not always fun, and work can be work. Refer to the tarot in your "low" moments, for it cures what bedevils you by removing the blinders that prevent you from seeing how far you have progressed. When climbing the dizzying heights of life, you can also get carried away, step over the edge, and then wonder where things went wrong. Tarot gets you back on course. It sobers you up and gives you clarity.

HIGH TAROT

Use the tarot also when feeling high and even intoxicated. Intuitive receptivity is enhanced by mind-altering lubricants. There is nothing wrong with playing tarot at parties and in mind-altered states. Amazing insights are often the outcome. To remember them, however, is another matter.

Tarot, itself, is a powerful intoxicant! It is easy to get hooked. It can become like any other addiction—a way to escape from yourself and avoid taking responsibility. There is nothing wrong with consulting the tarot frequently, if done in the right spirit, which is to always view the cards as simply a tool for dialoguing with yourself. To be ruled by the cards is to misuse them. It is like letting a drug, or another person, or an outside entity rule you.

XVI

TOWER

The Tower, symbolizing the law of purification, is a revolutionary self-cleansing. What is being purified is represented by the tower—a symbol of mankind's ego and the structures he builds to support his vanity. Standing tall and proud like the ego would wish, humanity creates a towering structure of beliefs and edifices. In reality this is but a "tower of babel," a house of cards and confusion destined to be destroyed. The Kabbalah letter-name for the Tower is *Peh*, which means "mouth and speech," and stands for the activity generated by words, words, and more words. Big mouths are always taken down in the end.

Struck by fire and lightning, the tower falls. The revolution beheads those who are on top or who believe they are on high. The Tower suggests the *I Ching* Hexagram #49, *Ko*/Revolution:

Fire in the lake: the image of REVOLUTION. (I Ching, p. 190)

As the fiery Mars, god of war and conflict, the "warrior of the soul," *leap from the tower to purge your ego by sacrificing your egotistical vanities to the purifying fire.* The fire of purification is symbolized by the tower because it represents the highest point of observation. From the unobstructed view on the tower you are able to see yourself clearly. This awareness is the fire itself. A clear view of your impurities burns them out naturally. That is why the Sun, representing the fire of your clear awareness, is above the tower. *Move away from your daily world of habitual living and see yourself with a new clarity.*

The fire caldron of purification is explosive (the fractured leaping warrior in the Tower card). This cathartic purgation is symbolically rendered as dismemberment, and is therefore associated with mythological dismemberment figures, such as Zagreus, Pentheus, Orpheus, and Osiris. This metaphorical dismemberment is in accord with the Tower's number, Sixteen. This number, a Six number like the Lovers, represents separation created by the duality of opposites.

Six is also a number of integration. It is through dismemberment or disintegration that union results. Like all the dismembered gods who were ultimately resurrected whole, the Tower represents a restructuring. The Rune for the Tower is *Kenaz.* This K-rune represents the "fire of sacrifice" that brings regeneration. Out of the fire of transmutation is fashioned a new soul and a new life. *Be a warrior. Sacrifice with courage, will, and discipline what needs to go, and you will be renewed.*

Your "Tower" Qualities

MENTAL

TOWER HEIGHTS AND SUN "EYE" ABOVE TOWER: Look at your beliefs and
values, and burn out the ones that keep your confined and limited.
Unevolved: Dark thoughts; Gloom and doom that creates the seed
for the dark ages.

EMOTIONAL

TOWER HEIGHTS AND SUN "EYE": Look at your feelings; Burn out the ones that
keep you feeling dark and block you from feeling joy.
Unevolved: Rage that hurts others; Out-of-control frustration that is
projected onto others.

PHYSICAL

TOWER HEIGHTS AND SUN "EYE": Look at your body and burn out what blocks your energy; Purify; Eliminate.

Unevolved: Physically burned out; Stress leading to migraines or ulcers.

ACTION IN THE WORLD

TOWER HEIGHTS AND SUN "EYE": Look at your life situation and burn out what you would like to change; Restructure.

Unevolved: Spur of the moment self-destruction; Tearing down, quitting, throwing away through pique of anger or momentary inability to deal with stress.

SPIRITUAL WISDOM

TOWER: Commit yourself to spiritual growth, ascent, and evolution.

Unevolved: Ego pride.

Your "Tower" Oracular Universe

ASTROLOGY

MARS: You will naturally experience conflicts within yourself and with others as your old order is brought down and changed.

ALCHEMY

FIRE: You will naturally experience pain, agitation, and passion during the transformation process; Instability.

TIME

LEAPING: Do it! Make changes now, quickly and immediately; It's high time; "I can't stand it anymore"; "Enough is enough"; Call to arms.

GEOMANCY

INFERNO: Work out your problems in the hell realms; Hot spots; Sweat lodge; Hot seat; Detox center.

TOWER: Seek the healing places for rebuilding yourself, such as a retreat, hospital, spa, monastery.

SHAMANISM

RED-WINGED BLACKBIRD AND MOTH: Take off; Create a new life by changing.

ORCHID: Beauty will come through difficult growth and unfoldment.

AURA

RED AND BLACK: Painful warring as you cut out the dark aspects of your life.

PSYCHOMETRY

BUILDING: You and your world are structures that periodically need cleaning and renovation.

Consulting the Oracle:

"Tower" Way

DEFINE YOURSELF THROUGH YOUR OWN STYLE OF TAROT

You are continually changing. The Tower is your drive to keep things alive and burning through change. Tarot has burned through the centuries because, like the Tower, it has transformed. Originally an Egyptian wisdom book, tarot changed into a medieval card game, and now into "new age" symbols of transformation.

The tarot has no certified bible, except for the canon to follow the universal laws in whatever way works. Like the Tower, tarot must be updated and made relevant to the times. It must be personalized by you and made relevant to your own experience.

Given this freedom of expression in the tarot, there are as many styles of its practice as there are practitioners. Or at least there should be. The tarot sanctions this for the wisdom of the Tower symbolizes a commitment to be yourself, to be authentic—to purge out that which is not you.

The following are some general styles that fit certain personality types. If you are of a psychological orientation, use the tarot as a mirror of the mind. For a spiritualist, express the tarot in terms of visions and voices from the metaphysical world. Down-to-earth types use the tarot for basic decision making. Nontraditionalists invent their own layouts, if they use them at all.

XVII

STAR

The Star symbolizes the law of luminosity. In fact, you are made of star dust and you shine like a star. Everyone radiates star light. *Recognize your star light, and you will succeed and star on all levels of being.*

Like the Star of Bethlehem, you are a guiding light in the darkness, *be a guide—an illuminator to others.*

The Star, symbolized by the oriental goddess, Kuan Yin, means to *give of yourself with compassion in service to others so they may find their star light.* As the Aquarius water-bearer and the water Rune, *Laguz,* you bring life-giving waters to others for their regeneration and healing. In helping others with your clarity and generosity, you help yourself achieve your destiny—to reach your star.

The *I Ching* Hexagram for the Star is #22 *Pi*/Grace, which is the kind of beauty associated with the Roman version of the Star Venus:

Tranquil beauty—clarity within, quiet without.
This is the tranquility of pure contemplation.
In this aspect the world is beautiful. (I Ching, p. 91)

In the Kabbalah, the Star is represented by *Tzaddi*, which means "fishhook." The Star's hook or attraction is an inner and outer expression of beauty, which is irresistible. The Star's hook of beauty attracts others and so the Star is capable of great power to influence others. *Use your beauty to serve others in finding their own beauty.*

The Star's number is Seventeen, which is the combination of Ten and Seven. Both ten (Fortune) and seven (Chariot) represent attainment. The Star has achieved the heights and is rewarded with fame and acclaim. Once having achieved stardom, the Star personality shines its light with an infinite radiance. This is symbolized by the infinity sign of the sideways number Eight (∞), which is what the Star's One and Seven add up to.

Your "Star" Qualities

MENTAL

STAR: Esteem your brightness and your ideas; Think beauty; Offer optimism and hope; Use your imagination; Think inspirationally.
Unevolved: Spaced out; Out of touch with ordinary reality.

EMOTIONAL

STAR: Radiate; Twinkle; Esteem your beautiful feelings.
Unevolved: Distant; Cold.

PHYSICAL

STAR: Make yourself beautiful and handsome; Energize; Be light.
AQUARIUS: Your ankles show your particular kind of beauty.
Unevolved: Vanity.

ACTION IN THE WORLD

STAR: Achieve; Esteem your accomplishments; Go for stardom; Be of service.
Unevolved: DISTANT STAR: Uninvolved; Uncaring; Ungiving; Patronizing; Selfish.

SPIRITUAL WISDOM

STAR: Aspire to see the light, to live in the light, and to be the light; Honor your own inner light; Recognize the star that you are; Esteem yourself.

Unevolved: DEAD STARFISH: Lack of self-recognition and esteem; Attachment to old achievements; Caught in the past.

Your "Star" Oracular Universe

ASTROLOGY

AQUARIUS: Be of the Aquarian age; Follow the stars.
COMET KAHOUTEK: Be swift, for you are only passing through.

ALCHEMY

AIR AND WATER: Watery aspect of air (Think with feeling); Airy aspect of water (Feel with wisdom).
JADE: You have strength to withstand pressure; Heal the kidneys.
EMERALD: Adorn yourself with healthy, eye-catching, beautiful, aesthetic jewelry.

TIME

STARLIGHT AND AQUARIUS: These are dark but hopeful times.

GEOMANCY

STAR: Stand in the limelight; Go to the heights; Be visible; Stand independently; Claim your own space.

SHAMANISM

PELICAN: Love (the pelican so loved her young that she opened her own breast to nourish them with her own blood).

AURA

WHITE: Follow the path of purity and light.

PSYCHOMETRY

CLOTHES, DRESS, COSTUME: Express your inner beauty by being beautiful on the outside; Make the world a beautiful place.

Consulting the Oracle:

"Star" Way

Tarot is for "Enlightenment"

Tarot is a path of enlightenment, a way to realize the starlight within you. It teaches you to see things as they really are, and you are really a light being. Use the tarot to see your enlightened nature. Your light essence is revealed through the tarot practice of viewing the cards as symbols of *inspiration, aspiration, upliftment, and affirmation*. By seeing the cards in this light, you are naturally enlightened.

"Inspiration" Reading

The tarot is a manifestation of the Star in the beauty of its images and concepts. As a reflection of yourself, the tarot is supportive of your own beauty—the star that you truly are. Like the illuminating star, tarot reveals your stellar qualities.

In moments of darkness, select cards face-down (which represents the dark night of our personal blindness) and see what light exists, what starry qualities you possess among the black holes.

Like the stars which inspire you, your spirit and energies are re-kindled by the radiant light of the tarot. Tarot cards give you optimism and hope. Use them for inspiration, particularly in the darkest of times.

"Aspiration" Reading

The Star is symbolic of aspiration, of your drive to reach the stars, to reach your star of destiny. Tarot cards are like stars. They represent what you aspire to. They show the beautiful ideals of life that you seek. Tarot reflects in its light not only who you are but who you can be. It reveals your attainable potential.

Select a card from the face-up deck that is particularly beautiful and inspiring to you. Let it represent a star within yourself that you would like to realize. Place it above your bed or on your ceiling. Looking up at the card is symbolic of your aspiration to become that star. Through continual sighting of that ideal, it becomes attainable.

Remember that even the most mundane and commonplace abilities are stars worthy of aspiration. Stars are everywhere in your life, in your reflection in mud puddles, in the eye of the beholder.

"Uplifting" Reading

In deciding how to interpret a card, select definitions that are most uplifting. Use interpretations that are inspiring, that are beautiful like the stars. Your whole self is uplifted. Your consciousness is raised and rarefied to the level of light. Enlightenment is to be light in spirit, not heavy and not dark. Uplifting values are essential in the process of becoming enlightened. Reading the tarot in an uplifting manner is a way of staying on the path of enlightenment.

"Affirmation" Reading

Tarot cards are affirmations. They affirm your enlightened nature. Read them as affirmations. Each cards says, "I am _____!" Select such an "affirmation card" every day. This helps you overcome the unenlightened beliefs about yourself that you are often innundated with by society. You need to combat negative self-image continually. Say the affirmation as denoted by the card several times. Write the affirmation down. Visualize yourself living the affirmation throughout your activities during that day or period.

XVIII

MOON

The Moon symbolizes the law of cycles and phases. This is represented by the phases of the moon, the tidal in's and out's of the ocean, the shifting sand dunes, and the emerging female Aphrodite and the receding male Apollo.

The *I Ching* Hexagram for the Moon is #32, *Heng*/Duration, which means

> ... *self-renewing movement taking place in accordance with immutable laws and beginning anew at every ending.The end is reached by an inward movement and this movement turns into a new beginning in which the movement is directed outward....a fixed law of change and transformation.*
> (I Ching, p. 126)

Inner changes through contemplation will in time quietly usher in a new phase.

The Moon is not a disruptive revolutionary force nor does it remain unchanging. It symbolizes conservative change, a preservation through "continuity transformation." The Moon signifies gentle evolutionary completions and beginnings. It is therefore associated with the growth and maturation represented by such goddesses as Ishtar, Hathor, Anaitis, and Artemis.

Centered amidst the moon cycles in the Moon card is Aphrodite, a symbol of equipoise (double dolphins) and centeredness during changes. Aphrodite plays the role of duality. Like the "Hermaphrodite," the Aphrodite moon goddess reflects the male light (hence the role of Apollo, the sun god, behind Aphrodite in the Moon card) and the night void waiting to be filled (female principle). The moon is therefore variously associated with Hecate and Diana—the feminine form of Janus, a symbol of duality. *Be changeable, able to flow with different phases and tides.*

As a result of its changeability, the Moon card represents illusion and delusion. What is real? Is "reality" dream or fact? This illusiveness often creates a kind of insanity called "lunacy," which is derived from the Latin word for moon, *luna*. Luna, the Roman goddess for the moon, means silver—the color of the moon, which reflects different colors and images. As a silver mirror, the moon mirrors the kaleidoscopic universe of change. Amidst this impermanence, what again is real? Enough to drive you crazy. *Remember that what is real is the ever-changing reality.*

Its hermaphroditic character makes the Moon a symbol of wholeness. This is indicated by its number, Eighteen. Eighteen, when One and Eight are added together, creates the number Nine—the number of completeness associated with moving through the full cycle. *Complete before you go on.*

The word Moon comes from the Indo-European root, *men*, meaning "moon month." So, Moon is associated with menses, the monthly female cycle. The Moon card symbolizes the mysteries and life-nurturing qualities of the feminine. As such, the Moon represents your *expression of the feminine, the passive, the internal, and the introspective.*

The Rune for the Moon is *Isa*. Representing the congealing force of ice, the I-rune stands for the magnetic force of stillness. *You have a natural force of attraction toward which others gravitate. Be still.*

The Kabbalah letter-symbol for the Moon is *Qoph*, meaning the "back of the head." This symbolizes the subconscious or that which is stored in the deep back recesses of the mind. The Moon card therefore represents your dreams, which reveal your personal subconscious. It also symbolizes past lives, people, or phenomena that recur in your life. The Moon subconscious conserves the old and brings it back to life. *Remember your dreams and you will know your past, which will help you understand your present.*

As Pisces, symbolized by the two dolphins, the Moon card represents not only the feminine and subconscious (water and ocean depths), but an extraordinary sensitivity of a psychic nature. The ability to pick up vibrations, even the most distant and subtle, is characteristic of the dolphin Moon mentality. The shadowy world of the occult and the hidden mysteries are capably probed and sounded out by the Piscean Moon nature. *You are naturally psychic, particularly at night. Cultivate your Moon dreams to psyche out your life.*

Your "Moon" Qualities

MENTAL

APOLLO IN BACKGROUND: Your logic and reason (traits of Apollo) take second place to feelings, intuitions, dreams, and imaginations.

Unevolved: LUNA: Deceptions of the moon; Lunacy; Illusions and delusions.

EMOTIONAL

APHRODITE: Be a romantic; Feel; Empathize.

Unevolved: OCEAN: Emotional instability of great ups and downs.

PHYSICAL

APHRODITE: Recognize your femaleness and maleness.

PISCES: Stay on the balls of your feet to stay balanced while shifting and changing.

Unevolved: Insomnia.

ACTION IN THE WORLD

APOLLO AND APHRODITE AND TWO DOLPHINS ON SAME WAVE: Resolution of relationship issues. Fulfill your karmic connections and attractions to others; Complete obligations and lessons with karmic partners such as family, old friends, lovers; Complete old karma when old relationships resurface.

Unevolved: Stuck in the same old cycle; Spinning endlessly in the same old patterns.

SPIRITUAL WISDOM

OCEAN AND MOON DREAMS: Be aware of your subconscious motivations and drives; Meditation.

WINGS: Spiritual wisdom; Evolution; Transformation.

Unevolved: Emotions get in the way of seeing clearly; Insecurity prevents flights of transformation.

Your "Moon" Oracular Universe

ASTROLOGY

MOON: Follow the feminine values, ways, and means; Complete old habit patterns, particularly in relationships; Be emotionally attached but also able to complete relationships; Reflect deeply before acting; Use your menstruation periods for inner knowing and strength.

PISCES: See patterns, cycles, and karma; Do not be afraid to be psychic.

ALCHEMY

WATER: Take the easy path; Go with the flow, move with the tides; Adjust; Mellow out.

MARBLE: Accept your streaky, changeable nature.

TIME

NIGHT: You receive knowledge in the night time; Dream time.

GEOMANCY

MOONLIGHT: Let yourself dream in half-lit places; Shade; Candlelight; Desert.

SHAMANISM

WOLF: Heed the longing of the "call of the wild" primordial animalistic drive and behavior.

COYOTE: Beware that all is not as it appears to be.

DOLPHIN: Be sensitive to sound and vibrations; Be intuitive.

OWL: See into what is hidden (darkness); see the dark, shadow side.

NIGHT FLOWER: Come alive and blossom at night.

AURA

SILVER: Reflect.

SILVER AND BLACK: Seek the mysterious and elusive.

PASTELS: Be sensual and soft.

PSYCHOMETRY

MIRROR: You mirror others; Reflect others by taking on their attributes and thus reveal their true nature.

Consulting the Oracle:

"Moon" Way

Tarot is a medium for understanding the qualities of the moon. Tarot is a "moon media." The following practices of Moon tarot help you express the Moon way of being.

FOLLOW THE MAGNETIC ATTRACTION

Subconscious magnetic fields, like the pull of the moon on your emotions and feelings, draw you toward certain decks, cards in readings, and interpretations of symbols. Assume a position of neutrality, a moonish passivity that allows the cards and symbols to move you. Do not try in tarot. Simply go with whatever pulls you. Do not resist. Tarot is meant to be easy.

SEE YOURSELF IN THE MIRROR OF TAROT

The tarot mirrors you like the moon which reflects the light of the sun stars. The tarot does not really tell you anything that you do not already know. If the tarot surprises you with new information, it is because you have chosen not to look at that aspect of yourself in your mirror. View the cards as a mirror.

LET THE SUBCONSCIOUS BE REVEALED

The moon, which appears at night, symbolizes the surfacing of your subconscious through dreams that are replete with visions of places you have been and states of consciousness you have experienced. Tarot symbolic imagery seeps into your subconscious and often strikes existent aspects of the subconscious. Memory is jarred loose. The past is raised.

Allow the light of the present to strike the darkened past and reflect back again to present awareness. Tarot, like our Moon dreams, is an invaluable tool for digging into previous experience.

In drawing up your early and even primordial past, your present patterns, phobias and skills are better understood. Like the Piscean water quality of the Moon, your life can open up and flow more easily as you unblock personality logjams and release potentials through the exposure of our past.

WAKING DREAM

Do not be surprised if tarot symbolism appears in your dream world. Tarot and dreams are similar processes of eliciting the subconscious. In the tarot, however, you engage your subconscious in an awakened state. The tarot may help you understand your dreams and your dreams may help explain your tarot cards. It is possible to establish a regular dialogue between your dreams and tarot.

XIX

SUN

As the emitter of light and heat, the Sun represents the law of radiance. The rays of the sun awaken and give life. The *I Ching* Hexagram for the Sun is #30, *Li*/The Clinging Fire. It stands for nature or sun in its radiance:

> *Through its radiance the four quarters of the world are illumined*
> *and its light spreads to penetrate the nature of man,*
> (I Ching, p. 119-120)

The radiant light of the sun brings consciousness, hence the association of the Sun with the "all-seeing eye." In India the Sun as Surya is the eye of Varuna; in Greece as Helios, the eye of Zeus; in Egypt it is the eye of Ra. In the Runes, the Sun is *Sowilo*, which represents the eyes of consciousness of the chakras. Your chakra wheels of awareness move you through your "will." *Move with purpose to be the Sun.*

With a turned-on consciousness, you will have the radiant fire of the Sun, a bright mind, a warm heart, an active body, and a fiery spirit. As the

Sun you will have a life vitality like the youthful Tutankhamun, the Sun king.

Full of the life radiance of the Sun, *become the Sun in your own world, a central figure of power that creates life.* This is in accord with the Kabbalah letter for the Sun, *Resh,* which means "head or face." *In the head and as the head is your power of authority and leadership, which you can openly express to radiate light and life throughout your world.*

Your "Sun" Qualities

MENTAL

MORNING SUN AND YOUTHFUL KING TUTANKHAMUN: Be awake, alert, conscious; Create a healthy and optimistic mind; See the bright side; Wake up others.
Unevolved: Overbearing intellect.

EMOTIONAL

CELEBRANT OF THE SUN: Life is sunny, joyous, and uplifting.
Unevolved: Burned out; Overindulgent.

PHYSICAL

MORNING SUN AND YOUNG KING: Maintain a youthful vitality and energy; Get heated up; Get your metabolism moving; Exercise for health; Go outdoors into the light.
Unevolved: Physical excess to the point of injury and illness; Sunburn.

ACTION IN THE WORLD

COUPLE WALKING TOGETHER AND UNION OF SUN AND EARTH: Co-creative synergistic partnerships; Mutual sharing of energies and talents.
SUN RAYS: Giving to others.
CELEBRANT: Playing with others.
BUTTERFLY AND FLOWERS: Working with others.
SUN AND FLOWERS: Loving others.
Unevolved: Dominating.

SPIRITUAL WISDOM

MORNING SUN, BUTTERFLY, AND FIRE: You have transformative/recreative ability—you can awaken the mind from sleep; the body from heaviness and fatigue; the heart from depression; and the spirit from oppression.
Unevolved: Ego.

Your "Sun" Oracular Universe

ASTROLOGY

SUN: You are a dynamic creative central figure of power, influence, leadership, and responsibility; Move, stimulate, and energize others.

ALCHEMY

FIRE: Be assertive, outgoing, active, worldly.
GOLD: Strive for your best.

TIME

SUN: Be active in day time.

GEOMANCY

SUN: Seek the center, the spotlight, the heat, and the sun.

SHAMANISM

MONARCH BUTTERFLY: Be light and playful.
POPPY: Phototropic (move to the light for nourishment); Be creative, fertile, sexy.
SUNFLOWER: Radiate your light to all; Be all-encompassing.
ORANGE: Take Vitamin C; Eat healthy foods.

AURA

RAINBOW SPECTRUM: Be colorful.

PSYCHOMETRY

COIN: Make money; Be fruitful; Share your abundance; Reward yourself.

Consulting the Oracle:

"Sun" Way

SEE THE SUN

Often, you cannot see the forest for the trees. Similarly, your own life is so obvious and close that you cannot clearly comprehend it. The same for the sun. It is the most obvious and dominating force of your day and yet you cannot look at it directly. Reading the tarot is like putting on a set of glasses that allows you to see yourself. Cards are like a lens through which you can understand your true nature. It is like understanding the sun through a picture (lens) of it. You can indirectly know yourself and your sun through an intermediary tool or medium.

What you cannot see clearly about yourself is the sun that you are. To see your Sun nature is blinding, and so you remain largely ignorant of your radiance. Through the medium of tarot, however, you can see that you are illumined, creative, and strong like the sun. The tarot through its dazzling bright symbols enables you to see your sun side. Tarot is a golden opportunity to imprint your consciousness with the reality of your Sun nature.

Consulting the oracle of tarot is a way of expressing your Sun nature: Through a reading you awaken, energize, heal, and clarify. This power is often too blinding, however. Beware that the radiant sun you are in a reading may be too strong for your own or another's system and serve to burn out and perhaps even cause pain. Be discriminating. Know when and how to moderate your Sun power so that it is acceptable and comforting.

XX

TIME-SPACE

Time-Space, traditionally known in tarot as Judgment or the Aeon, is symbolized in the *Voyager* by Xipe Totec, Aztec "god of spring." Wearing the skin of a sacrificed human, Xipe represents the *new life which comes after your judgment of death to old karmic patterns that are self-destructive.*

The law of karma (the law of laws) symbolized by Time-Space means that you can *direct the course of your life by examining and altering psychological and behavioral patterns*. This implies that you have the ability to see into past patterns that create present realities,which in turn predict future patterns. As the *Perthro*, Rune of time, karma, synchronicity, and divination, Time-Space symbolizes a total overview of where you have been, are, and are going. With this perspective, your karma can be consciously recreated.

As the "last judgment," Time-Space represents a significant Uranus-like transition period in your life. Your rebirths, both in this life and the afterlife, are determined by how you judge the prevailing direction of your life. Time-Space is associated with an *extraordinary* number of mythological figures, for this concept of judging karma is prevalent among all cultures. See Aeacus (Greek), Annukai (Babylonian), Ch'in (Chinese), Chitragupta (Hindu), Dharma (Hindu), Emma or Mirume (Japanese), Horus (Egyptian), Minos (Greek), Mahu (Hindu), Monker and Nakir (Moslem), Nergal (Assyrian), Osiris (Egyptian), Rashnu (Zoroaster), Rhadamanthus (Greek), Sinje-Cho-Gyal (Tibetan), Thoth (Egyptian), Taripaca (Inca), Tezcatlipoca (Aztec), Ts'in-Kuan-Wang (Chinese).

The Kabbalah letter-name for Time-Space is *Shin*, which literally means "tooth." As teeth are sequentially related, it symbolizes relationships in time and space. *Shin* is also associated with the Hebrew words *Ruach Elohim*, which means "Holy Spirit," the life breath. As the spirit, Time-Space represents the breath of fresh air, the new life that attends the breaking out of old habit patterns.

The *I Ching* Hexagram for Time-Space is #57, *Sun*/The Gentle.

> In nature it is the wind that disperses the gathered clouds, leaving the sky clear and serene. In human life, it is the penetrating clarity of judgment that thwarts all dark hidden motives. (I Ching, p. 220)

Time-Space as its number, Twenty, suggests, is a harbinger of new things to come. The number Twenty means the ending of the second cycle of tens and the beginning of the third cycle of ten. It is the departure point *in consciousness* for the sowing of new seeds that will result in higher synthesis (third cycle of ten).

Your "Time-Space" Qualities

MENTAL

THREE MEDITATING BUDDHA JUDGES: Be reflective in a judgmental, evaluative, critical, discriminating, and analytical way.
Unevolved: FLYER: Spaced out; Deluded.

EMOTIONAL

MEDITATOR: Be controlled, reserved, and dispassionate when making judgments.
Unevolved: STONE: Blocked feelings; Colorless; Bland.

PHYSICAL

MEDITATOR: Be physically still; Explore "out of body" experience; Feel your ethereal body.

Unevolved: FLIGHTS OF MIND: Ignorance of the body.

ACTION IN THE WORLD

ZEN GARDEN AND DESERT: Time of austerity and nonmaterialism; Reflect on your worldly situation; Do not act before evaluating.

Unevolved: FLIGHTS: Cannot bring ideas down to earth; Ungrounded.

SPIRITUAL WISDOM

THREE ROCK MONUMENT SEQUENCE; HEAD AND TAIL OF FISH; SUN AND MOON SEQUENCES: You have the ability to be anywhere in time and space simultaneously in consciousness; You are a seer of the past, present, and future, the here and there; You can see how the present is a product of the past and a seed for the future.

Unevolved: NUCLEAR REACTOR (BLUE RAYS OF RADIOACTIVE LIGHT): Destructive use of visionary power.

Your "Time-Space" Oracular Universe

ASTROLOGY

CYCLICAL PATTERNS: Understand how your life moves in cyclical patterns.

PHASES: Understand cause and effect relationships (karma).

ALCHEMY

AIR AND LIGHT: Your consciousness is truly boundless and infinite light.

TIME

MOVEMENTS BETWEEN: You see the changing patterns in transition times; Pisces to Aries transition; Winter to Spring transition; Timeless; Between ending and beginning.

GEOMANCY

MIND FLIGHT: Go to inner spaces and to placeless places.

DESERT: You have a vision in places of pure light and pure air; Unobstructed places.

SHAMANISM

BIRD: See your future.

FISH: See your past.

HUMAN: See your present.

ORCHID: Like the thousands of varieties of orchids, you have an ability to create out of yourself a new person, a new variety of human; Live off the air (or in your mind).

SEED: Be mindful of how every thought creates a seed for a future event or situation.

AURA

BLUES: Go deep and far with your vision and imagination.

PSYCHOMETRY

SPACECRAFT AND SUNDIAL: As instruments of enhancing awareness of your place in time and space, they represent revolutions in consciousness; Through physical explorations you discover inner spaces; Join physics and metaphysics.

CHIROGNOMY

CLASPED HAND: Introspect; Recycle your energy.

Consulting the Oracle:

"Time-Space" Way

OMNIPRESENCE

The Time-Space card tells you that tarot is a vehicle that takes you simultaneously into the past, present, future, and to the here and there. You can be omnipresent! Tarot confirms the power of your consciousness—its ability to be infinite in time and space and able to create the future. Practicing the tarot makes you aware of these powers and gives you the capability of exercising them.

Past, Present, Future. . .

The cards you select in a reading reflect the present. But the present is a product of the past. And the future is an effect of the present. The past and future are simultaneously contained within the present.

Time-Space reveals the law of karma, that you live according to sequential patterns of cause and effect. What you germinate today contains the seeds you have sown in the past and those that will blossom tomorrow.

In knowing your present, you can understand your past and future. Once you have seen the future, you can alter it by planting new seeds in your consciousness.

Here and There

Synchronicity is the explanation we give to understand that space, as well as time, is interconnected and one. You are a cause and a result of what is happening elsewhere. Linked as you are to another place in space, you are capable of seeing here and there. To be elsewhere, all you have to do is see in your mind's eye what is happening over there. You can even ask the tarot cards what is going on elsewhere. Every card selected in a reading represents what is the here and the there. To see what is happening afar or with another person, simply ask the cards what is occurring here.

"Relativity" of Readings

The theory of relativity suggests that reality is in the perception of the observer (which is symbolized in the Time-Space card by the different minds of the three Buddha judges who bathe in the light of a nuclear accelerator, a product of relativity). A reading is relative. There is no such thing for example of an inherent "good" or "bad" reading. Whether it is good or bad depends upon the eye of the observer. What is good for one could be bad for another.

Seed Ideas

Readings should not be judged in terms of goodness or badness. The utility of a reading comes from the ideas and visions they catalyze. It is your ideas that create your life situations. Your ideas are the seeds from which your life buds forth. Tarot helps you create your future by provoking ideas which, if planted strongly in your consciousness, will become manifest on the physical material level of reality.

XXI

UNIVERSE

The Universe symbolizes the law of universality. Each of us is a complete seed of the universe. You are a microcosm of the macrocosmic universe. *You are at one in consciousness with all phenomena.* The Runes for the Universe are *Mannaz* and *Othala*. *Mannaz* is the symbol for your wholeness, the archetypal complete person. The whole person is a child of the universe. As the offspring of the goddesses and gods, you are symbolized by the *Othala* Rune, which means you have inherited the gifts and qualities of the universe. *You carry the universe in your genes.*

Like the center stone in the Universe card, you possess within yourself a universe of possibilities. What you see in your mind's eye exists. Like a sculptor, you can sculpt out of yourself anything under the sun—a flower, a city, a god, a star.

Like the stone you are whole and perfect, but just like the unfinished sculpture by Michaelangelo, you are never finished. Life is never completed; it is a never-ending series of completions. Life is always a process of becoming. The evolutionary journey through the universe of being is the mark of your totality. The voyage itself is the universe.

The word, "universe," is composed of two Latin words, *unus* meaning "all together one" and *verse* meaning "turning." So universe means the "revolving totality." The Kabbalah letter-name for the Universe Card is *Tav*, meaning "cross." *Tav* therefore signifies the four corners, or totality, and everlasting life through death and rebirth. Again and again the symbols for the Universe suggest oneness and completeness through change, death and renewal, revolution.

The *I Ching* Hexagram for the Universe is #64, *Wei Chi*/Completion:

> . . . *a transition from chaos to order. This hexagram comes at the end of the Book of Changes. It points to the fact that every end contains a new beginning. Thus it gives hope to men. (I Ching, p. 252)*

The continuously revolving totality of the Universe card-symbol is supported by its number, Twenty-One. Twenty-One is the beginning of the third cycle of Tens and is the third completed phase of Sevens, which is a number of attainment. Three (Two and One) is a number of synthesis. One (thesis) plus Two (antithesis) creates Three (synthesis). In numerology, the right-hand digit can suggest the resolution of a situation implied by the left-hand digit (in this case the duality and multiplicity of Two is reduced to the unity of One). The Universe is a synthesis of multiplicity and of beginning and ending.

The archetypal concept of wholeness through diversity and change gives the Universe its astrological association with Saturn—the Roman version of the Greek mythological god, Cronus. Symbolized by the planet Saturn, Cronus is the father of gods, primal cause, supreme deity, destroyer and renewer of all life. Cronus or Saturn brings order out of chaos, material form out of spirit essence, finiteness within the infinite.

Other mythological associations of the Universe embodying this quality of all-encompassing wholeness are Alpha and Omega (Greek), Aum or Om (Hindu), Brahma (Hindu), Izanagi (Japanese), Janus (Italic), Orphic or Cosmic Egg (Egyptian), Panggu (Melanisian), P'An Ku (Chinese), Purusa (Hindu), Tai Kih (Chinese), and Ymir (Norse).

Your "Universe" Qualities

MENTAL

DIAMOND EYE: See a universe of possibilities; Be versatile in your perceptivity; See how to cut your raw potential into refined manifestation.

Unevolved:

UNIVERSE: Information overload creating confusion and indecision.

HEAD OF STONE: Mental rigidity.

EMOTIONAL

FOOTSTEP ON MOON: Do not be afraid to take the big step, or the first step, or the last step; Live your dream.

Unevolved: HEART OF STONE: Emotionally blocked, hard, closed.

PHYSICAL

CHIPPING AWAY OF STONE AND "AWAKENING GIANT": Death of the old body and birth of a new one; Sculpt your body; Recreate your physical self.

Unevolved: BODY OF STONE: Stiff; Sedentary.

ACTION IN THE WORLD

VOYAGER SPACECRAFT AND FOOTSTEP ON MOON: Travel; Go new places, meet new people, do new things; Live your fantasy.

Unevolved: Accumulative; Heavy; Dense.

SPIRITUAL WISDOM

MICHAELANGELO SCULPTURE: You are a goddess/god so play creator in creating your universe.

Unevolved: Cannot accept the mystery and magic of the universe; No faith in the inexplicable; Cannot see beyond the physical eye.

Your "Universe" Oracular Universe

ASTROLOGY

SATURN: Harvest your natural riches.

UNIVERSE: You have infinite vastness and smallnes, order and logic, continuity and change, death and rebirth.

ALCHEMY

ALL THE ELEMENTS: Become whole by using all your elements for creativity.

DIAMOND: You become richer and more beautiful through age, through the crucible of time and experience.

TIME

UNIVERSE: Your time is anytime; All times.

GEOMANCY

UNIVERSE: Your place is any place; All places.

SHAMANISM

BIRD, FISH, SNAKE: Be adaptable to all conditions.

LOTUS: All experience and all situations are opportunities for growth and reward; You become more beautiful and pure through experience and growth.

AURA

FULL SPECTRUM OF LIGHT: You are of one light but of many different colors, shades and tones that mark your individual uniqueness; You are the same as others but different.

PSYCHOMETRY

VOYAGER SPACECRAFT: Explore; Extend your consciousness through extending your world; Apply your knowledge.

CITY: Organize and communicate your knowledge, roles, interests, values, and styles into a synergistic whole.

CHIROGNOMY

BUDDHA'S FOUR HANDS: You are versatile; You can simultaneously plan, plant, nurture, and harvest.

Consulting the Oracle:

"Universe" Way

The Oracle of Tarot affirms that you are a micro-universe. Tarot shows that as a replica of the universe, you have the characteristics of its inherent structure and order within ever-present change and revolution.

STRUCTURE AND ORDER

The internal structure and order of your life is demonstrated through tarot layouts or spreads. Layouts are really mandalas. A mandala is a symbolic portrait of integrated parts that reveals an overall pattern of wholeness. Tarot mandalas show you the relationship between various aspects of yourself and your world.

Tarot layouts provide a sense of personal completeness which is a vital and satisfying urge that you need to recognize and experience. Enabling yourself to see your inherent order and structure provides a base that can be easily pictured and recalled. Such a personal map or structure gives you a self-image and an identity that can then be followed or sculpted (transformed) in any way.

Even if you do not use a formal layout or mandala in your readings, it is important to at least rearrange the cards at the end of a reading to compose an overall picture or order. If a layout is used, it is effective to have the layout copied on paper and to write in the cards as they selected for each position.

CHANGE AND REVOLUTION

As the universe is always changing, so are you. Tarot readings give a good indication of your personal revolutions. This is best seen by periodically performing the same reading (using the same layout). A comparison of the readings over time reveals continuities and changes. Performing the same reading on auspicious days, such as birthday, solstice, New Year's, etc., is an excellent practice. To know your "Year Cards" and how they change from year to year is a highly effective technique for realizing the potential of your annual revolutions.

CHAPTER SIX

Minor Arcana Qualities

The Minor Arcana cards represent the so-called "minor secret" principles of life, and they are divided into four suits—Crystals, Cups, Worlds, and Wands—with Ace through Ten for each suit. Each suit represents different qualities for a certain aspect of ourselves. For example, the Crystals suit symbolizes qualities of our *mental disposition*. The mind is like a crystal—full of multifaceted, creative, and structured light. (In the traditional Tarot, the mind is represented by the suit called Swords). The Cups suit stands for *emotional state*s. The heart is like a cup, full if we are emotionally fulfilled and empty if we feel drained and empty. The Worlds suit reflects our *worldly life*, our actions in the world, and our material physical being. (This suit is called Disks or Pentacles in the classic tarot decks.) The Wands suit represents our *spirit*— the magic of life that we hold in our hands.

The Minor Arcanas are the personality attributes of their corresponding Major Arcana Archetype Cards. The correspondence between Minors and Majors are *numerological*. For example, the number Three Minor Cards of each suit represent the attributes of the number Three Major Arcana Archetype Card. Thus, the Major Arcana Three Card, the Empress, has the qualities of the Three of Crystals—Creativity; Three of Cups—Love; Three of Worlds— Nurturing; and Three of Wands—Compassion.

BRILLIANCE

Ace of Crystals

Brilliance is your *Magician* state of mind (Aces have the value of One and therefore represent the attributes of the number One Major Arcana Archetype Card, the Magician). You have your own brilliance. It shines through whenever you have great passion and interest. You must believe in your mind's ability to be brilliant.

Brilliance represents the quality of insight. To see and understand insightfully comes with a driving curiosity. Follow your curiosity and it will bring you great "Aha's!" Insight also depends on your concentration. Intense focus on what interests you will bring insightful clarity.

Brilliance is the ability to be creative. Creativity is the product of your imagination. Imagine! Trust your imagination, for that is where your genius lies. Imagination does not work unless there is open-mindedness. Open your mind. Do not censor your imagination. Creative ideas are revolutionary. Revolutionary thoughts come from turning things around in your mind. Like a crystal, see things from different points of view.

Brilliance is manifested by your mind's ability to integrate and synthesize. Use your logical reasoning power and your natural intuition to organize your creative insights. Put your ideas into an intelligible and workable order.

Remember, your mind is like a crystal—it is naturally brilliant. Like a crystal, be sharp and penetrating. Spin ideas around and see through the multiple perspectives or many facets of your crystal intelligence. Put these facets of creative awareness into an organized whole, like a crystal.

Your "Brilliance" Qualities

EVOLVED:

DIAMOND: You have brilliant ideas.

CITRINE SUNBURST: Awaken your mind to flashes of insight—"Now I see, now I understand, now I get it."

CLEARING SKIES: You are facing a dawning of clarity.

SHARP CRYSTAL FACETS: You have piercing, insightful intelligence.

CRYSTALS ABOVE THE EARTH: Look at things with overview, big vision.

SPINNING CRYSTAL EFFECT: Generate creative ideas by spinning ideas around.

CENTER DIAMOND: Stay focused and centered.

CRYSTALS SET TOGETHER AND CUT DIAMOND: Organize your ideas.

UNEVOLVED:

DIAMOND: Powerful intellect that invites jealousy, envy, criticism.

EXPLOSIVENESS: Overbearing intellect; Wants to dominate with ideas.

Your "Brilliance" Oracular Universe

ASTROLOGY

SUNSTAR: Be a guiding light to others.

ALCHEMY

FIRE: Move your mind so that it does not get stuck; Consume new fuel or information; Give your mind freedom for expression.

DIAMOND: Keep striving for high, ideal, and lofty thoughts.

TIME

SUNRISE, SUNSET: Time to look at things from a new perspective; Time of transition and breakthrough; Newness.

GEOMANCY

MOUNTAINTOP, DESERT: Find a clear space of your own where there is nothing between you and the universe; Be alone with your thoughts.

SHAMANISM

CARBON INTO DIAMOND: Your brilliant ideas are relevant, down-to-earth, and practical.

AURA

AMETHYST: Open your top of the head crown chakra.
YELLOW-ORANGE: Find a way to stimulate and revitalize your mind.
WHITE: Maintain mental harmony and purity; No ill thoughts.

PSYCHOMETRY

CUT DIAMOND: Refine your ideas so that they appeal to others.

ECSTASY

Ace of Cups

Ecstasy is your *Magician* state of emotional feeling. It is possible to live ecstatically but you must believe so. Ecstasy is yours if you have the courage to completely live out the full range of all your emotions. Do not censor or deny any of your feelings, for they are all divine. Ecstasy is an emotional intensity that comes with truly living. Living is feeling. Feel everything. Express all your feelings.

Intensity of feeling comes with a love for life in its entirety. To live in ecstasy means to accept and revere all. Love life in all its passion and boredom, in all its pleasure and fear, in all its quiet satisfaction and raging anger, in all its ups and downs. Ecstasy means to be totally loving and living.

Your heart is like a cup of life. As the open cup, drink all of life in. Life is the source that nourishes and fills you. Like the cup, pour out all your feelings. Do not hold your emotions back. Let them out so that new emotional vitality may come back in. Ecstasy is continuous renewal. In the complete taking in and giving out of life, you flower. You become who you are. In truly being yourself, you are beautiful and ecstatic.

Your "Ecstasy" Qualities

EVOLVED:

CLOUDS OF FLOWERS: Feel yourself "up in the clouds"; Create pleasure.
BOUQUET OF FLOWERS: Feel special; Celebrate.
GARDEN PARADISE: Acknowledge your emotional abundance.
BUTTERFLY: As a flower with wings, feel light and soar high.
WATERFALLS: Pour out your emotional abundance to others.
RAINBOW: Completely express your feelings, from sunny to rainy.

UNEVOLVED:

FLOWER: Overly sensitive, unprotective of self; Emotional fragility; Extreme ups and downs; Egotistical need to be noticed and the center of attention; Caught up in physical, superficial beauty.

Your "Ecstasy" Oracular Universe

ASTROLOGY

RAINBOW: Sagittarius—Be emotionally expansive and explorative.

ALCHEMY

WATERY and AIRY: Do not block transcendent feelings of flying high.

TIME

BLOSSOMING: It is time to accomplish; Come out; Spring forward.

GEOMANCY

FLOWER-CUP: Be in the heart; Come from the heart; Follow the heart.
GARDEN: Gather flowers.

SHAMANISM

BUTTERFLY: Play; Dance
FLOWER: Be a flower; Wear a flower; Have flowers.

AURA

LIGHT: Express the rainbow of feelings.

WHITE: Be emotionally honest.

VIOLET: Feel a deep spirituality.

BLUE: Enjoy the peace of Equilibrium, and suffer the blues of Disappointment, Sorrow, and Stagnation.

GREEN: Be able to revitalize.

YELLOW: Radiate like the sun.

PINK: Love.

RED: Fully experience the excitation of Passion, Anger, and Fear.

PSYCHOMETRY

PERFUMES: Put on the scent of the flower; Be alluring, exotic, sweet, irresistible.

SUCCESS

Ace of Worlds

Success is your *Magician* ability to achieve your goals and succeed in the world. To succeed, you must first believe that you are a success and that you will continue to succeed. Success also requires synergy. Bring together all your internal and external resources and talents.

Success is an organic process. Set your goals and plan on the means for achieving them. Begin acting on your plan. Once the plan has been initiated, nurture it with patience and persistence. Complete the task and reward yourself.

True success is on-going success. Use the successes of the past to achieve again. You must, however, adapt to new situations and opportunities. Do not be afraid to change and innovate.

Part of success is overcoming adversity. Learn from mistakes and setbacks. Realize that every failure is a new opportunity. Be opportunistic and resourceful.

Success is represented by worlds or planets. Like the creation of these worlds, know that the successful creation of your material world is the result of mixing together your elements or faculties. Make sure that any endeavor you try has your mind, heart, body, and spirit in it. Worlds are not created overnight. It takes time to succeed. Take one small step at a time. As worlds revolve and evolve, be ready to adapt and make changes. Just as worlds undergo periodic natural upheavals, so may your plans. Like the forest, which is renewed by fire, convert one step back into two steps forward.

Your "Success" Qualities

EVOLVED:

INTEGRATED PLANETARY SYSTEM: Get it all together in the material world of work, money, relationships, health, and home.

SATURN: Succeed in the world of work, career, profession through Saturnian hard work and discipline.

JUPITER: Succeed in the world of money and finances through Jupiterean expansion, growth, and risk.

MOON: Succeed in human relationships through moon-like sensitivity, caring, and sharing.

SUN: Succeed in physical health through sunny exercise, outdoor activities, and play.

EARTH: Succeed in the home-world through stewardship of your earth home.

DYNAMIC INTERACTION OF PLANETARY WORLDS: Be creative and active in your worldly life; Get established but not stuck in a status quo situation; Juggle different worlds; Be at home in the office, the bank, the gym, the hearth, and community; Be a doer, a dynamo; Create while on the go.

UNEVOLVED:

MATERIAL WORLDS: Caught up in the material world to the exclusion of other values and perspectives; Inflated sense of self-importance from material successes.

Your "Success" Oracular Universe

ASTROLOGY

SOLAR SYSTEMS: Be systematic; See the big picture; Know how things fit together and work; Practice synergy, the capability of drawing different elements and resources together; Be a team player; Co-create; Cooperate in partnerships; Make alliances.

ALCHEMY

EARTH: Be practical, realistic, "earthmatic"; Practice the "art of the possible."

TIME

CONTINUOUSLY REVOLVING PLANETS: Be ready and prepared; Any time, all the time.

GEOMANCY

UNIVERSE: Go anywhere; Indoors, outdoors; In the office or at home; In the bed or at the bank; At home or away from home.

SHAMANISM

OUROBOROS: Like the mythical snake that bites its own tail, act in circular motion bringing together infinite possibilities and spinoffs. Think of success as a dynamic continuum.

FLOWERING TREE: See yourself as a tree with the wherewithall to create prosperity, security, protection, beauty, and service.

AURA

ALL COLORS UNDER THE SUN: Perform the brown, down-to-earth mundane duties and yet spectacular reds; Know how to be restful and neutral, and yet radiate great light; You are complex—full of many tones and shades.

PSYCHOMETRY

TELESCOPE: Dream and envision; Build the tools that enable humankind to explore new horizons and build new worlds.

ILLUMINATION

Ace of Wands

Illumination is your *Magician* state of enlightenment. You hold the wand of light in your hand. You are enlightened. To be truly enlightened, however, you must know that you are.

The wand of Illumination is understanding, which is never ending. Like the light, which radiates out through the darkness, continue to search for the truth and answers. Follow your curiosity. Trust your intuition. Holding the wand of light, you are already a guiding light. Illumine others.

The light of Illumination represents purity, clarity, and honesty. Purify to burn out any impurities of character. Use your light of awareness to clean out your dark or shadowy personal qualities.

Holding the light of Illumination means living in the fire of life. Live your life to the fullest. Know what gives you energy and vitality. Be passionate.

As you spread your light, you grow and are transformed. Have the courage to change and expand. In perpetual transformation, you are a revolutionary. Give others the understanding and energy to grow and evolve.

Your "Illumination" Qualities

EVOLVED:

LIGHT: Seek the spiritual, the awareness of the everlasting light of the spirit, the divine truth of life; Seek enlightenment.

SHAFTS OF LIGHT: Revere your revelations and visions; Create the conditions for dramatic insights that "blow your mind."

INFRARED VISION (HAND): See beyond or through the superficial, material reality.

MOON LIGHT: Follow your intuitions and dream messages.

RADIATING FIRE LIGHT: Hold the torch of personal revolution by burning out and breaking through entrapping old patterns, habits, forms, and perceptions.

RAINBOW LIGHT: Activate the seven chakras and the seven virtues.

LIGHT EXPLOSION: Live in the fire of life; Arouse the Kundalini.

UNEVOLVED:

FIERY: Burns up and burns out; Temper tantrums; No tolerance for the slow; Does not finish; Scattered; Unstable; Easily bored; Cannot do the routine, needs constant excitement; Drugs to get "high."

Your "Illumination" Oracular Universe

ASTROLOGY

STARBURST: You are at a new beginning, a new age, a new eon; Irrevocable change on all levels of being follows new insights.

ALCHEMY

LIGHTNING: Feel your electricity.

GOLD: Seek light (In Hinduism, gold means mineral light; The Latin word for gold is *aurum*, the same as the Hebrew word for light, *aor*).

TIME

NEW LIGHT: It is time to see anew; Inception; Conception; Dawning.

GEOMANCY

GALACTIC: Transcend your place; Go to another world; Move.

SHAMANISM

FIRE BREATHING DRAGON: Have courage over fear; Express your personal power, for "Dragon" comes from the Greek *drakon*, meaning "the seeing one whose glance is lightning."

FLOWER SHOOT: Aspire to the light, to upwards evolution and growth.

AURA

FIRE COLORS: Live with intensity; Burn white hot.

PSYCHOMETRY

TORCH: You are a savior and destroyer, a saint and sinner.

CHIROGNOMY

KNOTTY HAND: Analyze; Philosophize about the ideal, the absolute.

EQUANIMITY

Two of Crystals

Equanimity is your *Priestess* state of mind. Equanimity is a heightened state of balanced awareness. Objectively assess your alternatives, pros and cons, assets and debits. Be even-minded. Accept the good and bad equally. Mental stability is the sign of level-headedness. Maintain a positive and healthy mental attitude in this Priestess' condition of clarity and centeredness.

Equanimity is achieved through dispassionate analysis. Free of emotional attachments, fair and just understanding is possible. Physical moderation and relaxation contribute to your equanimous mind. Mental clarity and balance may require removing yourself from the action. Get away from it all to see the truth. In this state of detachment and noninvolvement, you can see with nonjudgmental awareness. This pure state of awareness transcends your thinking mind and allows your all-knowing consciousness to evaluate and decide according to the higher laws and values of the universe.

Your "Equanimity" Qualities

EVOLVED:

BLUE SAPPHIRE EYE: Be aware.

ON-TOP-OF-IT SAPPHIRE: Know what is going on at all times.

ABOVE-IT-ALL SAPPHIRE: See things from a higher point of view.

ABOVE-THE-JUMBLE-AND-CONFUSION SAPPHIRE: Amidst uncertainty and ambiguity, distance yourself to gain clarity.

LONE SAPPHIRE: Meditate; Contemplate; Trust your judgment.

SAPPHIRE ABOVE THE CLOUDS AND STORMS: Be positive and optimistic.

SAPPHIRE IN THE CENTER: Stay centered.

BIPARTITE SAPPHIRE: Keep your balance—an even-mind, a level head.

SAPPHIRE HARDNESS: Maintain your stability, your point of view.

UNEVOLVED:

LONE SAPPHIRE: Fear of involvement.

PERFECT SAPPHIRE: Only perfection and perfect order is acceptable.

HIGH SAPPHIRE: Haughty; "I am better than you" attitude.

Your "Equanimity" Oracular Universe

ASTROLOGY

SAPPHIRE: Libra and Venus—Think in terms of proportion, beauty, and balance.

ALCHEMY

AIR: Keep moving the mind to continuously adjust to new realities.

TIME

ON-TOP-OF-IT SAPPHIRE: Stay in the present.

GEOMANCY

HEIGHTS: Seek viewpoints, vantage point, high spots.

CENTERED SAPPHIRE: Assume the middle, midpoints, intersections.

SHAMANISM

SNOW LEOPARD: Be solitary and contemplate for understanding.
ALPINE VEGETATION: Seek aloneness and remoteness for clarity.

AURA

BLUE: Be at peace.

PSYCHOMETRY

CUT SAPPHIRE: Trust your fine hand and fine eye; Create with precision.

EQUILIBRIUM

Two of Cups

Equilibrium is your *Priestess* emotional state. Like the Priestess, keep your emotional balance. Ride the ups and downs of life equally, never going too high or too low. Do not resist or suppress your feelings. With a balanced equanimous awareness of your feelings, you will naturally keep your equilibrium. In this state of emotional stability, ride off any emotional storms. Equilibrium means emotional self-sufficiency. Keep your center of balance regardless of the turn of events in your life. Constantly monitor and regenerate your emotional vitality to keep it flowing evenly.

The mental quality of equanimity, equally accepting every new situation in your life, is the key to emotional balance. Equanimity is frequently associated with the equipoise of your physical energy level.

An even metabolism creates an even mind and and an even heart. Emotional equilibrium is the result of an even balance between involvement in the material world and a spiritual detachment from it. Be in the world but with an awareness that transcends the material life.

Your "Equilibrium" Qualities

EVOLVED:

CUP RIDING ON TOP OF THE WATERS: Stay on top of your emotional waters; Ride through any emotional situation including the "blues."

CUP RIDING ATOP THE WINTRY COLD AND SPRING GREEN: Maintain your emotional stability amidst wintry emotional barrenness and iciness, spring torrents of feeling, summer tranquility and peace, and fall dryness and endings.

CUP RIDING ATOP THE RIVER OF LIFE: Keep emotionally balanced amidst the ever-changing conditions of life: the twists, turns, shoals, and bogs.

ON THE RIVER: Go with the flow of feelings; Do not resist emotions.

DUCK: Fly over your emotional waters; See your feelings, understand, and accept them.

DUCK FEATHERS: Ward off and protect yourself from undesirable feelings; Weather the storms of other's emotional outpourings.

CACTUS: Seek emotional self-containment (Be like the cactus which needs very little water, or emotional fulfillment, from the outside world to blossom).

PRICKLY CACTUS: Deter unwanted feelings arising from undesirable external situations.

WATERSHED/RESERVOIR: Be like the mountain watershed, continuously full of emotional reserves; Your inner self is a spring of emotional fulfillment; Be nondependent on external events for emotional vitality and satisfaction; self-sufficient.

YELLOW CACTUS FLOWER: Glow with emotional sunnyness.

GREEN: Emotionally regenerate and revitalize yourself.

UNEVOLVED:

CUP RIDING ATOP THE EMOTIONAL WATERS: Unfeeling; Uncaring; Emotional repression; Coldness.

Your "Equilibrium" Oracular Universe

ASTROLOGY

AQUARIUS (AIR-WATER SIGN): Like the duck, symbolize your lofty thoughts and airborne visions that are inspiring and emotionally fulfilling.

SCORPIO: You are capable of emotional transformation, able to let go of certain feelings in order to maintain your equilibrium.

ALCHEMY

WATER: Be easy-going like water, which flows downhill.

MARBLE: You can feel deeply, yet like cold marble be unmoved.

TIME

ALL SEASONS: Be versatile and adaptable.

GEOMANCY

MOUNTAIN HIGHS AND RIVER LOWS, DESERT DRY AND JUNGLE WET: Go to places of extremes and everything in-between; Anyplace.

SHAMANISM

WATERBIRD: Dwell on the water of feelings and yet be capable of flying above or transcending the feelings.

CACTUS: You are capable of great happiness (blossoming) in the driest (desert) of times.

AURA

GREEN: Transform your "blues" into sunny yellow; Regenerate.

PSYCHOMETRY

VASE: Hold your emotions (waters) in control.

REFLECTION

Two of Worlds

Reflection is your *Priestess modus operandi* in the material world. Think before you act. Reflect before you run. Contemplate before your consume. Introspect before you extrovert. Reflection is time off to take a good look at your situation. Be patient. Let time and reflection reveal how you are doing and what your next move will be.

Reflection can be thoughtful evaluation, contemplative meditation, or creative envisionment. All require peace of mind uncluttered with the demands of worldly life. Get away from it all, even if for a moment. Emotional tranquility brings clarity. You cannot see to the bottom of things if the surface is all stirred up. Understanding and insight come by looking deeply. Ask yourself, "who am I," and "what do I want." By reflecting on your true nature, you find your way—the right way.

Your "Reflection" Qualities

EVOLVED:

REFLECTING POOL AND MOON: Reflect; Contemplate.
WINTER CLARITY: Get clear; Be clear; Evaluate; Plan.
WINTER BLUE: Be at peace.
NIGHT AND MOON: Dream; Imagine.
COMET AND LIGHTBURST: Look for new visions, new ideas, new inspiration.
NIGHT AND WINTER: Hibernate; Take it easy; Relax; Lay off; Recuperate;
    Give the body a rest; Fast; Heal; Conserve; Rest.
SNOW COVERING: Be austere and simple; Don't move; Not a time for
    action; Wait.

UNEVOLVED:

REFLECTING POOL: Overly reflective and passive to the point of being
    chronically inactive; Always waiting and watching; Afraid to jump
    into the heat and passion of life.

Your "Reflection" Oracular Universe

ASTROLOGY

MOON: Go inward into yourself; Be receptive, a receiver.

ALCHEMY

FROZEN WATERS: Be still; Pause.
SILVER: Self-reflect.

TIME

WINTER: Reserve; Hold in; Contract.

GEOMANCY

MOUNTAIN LAKE: Find a place of refuge, a hermitage.
HIGH ALTITUDE: Find an uncluttered environment with clear air and light.

SHAMANISM

WOLF: Calculate; Hunt (seek, search).
PINE TREE: Go on a vision quest.

AURA

WHITE: Assume a position of neutrality and openness; Be virginal.

PURITY

Two of Wands

Purity represents how the *Priestess* sees and is. Like the Priestess, see yourself purely or honestly as you truly are. With this clarity, see who you really are as opposed to who you are supposed to be or were taught to be. Purity means to live authentically, to be you, uncontaminated by conditioning inappropriate to the real you. In being pure or true to yourself, you are cleansed, pure of negative mental, emotional, and physical states. Purity is your own morality. You are clean, or moral, if you live in truth with yourself.

Self-purification, or self-realization, begins with pure and honest self-observation. Clear awareness of self is established through a peaceful mind and a calm heart. A body unadulterated by stimulants, chemicals, and drugs brings clarity. A meditative place of tranquility and solitude creates the material conditions for self-clarification.

Your "Purity" Qualities

EVOLVED:

CRYSTALS, WINDOW, LOTUS REFLECTION: See with crystal clarity your own true nature; See it as it is; See without prejudice or preconception, without previous conditioning.

NATURAL CANDLELIGHT: Be authentic, true to yourself without falsity or artificiality.

NATURAL WHITE LIGHT: Return to your own natural goodness; Live in the perfection of your great spirit—the light.

SNOWY WHITE, HERON, SNAKE: Your true nature is untainted, without fault; Be incorruptible; Act with absolute honesty and integrity.

PATH IN SNOW: Follow your own path.

UNEVOLVED:

PURITY: Confined by moralities that are not universal moralities; Puritanical and moralistic in a sense that inhibits total personal expression and liberation of human potential.

Your "Purity" Oracular Universe

ASTROLOGY

STARS: Follow your own star path; Create your own destiny.

ALCHEMY

AIR, WATER, and FIRE: Clean up and clear out all falsities; Allow no dust upon your lens of perception.

TIME

DAWN'S EARLY LIGHT: Trust your innocence; Freshen up; Lighten up by letting go of yesterday; Be spontaneous; Follow your intuitive inspiration.

GEOMANCY

EXPANSES, VIEWS, VISTAS, WINDOWS: Find space, openness, tolerance.

SHAMANISM

SNAKE: You are infinite, able to shed the old skin and regenerate through purity of perception.

HERON: Fly with your own ideas; Your original ideas are beautiful; Mental innocence is power.

HORSE: Move the way your body wants to, regardless of learned patterns.

LOTUS: You are capable of unfolding into great beauty if you follow your own inherent potentials.

AURA

WHITE: See life through the white light of purity and you will be pure.

PSYCHOMETRY

WINDOW: Look without to see within; How you see the outside world is how you see yourself.

CREATIVITY

Three of Crystals

Creativity represents your *Empress* creative mind. Like the mother-Empress, you are inherently pregnant with ideas. New ideas are right now germinating within you and are awaiting their birth. Be creative. Let your ideas out.

Creativity is born out of love, love for what you have to offer the world. You have been given the great mothering ability to create new life through new ideas. Love your creations for they are life and life-giving.

Creativity flourishes when you place yourself in interactive situations with different environments and people. Creativity is the product of synthesis, of your union and communication with energies outside of yourself. Treat your life as a continual mating with the world and you will create the world.

Your spirit is naturally creative. Give your spirit freedom, and you will discover an endless source of new life through your creativity.

Your "Creativity" Qualities

EVOLVED:

CRYSTAL EGG, CIRCLE, CAVE, WOMB: You possess an inherent source of ideas that dwell within yourself.

ABSTRACT, AMORPHOUS CRYSTAL MATTER: Ideas are germinating, awaiting birth in your crystalline, primordial brain matter; Ideas lay fallow in the cellular self of your genetic heritage; Ideas await regeneration in the unconscious.

TOURMALINE CRYSTALS SURFACING: Tap your idea-source; Give birth to an idea; Allow new ideas to surface.

THREE TOURMALINE CRYSTALS (TWO IDEAS TO CREATE A THIRD): Create through synthesis; Engage in the mating of ideas and minds.

TOURMALINE CRYSTALS EMERGING FROM INNER SOURCES INTO THE WORLD: Let your inner consciousness meet external influences and create ideas (Try out an idea on someone else).

TOURMALINE CRYSTALS BETWEEN AIR AND EARTH: Take your conscious awareness (air) into the subconscious (earth) and create ideas (Ask for an answer through your dreams).

VERTICAL CRYSTAL MEETS CIRCULAR EGG: Let your male creative intention meet your female receptivity and openness and new ideas will be conceived.

TOURMALINE PINK AND BLUE: Your pink sexual creativity is transmuted into creativity on the blue mental level.

ORGANIC COMPOSITION AND FLOWING RIVER ON UPPER RIGHT OF CARD: Free associate with raw and unrefined ideas; Allow an organic flow of thoughts.

ABSTRACT CRYSTAL MATTER: Engage in abstract thought; Ideas for ideas' sake; Use your pure imagination.

HALLUCINOGENIC CRYSTAL MATTER: Altered states of consciousness may give you creative breakthroughs.

EARTHINESS: Create down-to-earth ideas; Be a creative problem solver.

UNEVOLVED:

Unawareness of natural inner sources of creativity; Dependence on others, books, or authorities for ideas.

Your "Creativity" Oracular Universe

ASTROLOGY

EARTH SURFACE and EARTH INTERIOR: Generate creativity by the mating of night (introspection and subconscious) with day (extrovertion and logic).

ALCHEMY

FOUR ELEMENTS: Let your fire spirit ignite your earth-matter brain to mix with the ocean of the collective unconscious to create an idea (air).

CRYSTAL (THE ONLY MINERAL THAT GROWS): Grow through new ideas and points of view; Move ideas up and out.

TIME

CHAOTIC CRYSTAL MATTER: Form new ideas out of creative chaos, when everything is mixed up, inchoate, and formless.

GEOMANCY

INTERIOR CRYSTAL MATTER and EXTERNAL TOURMALINES: Be in-between and interstitial (where different influences meet and mix); Go to frontiers, borders, edges, confluences, and conclaves for creative ideas.

SHAMANISM

SNAKE: Let go of old ideas to regenerate new ones; Go inward to find inspiration; Let certain ideas hibernate and germinate.

AURA

PINK, ORANGE, GREEN, AND BLUE: Mix together a variety for an interesting and distinctive creativity.

LOVE

Three of Cups

Love represents the heart of the *Empress*. Open your heart like the Empress and receive love. See how much love the universe is giving to you. Recognize how worthy of love you are. In return for all the love you are receiving, give your love to others. Love is an exchange, a giving and receiving of your passion for life and for co-creation. Out of love is born community. Love is a relationship. Share your ideas, your touch, your projects, and your growth. Follow the heart and you will create a world of love. With love you can trust and you can grow. Love is what makes all things possible. Love is the life essence that holds all things together and moves everything forward. Loving is living. Love is reverence for all that lives, unconditionally.

Your "Love" Qualities

EVOLVED:

RECEIVING CUP: Receive love; Love what is given you; You are surrounded by love at all times.
POURING CUP: Give love; Share yourself.
PINK ROSE: Love yourself, for you are a product of love; Love is perfect, you are perfect.
WATERFALL: Fall in love; Be passionate in your living; Let go of fear.
CAMELLIA "EYE": Follow the heart, the path of love.
FLOWERS: Express your feelings for they are beautiful.
NAUTILUS: Love will bring you changes and growth.
FISH: Love your community; Love through sexuality.
MOON: Love your family (karmic love).
FULL CUPS: Deep fulfillment is realized through love.

UNEVOLVED:

WATERFALL AND CRASHING WAVES: Invasion of others' sentiments; Overbearing expression of love; Conditional love.

Your "Love" Oracular Universe

ASTROLOGY

VENUS (MOTHER OF CUPID): Be in love with all of life.
MOON: Be a romantic; Lovestruck.

ALCHEMY

WHITE WATER: Transform any situation by love.
GLASS: Love is beautiful but fragile; Take special care of love or it breaks.

TIME

UNION OF CUPS AND FISH: Seek a meeting time.

GEOMANCY

UNION OF CUPS AND FISH: Find a meeting place.

SHAMANISM

FISH: Love through touch; Get wet (express your primordial emotions of joy, love, sorrow, sex, salivation, surprise).

RED CAMELLIA: Realize your inherent perfection; You are naturally beautiful.

AURA

PINK: Heal yourself through love; Get into the "pink of life," which brings love.

TURQUOISE: Protect love.

GOLD: Your love is golden.

PSYCHOMETRY

CUP: Hold but do not possess; Let out and let in; Openness; Love is relationship yet freedom.

NURTURING

Three of Worlds

Nurturing represents the *Empress* role in the world. Like the Empress, be a nurturer. Support your creations with patience and tender loving care. Nothing grows overnight and without help, so exercise discipline, vigilence, and creativity to insure the growth of what you have given birth to. Lend a helping and guiding hand that gives your "babies" their natural inclinations to flower and flourish in their own time and way. Nurturing means not to be too overbearing or zealous in your attention so that you stifle growth, nor does it mean to be so *laissez faire* that your harvest dies on the vine. Love with wisdom and hard work with play are the keys. With a proper nurturing attitude, your creativity will pay off and you will reap the harvest.

Your "Nurturing" Qualities

EVOLVED:

MOTHER ELEPHANT AND MOTHER BIRD: Nurture new births and material creations into flower, maturity, and full growth; Parent.

RANCHER'S HAND AND ELEPHANT'S TRUNK: Lend a hand; Be supportive.

RANCHER'S HAND: Tend to business; Take care of responsibilities; You are like a gardener or farmer.

NEST: Nurture yourself through your homelife, proper diet, and exercise.

UNEVOLVED:

Stifle the young by imposing standards and values to the extent they cannot be themselves (the "smothering mother").

Your "Nurturing" Oracular Universe

ASTROLOGY

VENUS: Love your creations; Create beauty.

TAURUS (ELEPHANT): Provide nourishment; Be a provider.

SATURN: Work with diligence and discipline—one step at a time.

ALCHEMY

EARTH: You are a manifester and materializer; Produce.

TIME

SUMMER: Keep going; Don't give up; Your creations are ripening and blossoming.

GEOMANCY

MEADOWS, FIELDS, GROVES, GARDENS: Nurture where there is beauty, fecundity, peace, and cultivation; Seek a mothering environment.

SHAMANISM

ELEPHANT: Take responsibility for the family you have created; Pay attention to the areas that are hurting.

APPLES: Keep your creations healthy for health is wealth.

AURA

GREEN: Maintain your youth and vitality.

YELLOW: See how others are nurturing.

PINK: Enjoy the fruits of your labor as you nurture them into complete fruition.

PSYCHOMETRY

NEST (HOME OR POCKET): Provide a protective warmth and love.

COMPASSION

Three of Wands

Compassion represents the healing spirit of the *Empress* mother. Like the Empress, be open to helping all, including yourself. Know that everyone is suffering in some way. Accept everyone's frailties and shortcomings with tolerance. Commit yourself with unconditional love to help others and yourself to become whole. You have the ability to heal through your understanding love and healing hands. Be gentle. Be patient. Take it easy. Compassion is nurturing and loving. The result is a renewal of the creative spirit.

Your "Compassion" Qualities

EVOLVED:

BUDDHA'S GOLDEN HAND: Understand with tolerance the human condition of frailty and suffering.

BUDDHA AS BODHISATTVA: Help all life forms grow.

HAND WITH BUTTERFLY: Accept others regardless of their condition.

FIVE-FINGERED HAND: Five is a number of wholeness, so restore your body and soul, mind and heart into creative unity and wholeness.

RED AURIC HAND OF HEALER OLGA WORRALL: Use your hands to heal; Let your hands guide you.

BUDDHA'S FIFTH MUDRA (POSTURE OF THE HAND): Recognize the perfection of the spirit and do what you can to recall for yourself and others that perfection; In your own way you can be of great service to others.

UNEVOLVED:

OPEN HAND: Over-giving; Allowing yourself to be taken advantage of; Martyr complex.

Your "Compassion" Oracular Universe

ASTROLOGY

SUN: You are a giver of new life; You have the power to awaken and recreate.

ALCHEMY

FIRE: Energize; Your healing warmth comes from your passion to purify and mend.

GOLD: Honor your own strength, health, beauty, and perfection.

TIME

SUNRISE: Know when to awaken your energies and regain your youth.

SUNSET: Know when to rest and relax.

GEOMANCY

UP IN THE AIR: Healing makes you feel high; Go where you feel fresh, young, vital, alive, restored.

SHAMANISM

BIRD: Follow your spirit guides or intuition; Trust.

BUTTERFLY: Unfold, transform, and transmute; Every moment holds the possibility of metamorphosis.

ROSE: Love is the divine healing power; Use flower remedies.

AURA

RAINBOW: Be optimistic amidst despair, for there is always wholeness and goodness in the stormiest and darkest of times.

PSYCHOMETRY

SCULPTURES OF SAINTS: Remember your virtuousness and your own saintliness.

CHIROGNOMY

SQUARE HAND: Use the healing abilities of your hands.

LOGIC

Four of Crystals

Logic represents the *Emperor's* way of thinking. Like the Emperor, be logical. Use your discriminating intelligence to classify. Prioritize. Let go of aspects and ideas that do not fit. Put things into a workable whole. Structure. Create a practical system. Build a solid foundation upon which you can expand. Think and plan. See how every piece is related to the whole. Integrate and unify. Reason holistically. See how all the domains of your life require organization and order. File. Plan ahead on your calendar. Throw away. Tidy up. Tighten up. Be efficient.

Your logic is sharpened by being in a state of emotional and physical balance. By recognizing that all phenomena in the universe have an order, you can better establish your own sense of order, harmony, and proportion.

Your "Logic" Qualities

EVOLVED:

CRYSTALS COMING TOGETHER INTO A FOUR-SIDED SQUARE:
> Ordering—See how things fit together; Use your left brain.
> Classifying—See relationships and classify; Categorize.
> Systematize—Make an organized whole.
> Patterning—See structure and patterns.
> Concentration—See the essential; Focus.
> Prioritize—Leave out the nonessential.
> Holism—See the big picture and how details fit in.
> Integration—Bring differences together.
> Structuring—See the underlying similarities and differences and how they work together into a system.
> Evaluation—Apply your critical discrimination.
> Decision making—Decide.

BACKGROUND REPETITIONS: Be linear and sequential in your thinking.

UNEVOLVED:

LOGICAL STRUCTURE: Unable to deal with randomness, chance, the organic; Cannot tolerate mystery and the idiosyncratic; Unoriginal; Strictly a technocrat and not an inventor; Everything must be pigeon-holed, planned, budgeted; Lacking spontaneity; Believing the universe will run according to our logical mind and its plans.

Your "Logic" Oracular Universe

ASTROLOGY

ASTROPHYSICS: Inquire into the structure of matter and the organization of the universe.

ALCHEMY

AIR: Think. Think. Think.

CRYSTAL: Structure your ideas into a beautiful, open, and enlightened system; Organize things like a crystal.

TIME

CRYSTALS COMING TOGETHER: It's time to meet, plan, and make decisions.

GEOMANCY

SQUARE: Find your center; Office; In squares.

SHAMANISM

FOUR SIDES (FOUR WINDS, FOUR POLES, FOUR DIRECTIONS, FOUR SEASONS): Make whole; Heal; Communify; Synergize.

AURA

RAINBOW: Compose and harmonize according to the rainbow color range; Bring together opposites; Reconcile; Blend.

PSYCHOMETRY

COMPUTER: Program; Set up.

ANGER

Four of Cups

Anger symbolizes the *Emperor's* emotional nature. Like the Emperor, you are angry whenever you have not reached your goals. Anger is great energy, however, and so use it productively. Use your frustration to move ahead. Convert your anger into progressive energy. Release your rage by actions that get you to your goal. Act. Move. Breakout. Get going. If you apply your anger correctly, it is purifying, catalytic, and effective.

Anger can also be a destructive energy. To hate and turn your insecure envy and jealousy into a hurtful tantrum toward yourself or another is completely self-defeating.

Your "Anger" Qualities

EVOLVED:

RED: See red; Energize; Act.

SMASHED CUPS: Revolutionize; Breakout.

GREEN: Use your envy as a role model for what you want to create.

RUSHING STORMY RIVER: Purify by releasing emotions as you rush ahead
toward your goals.

ANGER: Use your anger to understand what you fear, for anger is a product
of fear and insecurity.

UNEVOLVED:

BROKEN GLASS: Hurting others; Breaking down what you have built
in a pique of anger.

RED: Hatred.

PRICKLY CACTUS: Defensive.

ANGER: Unable to see that whatever happens has a cosmic justice and
built-in opportunity.

Your "Anger" Oracular Universe

ASTROLOGY

MARS AND ARIES: Honor your ego-will; Be assertive.

ALCHEMY

FIRE: Burn with desire; Use your burning desire as the fuel to realize
your passions; Recognize that you are volatile and dangerous.

ROCK: Do not give in; Be rock hard.

TIME

IMPACT: Be ready for sudden change; Things happen in a flash.

GEOMANCY

CLASH: Your energy rises in combat zones; Conflict spots.

SHAMANISM

AROUSED BULL: Be stubborn; Single-minded drive.

CACTUS FLOWER: You feel prickly; Others better watch out.

AURA

RED: Use your primitive, animal-like, lower chakra energies to create changes.

PSYCHOMETRY

GLASS CUP: You are emotionally fragile.

COMMENCEMENT

Four of Worlds

Commencement represents the *Emperor's* way of behavior in the world. Like the Emperor, act! Do it now! There is no time like the present to set your plans in motion and do what you want to do. Get the ball rolling! Do not be afraid to come out and take the leap. Ram ahead! Give it a go! Once you have started, keep going. Get it done! Be a doer.

To give birth, or to manifest anything, is always laborious and a struggle. Set your mind with determination and resoluteness. Charge up emotionally. Follow your enthusiasm. Build up your physical energy. Realize that in action you are living in accordance with the great creative spirit. Manifest your world and your dreams by putting your spirit into action. Mobilize all your powers. Gather your strength and jump into it!

Your "Commencement" Qualities

EVOLVED:

LIGHTBURST: Move your energy with swiftness.

GREEN: Treat each action as a brand new action.

LEAPING ANIMALS: Exercise and express your talents and your dreams.

SPRING: Sow new seeds; Start again and again and again; Try it out.

FOUR MARS: Assert yourself; Let nothing stop you.

RAM AND STAG: Ram ahead; Take the leap; Spring forward.

BIRTH OF CROCODILE AND ISLAND OF SURTSEY: Create; Come out; Give birth;
Procreate; Move through labor pains; The first step is the hardest.

MALE GENITALS: Express yourself sexually.

UNEVOLVED:

Injudicious emotional excess; Leaping before looking; Acting before
thinking; Irresponsible action; Addicted to the thrill of commenc-
ing but never completing.

Your "Commencement" Oracular Universe

ASTROLOGY

MARS and ARIES: Take the initiative; Be a self-starter.

ALCHEMY

FIRE: Be swift, fiery, and expansive.

SULPHUR: Be active.

TIME

SPRING: Begin in Aries (March-April).

GEOMANCY

BIRTH: Seek new places, new air, new environments.

SHAMANISM

RAM: Have the courage to do battle and lock horns.

SPROUTS: Be fresh, new, light, and airy.

POPPIES: Express your fertility, the creativity you are full of.

AURA

RED: Arouse your metabolism.

GREEN: Recognize that you are young, inexperienced ("green horn"), and unseasoned, but that you make up for it with energy and enthusiasm.

PSYCHOMETRY

SPADE: Plant the seed; Propagate.

ASPIRATION

Four of Wands

Aspiration represents the *Emperor's* spirit. Like the Emperor, aspire to fulfill all the potentials of your being. Aspire to the heights! Free yourself from whatever is keeping you back from being all that you can be. Reach out for help from the great spirit as you strive to help yourself. Empower yourself to become the master of your own destiny. With this aspiration, you can achieve victory!

For aspiration to become attainment, it must be accompanied by willpower and concentrated focus on your goal. You must be courageous and emotionally and physically aroused. You must stand up for your rights and act on your ideals. To realize your potentials, you must be a spiritual warrior. Ready to do battle for your highest good, you will break through the forces of entropy and oppression. Onward and upward!

Your "Aspiration" Qualities

EVOLVED:

SPIRE: Aspire to the heights of personal attainment; Aspire to fulfill your noblest ideals and highest potentials; Act with inspired idealism.

HANDS, SPIRES, MONUMENTS BREAKING OUT OF THE EARTH: Your spirit cannot be contained; Free yourself from enslavement to your present situation by rising above it.

LIGHT: Live in the light of the free spirit.

STATUE OF LIBERTY: Liberate for justice's sake.

OPEN HAND: Reach out for new life; Call on the higher powers for support.

FIST: Become self-empowered; Struggle for self-determination.

RED SKIES AND BLUE SKIES: Struggle; Out of conflict comes peace.

BREAKING THROUGH THE CLOUDS: You are already victorious and realized, but you must ever seek higher attainment.

UNEVOLVED:

Inflexible; Narrow-minded; Too forceful; Macho; Impatient; Egotistical.

Your "Aspiration" Oracular Universe

ASTROLOGY

URANUS: You are a revolutionary.

MARS: Stand up to conflict and warring for your ideals.

ALCHEMY

FIRE: Purify injustices; Burn out oppression.

GRANITE: Be unyielding and steadfast.

IRON: Be hard and strong.

GOLD: Seek perfection.

TIME

DAWN'S EARLY LIGHT: Awake at dawn; A new dawn.

CALL TO ARMS: Make decisions to go ahead; Start.

GEOMANCY

STRIKING OUT AND BREAKING THROUGH: Be at the frontlines; In the forefront.

SHAMANISM

MOUNTAIN LLAMA: Live your life at your top potential; It is the only life worth living.

AURA

ORANGE TO YELLOW: Advance through struggle to your place in the sun.

PSYCHOMETRY

MONUMENT: Use symbols for inspiration.

CHIROGNOMY

SQUARE HAND: Enjoy order and regularity rather than risk the heights; Ask for help rather than trying to do it yourself.

NEGATIVITY

Five of Crystals

Negativity is the mind of the *Hierophant*. Like the Hierophant, "revealer of the light," be aware of your negativities and negate them. See how your mind creates doubt and pessimism. Look at your defeatist thinking.

Know that how you view yourself and the events in your life is based on your mind's interpretation. Realize that a defeat in your mind may be a victory from somebody else's point of view. Negative interpretations are culturally conditioned—they come from all the ways in which society has said that you have not done well enough. Transcend this negative outlook by using the critical and discriminating quality of your mind to cut out defeatist thinking.

To overcome the negative mind is the most important lesson you can learn. Indulgence in negativity creates emotional stress and physical breakdown. It leads to worldly setback and failure. Negativity can break your spirit. All things bad are created in the dark mind.

Your "Negativity" Qualities

EVOLVED:

RED AND BLACK CRYSTALS: Have the red light warning of your mind ready whenever you detect the slightest bit of dark negative thinking.

CUT CRYSTAL: Cut out and slay negative thinking.

UNEVOLVED:

BROKEN CRYSTAL: You interpret events negatively; you see tornadoes, valleys, floods, quakes, and disasters everywhere; You defeat yourself with pessimism, doubt, and skepticism.

CHAOTIC CRYSTALS: Negative thinking creates confusion and conflict.

OPAQUE CRYSTAL: Negative thinking creates dull-mindedness.

DARK CRYSTAL: Negative thinking creates a closed and narrow mind.

FOOL'S GOLD CRYSTAL: Negative thinking creates delusion and the pursuit of illusions.

Your "Negativity" Oracular Universe

ASTROLOGY

PLUTO AFFLICTED: You are prone to violence, accident, and mistake because of negativity.

ALCHEMY

FIRE: Negativity leads to explosions; Burn up and burn out.

TIME

You are not in the present, but before or after the fact.

GEOMANCY

TORNADO, FLOOD: You see your life as a disaster zone.

SHAMANISM

SCAVENGERS: You feed off pain and defeat.

AURA

RED AND BLACK: You fear evil, death, and destruction.

PSYCHOMETRY

BROKEN TOOLS: You are unbalanced; Full of rage.

DISAPPOINTMENT

Five of Cups

Disappointment is the *Hierophant's* emotional barometer. Like the Hierophant, let your disappointment reveal your state of spiritual maturity. Disappointment is the result of your emotional attachment to an expectation that is unfulfilled. The "negative" mind views this as a loss. The outcome is sadness and heartache. A truly evolved person like the Hierophant, the master of life's lessons, is free of attachment to expectations. So, set your goals, but live in the moment. Be equanimous about the outcomes. Do not live for the expected outcome, for you may be disappointed.

The broken heart of disappointment leads to physical fatigue and illness. It creates setbacks on the worldly level and a loss of spiritual vitality. When disappointed, work harder at realizing your goals, but also work harder at letting go of your emotional attachment to the outcome. Staying in the present and working hard will insure your success, but do not emotionally depend upon it.

Your "Disappointment" Qualities

EVOLVED:

ROSE: Be grounded in the present reality; Beauty and success grow out of being down to earth.

UNEVOLVED:

SHATTERED CUPS AND BROKEN SHELLS: Dreams dashed and broken.
WILTED ROSE: No hope; Promise dies; Disillusionment.
SETTING SUN: Waning hope that comes with your disappointment.
CRASHING WAVES: Anger that attends disappointment.
SADDENED ROSE: Sorrow resulting from disappointment.
DARK AND SWAMPY WATERS: Fear catalyzed by disappointment.
BARREN, EARTH COVERED CUPS: Emotional state is dried up and stagnant from disappointment.

Your "Disappointment" Oracular Universe

ASTROLOGY

MOON AFFLICTED: Your emotional disappointment creates passivity.

ALCHEMY

STAGNANT WATER: You feel no emotional vitality, change, or movement.
SEDIMENT: You feel run down; No reserves.

TIME

SUNSET: You feel finished; Dead.

GEOMANCY

CUPS: You are in your cups with sadness; Teary and sad.

SHAMANISM

SHELLFISH: You are overly sensitive and attached.
ROSE: Accept the fleeting and impermanent nature of beauty and perfection.

AURA

MUDDY BLUES: You feel the blues.

PSYCHOMETRY

"DEAR JOHN" LETTER: You feel let down; Betrayed.

SETBACK

Five of Worlds

Setback represents the *Hierophant's* understanding that a new opportunity awaits. Like the Hierophant, know that one step back can mean two steps ahead. For every so-called "setback" there exists a new possibility. A setback in your world simply means that there is another way, a better way. Out of setback comes learning and new growth. Setback means you are being tested. You cannot master life unless you pass this test.

To consider setback negatively as a failure is to risk real failure for which there may be a long and difficult road to recovery. A setback is simply a matter of interpretation. A negative view of setback leads to truly negative results. A positive yet realistic understanding of "setback" leads to success. Keep this in mind: you cannot be set back unless you are moving ahead. Strategic review, retreat, regrouping, realignment, and redirection are all necessary steps of forward progress.

Your "Setback" Qualities

EVOLVED:

RAINBOW: For your every storm there is a rainbow.

FOREST FIRE: For your every fire there is reforestation.

STORMS, DROUGHTS, FIRES, ERUPTIONS: All your sebacks create conditions for necessary purifying, cleansing, and rebalancing.

EARTHS AS SEEDS: New seeds and opportunities are created by your setbacks.

DYING CORN: You will have business setbacks and financial difficulties.

CIRCULAR MOVEMENTS OF EARTHS: Be prepared for adverse turns of the wheel of fortune.

HURRICANE, FOREST FIRE, VOLCANIC ERUPTION: Unforeseen and sudden disaster and ruin.

WALL: You feel up against the wall.

DROUGHT: Prepare yourself for a drying up of resources.

SCORCHED EARTH: Ill health will occasionally happen.

FIRE: Fever, pain, and nerves are part of your life.

DROUGHT: Skin irritatons and stiffness can be expected.

CAVE AND VOLCANO: Digestive problems come with upsets.

EARTH ("BLUE WATER" PLANET): You need liquids; Heal yourself through water.

UNEVOLVED:

ABANDONED VILLAGE: Giving up; Unable to see the new opportunities created by setbacks.

Your "Setback" Oracular Universe

ASTROLOGY

EARTH: See the perfection of imperfection; The health, abundance, beauty, and creativity of the   planet is in part due to its inherent imperfection of illness, poverty, death, disaster.

ALCHEMY

FIRE, AIR, EARTH, AND WATER: Create wholeness through the conflict of opposites.

DUST: "Ashes to ashes and dust to dust"; Adapt, because everything decays over time.

TIME

TEMPORAL (EARTH AND HUMAN TIME): You are only a sand of time in the timeless cosmos, so relax, for it will pass in no time at all.

GEOMANCY

VILLAGE: You may experience setback in your home.
CORNFIELD: You may experience setback in your office.
FIRE: You may experience setback in your body.
HURRICANE: You may experience setback in your environment.

SHAMANISM

MOLE: Hunker down; Let it pass over.
CORN: Success comes through good fortune, which is the hard work that prepares you for every opportunity and contingency.

AURA

ORANGE-BROWN: Color of soil—Rotate, recycle, replenish; Diversify.

PSYCHOMETRY

GRAIN STORAGES: Hold onto the fruits of work; Preserve and guard against misfortune and ill wind; Be prudent and prepare.

OPPRESSION

Five of Wands

Oppression is the *Hierophant's* constant reminder that life is about liberation of all your potentials. Every form of oppression is an opportunity for liberation. To recognize your oppression is to understand the freedom of yourself. You cannot know freedom without knowing oppression. In knowing your oppression, you automatically know your way to liberation.

Oppression is always self-created. You create your own oppression through your ignorance, through your lack of self-awareness. Your limited self-understanding is your barrier. Increase your image of yourself and you will unlock all your talents. Free yourself from limitation by seeing yourself accurately. You are truly the universe. All things are possible if you see the possibilities. See yourself in a new light, and fly!

Your spirit is limitless and free. Your negative mind, however, only sees your limitations. The negative mind sees no way through setbacks and wallows in disappointment. Negativity perpetuates itself to the confinement of your spirit. Live in the radiance of your spirit and you will soar!

Your "Oppression" Qualities

EVOLVED:

EYES AND WINDOWS OF LIGHT: See your infiniteness; The greater your self-image, the more expansive your self-expression.

BARS: Be reminded of your oppression and thus of your way to liberation.

UNEVOLVED:

ECLIPSE OF SUN: Your light, your spirit, is oppressed.

BROKEN HAND: Your spirit is broken.

EXTINGUISHED CANDLELIGHT: You are ignorant in your self-unawareness.

DENSE BARS: You have a perceptual block—don't see yourself in a true light;   False-image; Misperception of self; Self-entrapment through this obscured self-view.

Your "Oppression" Oracular Universe

ASTROLOGY

SUN IN ECLIPSE: You have no energy; No creativity; You are in the dark.

ALCHEMY

EARTH: You are restricted by your density (lack of illumination and vision); You cannot see the forest for the trees.

IRON: You have sense of heaviness and finality.

TIME

DARK NIGHT: You are asleep in consciousness; Nightmares and bad dreams arise from your subconscious fears and memories of oppressiveness.

GEOMANCY

CONFINED SPACES: You are restricted and entrapped.

SHAMANISM

CAGED BIRD: Unnatural—you are unable to be yourself.
DEAD TREE: You are alive only on the surface and not in spirit (living death).

AURA

GREY-BLACK: You sense that there is no way out; Hitting the wall.

PSYCHOMETRY

HANDCUFF, FENCE, JAIL, TRAP, KNOT: You possess, control, or manipulate others to oppress them and yourself.

CHIROGNOMY

SQUARE HAND: You are oppressed by order and regularity.

CONFUSION

Six of Crystals

Confusion represents the Gemini *Lovers'* state of mind. Like the dance of opposites, let your mind play between ideas. Brainstorm. Allow the creative chaos of competing ideas and points of view. Do not censor anything. In this state of extreme mental activity and agitation, great ideas are born.

Maintain the ambiguity and indecision that attends this state of mental conflict, for out of conflict comes resolution and synthesis. Think with an open mind. Investigate all possibilities. Only by knowing the parameters can you intelligently know your values and make your decisions.

By seeing the opposites, you will understand the inherent duality of life, which is really created through the relativity of the mind. Knowing that everything is relative to one's viewpoint, you can see the truth as

219

transcending the thinking mind and comprising the opposites. Exercise the mind like this and you will have great wisdom and keep vital and young.

When you resist the inherent nature of the mind to create opposing ideas or to investigate a new subject, you close the mind down. Your mind atrophies. In keeping your mind and beliefs in check, you suffer headaches and loss of energy and/or you engage in unhealthy behavior to relax the mind.

The mind is in chaos during periods of great intellectual revolution or when your personal life is in flux. When things are coming apart in your world, let the mind wander and bend—otherwise, mental stress or breakdown may result. Time of change is chaotic but creative. Let the interaction of different ideas recreate your life.

Your "Confusion" Qualities

EVOLVED:

MANY CRYSTALS: Be mentally active.

PROFUSION OF CRYSTALS IN CHAOS: Let in many ideas; Allow the mind to battle amongst conflicting ideas.

BROKEN CRYSTAL: Open your mind; Be curious.

CRYSTALS IN OPPOSITION: Transcend the thinking mind by holding opposite ideas as simultaneously true.

UNEVOLVED:

BROKEN CRYSTAL: Mental breakdown due to oppositions; Mental paralysis and indecision because of information overload.

PROFUSION OF CRYSTALS: Addiction to new ideas; Overly cerebral; Lacking mental organization, focus, concentration, and discrimination.

Your "Confusion" Oracular Universe

ASTROLOGY

GEMINI: You are of two minds.

LIGHTNING: You are swift of mind with quick insights and revelations; Volatile.

ALCHEMY

EARTH INTO AIR: Old beliefs and thus old forms and structures are breaking down.

CRYSTAL: Be multifaceted in your awareness; Suggest another point of view.

TIME

GEMINI: May-June is a time for brainstorming.

LIGHTNING BOLT: Think quickly, swiftly.

GEOMANCY

OPPOSING CRYSTALS: You are in-between opposites in conflict.

SHAMANISM

HUMAN: You have the ability to create by considering different points of view.

AURA

RED AND BLUE: You blow hot and cold depending on your ideas; Fickle; Inconsistent.

PSYCHOMETRY

KNIFE, SWORD: Cut through and into to see the light; Investigate; You can be contrary, to oppose in order to criticize and hurt.

SORROW

Six of Cups

Sorrow is the *Lovers'* emotional state of expressing sadness or grief. Let your tears flow and you will be regenerated. Sorrow is a purification. Through the catharsis of sorrow you are revitalized. Sorrow is a liberation that comes with the release of emotions. Like an emotional death, you will be reborn. Let the anguish out. Pour out your feelings. Let go.

Have the courage to express your grief and you will not hit rock bottom and languish in despair. Loss of life vitality in a state of depression comes when you close up to defend your emotional sensitivity. Where there is water there is life. Cry and your light will shine again.

Your "Sorrow" Qualities

EVOLVED:

RIVER, FLOWER, WATER: Allow your river of tears to flow.

POURING OUT OF PURPLE FLOWERS: Show your grief.

TIPPED VASE: Cathart; Release; Let go.

VASE WITH ELEPHANTS, LIGHT, AND PALM TREE: Rebirth and regeneration come after purification or expression of sadness.

UNEVOLVED:

EARTHEN CUPS: Drying up emotionally; Trying to stay rock hard.

BLACKNESS: Continued depression.

DOWNWARD FLOW: Dropping to the depths and staying down.

SETTING SUN: Prolonged loss of life and vitality.

Your "Sorrow" Oracular Universe

ASTROLOGY

SCORPIO: Liberate your feelings and you will liberate your spirit.

ALCHEMY

WATER: Change the form of your emotional expression by showing your feelings (let it rain) and your emotional state will be transformed into sunlight.

GLASS: Your emotions are fragile; Strengthen yourself by pouring your feelings out.

TIME

MIDNIGHT: This is the "dark night of the soul."

GEOMANCY

RIVER: The river of life is where "all things must pass."

SHAMANISM

ELEPHANT (ELEPHANT BURIAL GROUNDS): Anguish over your loss like the elephant.

PALM (TREE OF LIFE): Have faith and hope, for all things are physically mortal but immortal in spirit.

AURA

BLACK: Mourn.

PSYCHOMETRY

VASE: Retain life by letting your emotional waters out so that new waters
can come in.

SYNERGY

Six of Worlds

Synergy represents the *Lovers'* worldly ability to bring resources together to create an alliance of power and success. Synergy is the combination of energies such that the whole is greater than the sum of each of its parts. Combine your own inner resources and abilities. Combine these with outside resources and with others. Combine this partnership into even a greater cooperative. Keep partnering, allying, and networking in ever-expanding circles. The collective has power. Organize. Co-create. Work in teams. You have the power to build your world and achieve your goals if you coalesce. Make it happen by using all available ways and means.

The mental conditions for success through synergy embody the ability to think holistically and creatively. Synergy requires emotional courage and physical vitality. Put your ego aside. There will be plenty of personal recognition when your team wins. In synergy, everyone wins.

Your "Synergy" Qualities

EVOLVED:

WEAVING TOGETHER OF RESOURCES: Energy, power, and productivity result from gathering and mixing your resources.

WHEEL: Work; Produce with a goal in mind.

SOLAR DISK TURBOCHARGER: Give it the works; Exercise your power.

INTEGRATING RESOURCES: Everyone and everything is an opportunity and a resource for gain.

UNEVOLVED:

Selfishness; Win-loss attitude (my win is your loss); Defensiveness.

Your "Synergy" Oracular Universe

ASTROLOGY

EARTH: Apply your broad knowledge and knowhow.

SATURN: Be patient and disciplined; Persevere.

JUPITER: Be expansive; Risk take.

SUN: Be creative in your leadership.

MOON: Follow your intuitions, dreams, and visions.

VENUS: Create with a sense of beauty and high ideals.

URANUS: Be a revolutionary by creating a unique blending together of different energies.

ALCHEMY

FIRE (SOLAR DISH): Go with your drive and ambition.

AIR (WINDMILL): Spin new and revolutionary ideas.

WATER (WATERWHEEL): Move with your churning passions.

GOLD AND PETROLEUM: Create wealth; Capitalize; Get investors.

TIME

WINTER: Reflect; Contemplate; Plan.

SPRING: Commence; Act.

SUMMER: Nurture; Cultivate.

FALL: Complete; Harvest.

GEOMANCY

CIRCLE: Opportunities are places where people and resources come together, such as communities, cooperatives, teams, unions, partnerships, associations, conventions, conclaves, intersections, medicine wheels, alliances, pow wows.

SHAMANISM

SWANS: Create faithful and loyal partnerships.

SUNFLOWER AND GRAPES: Use the same source in many ways (fruit/seeds/oil).

AURA

RED AND BLUE: Integrate masculine and feminine energies.

PSYCHOMETRY

MACHINES: Be inventive and efficient.

BASKET: Weave talents and resources together.

TRUST

Six of Wands

Trust represents the *Lovers'* belief in one's self and in the universe. Trust yourself. Be confident that you have been given the abilities and opportunities to realize your goals and dreams. Have faith in yourself and the courage to be yourself. Relax and simply concentrate on the task at hand and you will succeed.

Trust in the goodness of the universe. The universe is friendly and will support you. You are in good hands. Lend a supporting hand to others. Do not be suspicious, doubtful or uptight. Trust begets trust. Know that others can trust you. Without mutual trust, everything falls apart. The world is built on trust, so build *your* world on trust.

Trust your instincts and intuitions for not everyone and everything is trustworthy. But approach everything in a state of open trust. You will *feel* when something is not right. Trust that.

Your "Trust" Qualities

EVOLVED:

HAND OF GOD HOLDING THE RING OF LIFE WHICH HOLDS THE ACROBATS: Trust the universe.

BRIDGE AND PARACHUTISTS: Trust the laws of the universe.

CLASPED HANDS: Trust yourself; Trust the human spirit.

CIRCLE OF HANDS: Trust humankind, for we are all in the same family; There is a human bond, bridge, circle; Synergize; "Communify."

LINKING OF HANDS: Believe in synchronicity—that we are all in an invisible interrelationship and interdependent.

OPEN HAND: Be open, accepting, tolerant, ecumenical.

ETERNAL LIGHT: Maintain fidelity and allegiance in friendships, kinships, marriages, agreements, contracts.

ADULT HOLDING CHILD: Take responsibility; Be trustworthy.

CHILD BEING HELD: Trust; See the goodness in others; Let go and be held.

UNEVOLVED:

CLASPED HANDS: Grasping; Insecure; Oppressive; Possessive.

Your "Trust" Oracular Universe

ASTROLOGY

UNIVERSE: Trust that the universe is whole and perfect.

ALCHEMY

EARTH: Trust that things are cohesive, together, and solid.

DIAMOND: Trust your love, your light, your beauty, your richness.

TIME

ETERNAL FLAME: Trust that everything changes yet maintains continuity; Past, present, and future are different yet the same.

GEOMANCY

COMMUNITY CIRCLE: Find places of trust, such as earth, society, community, family, meeting grounds, partnerships.

SHAMANISM

DOG: Be a faithful companion; Have a faithful friend.

FLOWER: Trust that you can express yourself; Be open and vulnerable.

AURA

BLOOD RED: Be loyal.

PSYCHOMETRY

BRIDGE: You are a bridge for others; Do not be afraid to cross over and meet the unknown; Trust your curiosity.

CHIROGNOMY

DIFFERENT HANDS: It takes all kinds to build a world; Trust in diversity; Everyone has their own unique destiny to fulfill and this is what creates the web of oneness; Live and let live and everything will work out best; Do not interfere.

DULLNESS

Seven of Crystals

Dullness represents the *Charioteer's* stable state of mind amidst great movement. Like the Charioteer, make sure of your mental foundation. Make sure that the path you are following is conceptually solid. Dullness is the "philosopher's stone," for it symbolizes the philosophical underpinning on which you base your life. Your belief system is your grounding. Have a philosophy of life that is down-to-earth. A practical and dependable philosophy of living is your mental base. From that base you can take great leaps of consciousness.

Dullness is your refuge. Not only a philosophical home, it also represents a chance for you to rest your mind. Let your brain wind down. Be dull. In mental rest there is regeneration. Give your mind the opportunity to regroup and renew.

Watch that you are not becoming dull in your curiosity. The mind that degenerates is one that finds nothing interesting and stimulating to pursue. Boredom, the lack of curiosity, is antithetical to the life spirit. Keep your mind open, inquiring, and imaginative, but do not forget to rest it.

Your "Dullness" Qualities

EVOLVED:

STONE: Mental base of your values, beliefs, and philosophy.
DULL STONE: Mental rest.

UNEVOLVED:

DENSE CRYSTAL: No curiosity; No imagination; Boredom.
STONE WALL: Closed mind; Blocked.
HEAVY STONE: Set in your ways ("etched in stone"); Slow minded.
STONE: Stoned.
WALL OF STONE: Feeling blocked.
STONE WALL: Closed; Immovable; Defensive; Insecure.

Your "Dullness" Oracular Universe

ASTROLOGY

MOON: You are barren of your own ideas.

ALCHEMY

EARTH: Be conventional; Use practical wisdom.
GRANITE: You have an impenetrable mindset; Unreceptive mind.

TIME

HEAVY DULL ROCK: You are asleep; Sleepy time.

GEOMANCY

STONE WALL: Enclosed and dark places, such as cells, rooms, caves indicate that you are not seeing, but are in the dark.

SHAMANISM

STONE WALL: Your mind is in hibernation.

MOSS: Assumed and unnoticeable beliefs direct your life.

AURA

GRAY-BROWN: You feel commonplace; Dull.

PSYCHOMETRY

STONE: Stone Age tools—You are behind the times with outdated beliefs.

FEAR

Seven of Cups

Fear is the *Charioteer's* emotional state that drives him/her on. Like the Charioteer, go where there is fear. For where fear exists, there is the opportunity for growth. The greater you stretch yourself, the more fear there will be. Doing the fearful is an indication of your commitment to personal development.

Fear is what stops you, limits you, and holds you back. Don't hold back. Move on. See where your fears are so you can understand where your blocks are. Use the adrenaline energy of fear to catapult yourself forward through your hangups. Know that you will not be able to get rid of your fear until you go into it. Feel your fear and use its energy to move through it.

Watch that you are not "living in fear," in the sense that you "hunker down" with your life—always defending, protecting, enclosing, hoarding, holding onto. To close up and shut down your life because of fears is to stop growing, which is not the way of your spirit. Be prudent, careful, and watchful, however, for there are reasons for fear. But do not react impulsively with fear. When afraid, stop and reflect. It may be a moment to be prudent or a sign to go ahead.

Your "Fear" Qualities

EVOLVED:

WAVES OF FEAR: Ride with the fear through the fear; Dive into your fears.

UNEVOLVED:

OVERTURNED GLASS AND PASSED WATER: Worry, anxiety, terror.

ALL CUPS ARE CLOSED: Timid; Insecure; Not confident; Closed up emotionally; Defensive; Self-protective; Unexpressive.

BARRACUDAS, PIRANHA, LION, INSECT, SEA MONSTER, PRICKLY CACTUS, LURKING MEN, TIDAL WAVE: You are phobic; Feel fear everywhere.

MENACING LOOKING ORCHIDS: You are paranoid; Feel monsters where none exist.

Your "Fear" Oracular Universe

ASTROLOGY

MOON: Reflect on how much you carry the fears of your past life of animal survival instincts.

ALCHEMY

OCEANIC: You fear the unknown, dark, deep, death.

GLASS: You feel unprotected; Vulnerable.

TIME

OCEANIC DEPTH: You are experiencing a past life inheritance.

OCEAN MYSTERY: Your future is unclear.

BIG WAVES: Now is high time; Time of reckoning.

GEOMANCY

OCEAN BOTTOM AND CLOSED CUPS: You find places of hiding in fear.

SHAMANISM

BARRACUDA: You are aggressive because of fear and insecurity.

AURA

RED: Move with your adrenaline rush of energy; Have courage; Notice the warning signs.

PSYCHOMETRY

INCENSE BURNER: Purify evil spirits; Gather courage.

BREAKTHROUGH

Seven of Worlds

Breakthrough is the way the *Charioteer* expresses his/her energy in the world. Like the Charioteer, break through blocks that prevent you from achieving your goals and aspirations. Free up your talents and resources. Break out! Revolutionize your life. A breakthrough is not only a liberation but a purification, a cleaning out. Breaking through allows you to shed the weight of psychological and emotional resistance by expunging the fear blocks that kept you tight, rigid, and on the defensive. In exercising your strength, you work out the lethargies caused by inertia. Give your spirit a new spark by letting in fresh air as you let out your inner fire.

Breakthroughs require power. Be clear with your vision. Use your energy of fear to propel you forward and concentrate your physical strength. Act with will and determination. Do not be denied. Work hard with all your body and soul. Sweat. Breakthrough is labor but a labor of love and passion.

Take care that you do not burn others with your energy. Do not burn out yourself. Watch that you manage your impatience and intemperateness. Beware of blowing up.

Your "Breakthrough" Qualities

EVOLVED:

VOLCANO: Act with power to express your drives and visions.

BREAKING THROUGH: Break through difficulties, blocks, hangups; Solve the problem; Manifest the potential; Move forward; Come out; Emerge; Liberate yourself.

HORSE: Strengthen yourself; Exercise; Run free.

SUN: Express your energy, vitality, and sexuality.

BREAKING OUT: Purify the mental and emotional negativities by expressing yourself.

UNEVOLVED:

EXPLOSIONS: Blowing up; Hurting others.

Your "Breakthrough" Oracular Universe

ASTROLOGY

SUN: Be assertive, dynamic, yang; Project.

ALCHEMY

FIRE: Express your heat and passion.

HOT LAVA: You are dangerous, seething, and searing.

TIME

RISING SUN: "It's high time"; "Now or never"; Sunburst; Dawn; Spring Equinox.

GEOMANCY

VOLCANO: Find places of inspiration; High energy zones; Hot spots; Where the action is.

SHAMANISM

HORSE: "Feel your oats"; "Get on your high horse."
FOREST FIRE: Destroy the old; Revolt; Cleanse.

AURA

RED: Dare to be noticed and exposed; Dare to succeed.

PSYCHOMETRY

TORCH: Carry the torch; Lead the way; Start the fire.

COURAGE

Seven of Wands

Courage represents the *Charioteer's* spirit. Like the Charioteer, have the courage to face your fears and face them down, for fear can kill your spirit. Have the courage to look at your inner demons and strike them down. Clearly look at your fears, and they will dissipate in your light. Throw the light of your awareness on your shadow side and it is actually no longer dark. Have the courage to study your fears and you will naturally be enouraged and have the courage to act.

    Wherever there is fear, there is courage. You cannot know fear unless you have had the courage to experience it. The path of fear is the path of courage. Transform your fear into courage. Do not fear fear. Fear is your ally, your tool to realize your highest destiny through courage. Take heart. Trust. Be a warrior. Encourage yourself.

Your "Courage" Qualities

EVOLVED:

DEMON FACES: Your enemies are your inner demons.

FACES: Have courage; Face fear in the face; Face up to your fears; Face down fears.

DEMON CARVINGS: Exorcise fear through exposure of demons.

HAND HOLDING THE AXE, KNIFE, SWORD: Take dominion over your fears.

UNEVOLVED:

Discouraged because of fear.

Your "Courage" Oracular Universe

ASTROLOGY

MARS: Do battle with fears; Do battle with arms.

ALCHEMY

FIRE: Burn out your fears through awareness of them.

EARTH: Bury your fears (wood); Cut your fears apart (glass); Smash your fears (stone).

OBSIDIAN: Cut into the heart of fear and exorcise it.

TIME

MIDNIGHT: Let your subconscious fears be revealed in your dreams.

GEOMANCY

JUNGLE: Journey into your "heart of darkness"; Frightening places.

SHAMANISM

DRAGON: Guard against the dark forces of fear.

TREE: You are always protected; You have refuge.

AURA

BLOOD RED: Do not be afraid to be wounded (Red badge of courage, Purple Heart).

PSYCHOMETRY

TOTEM POLE, MASK, WINDOW, TAPESTRY: Exorcise demons through their symbolic externalization; Purify through the creative process; Art is therapy.

WEAPON: You have many tools to face demons and to deter them.

SYNTHESIS

Eight of Crystals

Synthesis is the *Balance* of the mind's abilities. Like Synthesis, use your whole brain. Synthesis is the full and integrated use of all your mental faculties.

Balance your mind by using equally your right-brain hemisphere of creativity and imagination and your left-brain logic and reason. Dream and analyze. Envision and think. Invent and evaluate. Draw and write. Sing and speak. Daydream and focus. Meditate and calculate. Be a poet and a reporter. Be a scientist and a technician.

Integrate these opposite poles of consciousness. Structure your creative visions into a meaningful order of thought and language. Imagine how you can make your logic appealing to the mind's need for magic and mystery. Balance your mind through "practical fantasy."

As a synthesizer, be a unifier and harmonizer. See both sides of any issue and find their points in common. See how all aspects are part of a bigger picture. Bring together oppositions. Be a creative problem solver. Moderate. Conciliate. Mediate.

Your mind is whole. View it all holistically and you will create wholeness in yourself and in the world. Heal yourself and others through the natural synthesis of the mind.

Your "Synthesis" Qualities

EVOLVED:

UNCUT, ORGANIC CRYSTAL: Use your right brain imagination, creativity, vision; Draw out ideas from your inherent creative source.

AIR: Pull ideas out of the air.

CUT DIAMOND, CALCULATOR, SCROLLWORK: Use your left brain logic, structure, organization; Put your ideas into practical application that have value and use for others.

CENTRAL CRYSTAL: Unify right and left brains; Heal, join, make whole; Be fair; Moderate.

UNEVOLVED:

DISTINCTION BETWEEN RIGHT AND LEFT BRAINS: Compartmentalizing the different functions of the mind; Unable to integrate; Being one or the other but never both simultaneously.

Your "Synthesis" Oracular Universe

ASTROLOGY

LIBRA: Keep the proper proportions; Mix evenly.

ALCHEMY

AIR: Move the mind.

CRYSTAL: Your genius is the unique way you integrate thoughts and visions.

TIME

BALANCE OF OPPOSITES: Past and future come together in the present; At the same time; Simultaneously.

GEOMANCY

IN-BETWEEN CRYSTAL: Be confluent; Straddle points.

SHAMANISM

CRYSTAL: Be light in matter (down-to-earth dreams, useful visions).

AURA

BLUE: Clear away confusion; Clarify; Make peaceful.

PSYCHOMETRY

CALCULATOR: Use your analysis to trigger new ideas and visions.

STAGNATION

Eight of Cups

Stagnation represents the emotional state of *Balance* when things have reached a point of stasis or stillness. Stagnation is when you have completed it all or gone all the way and are now waiting for the new inspiration and energy. Allow yourself to be in this swamp of emotional lethargy. Let yourself feel the blahs. Out of the swamp comes new life. Rest and you will regenerate. Know that new seeds are germinating under the surface of your indolence.

Do not let yourself stagnate, however, in the middle of a project, or when you have not "done your thing" all the way to completion. Stagnation is your reward for having reached the end. Sleep. Be dull. Pig out. But do not let yourself get stuck in your swamp of debauch. Too much stagnation may suffocate your creative spirit. Go to the swamp of sloth but get out!

Your "Stagnation" Qualities

EVOLVED:

EMPTY CUPS, FALLEN LEAVES, MUD FLATS: You feel emotionally dried-up, indolent, burned out, fatigued, dead, but you know that death leads to rebirth.

SWAMP: Germinate new life; Regenerate; You feel depressed; You've got the "blahs."

FROZEN WATERS, CLOSED CUP: You feel emotionally frozen, stuck, blocked, closed; Take care of your emotional energies by protecting yourself; Find your refuge; Retreat.

UNEVOLVED:

OOZE: Drowning and suffocating your emotional vitality; Feel overwhelmed and cannot get out or unstuck; Debauch to compensate for emotional loss; Self-destructive; Feel hopeless.

Your "Stagnation" Universe

ASTROLOGY

NEPTUNE: You have bottomed out and are waiting to start resurfacing.

ALCHEMY

WATER AND EARTH (SILT AND SEDIMENT): Let go and fall to the bottom; Do not resist; Slip and slide.

TIME

ICE: Slow-motion time; "Seems like forever."

GEOMANCY

SWAMPS AND FROZEN RIVERS: Restore your energy in still, motionless places; Places of quiet and solitude.

SHAMANISM

SLUGS: Be a slug.

HUMUS: Decay creates the conditions for new life; Life grows from the compost.

AURA

GREENISH BROWN: Return to earth (the mundane) to create conditions for a new spring.

PSYCHOMETRY

EMPTY VASE: You are waiting to be refilled.

CHANGE

Eight of Worlds

Change is the *Balance* way of keeping the balance. Staying healthy and whole requires constant change. The only constant in life is change, so adapt to your ever-changing realities. Move your mind, heart, body, and spirit in accordance with the changes. Change to keep up with change. Be flexible, be versatile, be adaptable. Do not get fixed or overly protective of the status quo. Conserve through change. Change sometimes just for the sake of change. Keep yourself renewed, alert, creative, and stimulated by changing up. Change prevents stagnancy. By changing, you unfold and branch out. Call upon skills and resources that you have seldom tapped. Grow through change.

Your "Change" Qualities

EVOLVED:

CHAMELEON, LEAF BUG, DOE, GRASSHOPPER, MOTH: Adapt to new realities by
transforming your attitudes, feelings, energies, and situation;
Blend in; Fit in; Keep up.

CHANGE OF SEASONS: Stay supple and malleable; Be soft and receptive.

EARTH CHANGES: Change your home environment.

VENUS CHANGES: Change your relationships.

SATURN CHANGES: Change your work situation.

JUPITER CHANGES: Change your financial status.

SUN CHANGES: Change your physical state, health, appearance.

COLOR AND SKIN CHANGES: Change your appearance.

MARS CHANGES: Change your life style.

UNEVOLVED:

Fickle; Unaccountable; Unreliable.

Your "Change" Oracular Universe

ASTROLOGY

REVOLVING SOLAR SYSTEM: Be aware of cycles; Change is cyclical.

ALCHEMY

FOUR ELEMENTS: One thing leads to another; Succession of cause and
effect; Changes will create changes; You cannot stop change.

MERCURY: You stay free by constantly transforming—breaking apart
and remerging; Move quickly; Act swiftly.

TIME

CHANGE: "Time moves on" so accept that nothing lasts; Everything is
here and gone, fleeting, impermanent.

GEOMANCY

CHANGE: Look for in-between places; Transition zones; Communication links; Places of movement.

SHAMANISM

CHAMELEON: Survive through adaptation.

TREES, PLANTS, FLOWERS: Lie fallow, sprout, branch, bud, flower, die; Follow the birth, death, and rebirth cycle.

AURA

CHANGING COLORS: Change your colors.

PSYCHOMETRY

CLOTHES, MAKEUP: Change your appearance.

HARMONY

Eight of Wands

Harmony represents the unifying spirit of *Balance*. See how everything fits together. See the perfection and order in life. Bring your own life into harmony. Blend all of your opposite traits and skills into a harmonious whole. Do not ignore any of your facets. Keep your center by bridging each of your aspects even if they appear in opposition to each other. Censor nothing. The inherent balance within you will always want to balance out any extremes. Allow this to happen. Establish and keep in your own mind the vision and affirmation of being in perfect harmony. Let your spirit orchestrate this harmony.

Harmonizing is playful creativity. Express one aspect of yourself and another wants to come out in response. Together, they synthesize and create a third, which in turn provokes another side. Let this action-reaction-synthesis syndrome play itself out.

In relation to your world, understand your unique qualities and life situation. See the uniqueness of others and their situations. Recognize how you can harmonize with the world and with others to create beauty. Life is a dance, a score. Learn how to play within yourself and with others. Know yourself, let go of competitive ego, and enjoy the music.

Your "Harmony" Qualities

EVOLVED:

BRIDGE: Bridge together all your different qualities and different selves.

GOLD MUSIC STAND: Follow the "golden mean," which is the creation of yourself into golden richness by mixing your inner dualities.

SOUND: Know your sound (your unique qualities).

WIND AND STRING INSTRUMENTS: Unify your inner self (wind) and release your outer expression (strings) in the world.

DRUM AND HARP: Integrate your physical world (drum) with the spirtual and ethereal (harp).

CLARINET/TRUMPET AND HARP: Harmonize your inner male (trumpet) and inner female (harp).

RAINBOW: Unify your seven chakras.

BEAUTY: Be an idealist; Seek to create absolute beauty.

MUSIC: Heal yourself through different kinds of music.

UNEVOLVED:

Dissonance; Disorder; Disproportionate; Disease.

Your "Harmony" Oracular Universe

ASTROLOGY

LIBRA AND AQUARIUS: Think in terms of balance and beauty.

ALCHEMY

AIR AND WATER: Be sensitive to vibrations; Hear the echos and reverberations; Follow ideas that make you feel lofty; Be lighthanded on yourself.

GOLD: Synthesize to produce the best.

TIME

MUSICAL: Follow the beat; Rhythmic timing; Fine timing.

GEOMANCY

AIR: Look for airy regions; Space; Heights; Expanses.

SHAMANISM

BIRD: Sing.
BAMBOO: Be yin and yang, soft and hard.

AURA

GREEN: Create by mixing the opposites of your yellow-hot and blue-
cold sides.

PSYCHOMETRY

MUSICAL INSTRUMENT: Find your instrument (your genius); You are like
a musical instrument that can inspire, relax, and heal others; Use
your power to influence the mood and spirit of others to help
bring them into their own harmony.

NARROWNESS

Nine of Crystals

Narrowness represents the *Hermit's* state of mind. Like the Hermit, focus on your priorities. Concentrate on what is most important for you to complete. Use tunnel vision to remove any distractions from achieving your goal. Pursue your objective with single-minded discipline. Stay out of the public limelight. Keep to yourself. Gather in your power to reach the light at the end of your tunnel. Keep to the straight and narrow. Go deep. Get totally into your work. Immerse yourself. There is no turning back. There is no exit except for attainment. Commit. Trust yourself and the course that you have committed to.

Narrowness can also represent narrow-mindedness, a closed mind that is caught in the blinders of its narrow beliefs. Look at your belief system and philosophy of life. Make sure that your mind is open, and that your philosophy allows for new values, ideas, and beliefs. A closed mind does not grow, but atrophies in dogmatism and ideology. See the light in other points of view. Be tolerant, receptive, and flexible to different perspectives.

Your "Narrowness" Qualities

EVOLVED:

TUNNEL, CAVE, NARROW APERTURE WITH LIGHT AT THE END OF THE TUNNEL: Focus; Concentrate; Stay resolved and disciplined; Do not waver; Complete; Go all the way; Set a deadline.

CAVE: Trust your focus; Have the courage to be insular, isolated, individualistic, and even eccentric in point of view; Be mentally self-sufficient; Stay true to your point of view.

UNEVOLVED:

TUNNEL, CAVE, NARROW APERTURE: Seeing only one perspective; Closed-minded; Inflexible; Fixed in your ideas and beliefs; Intolerant; Dogmatic; Ideologue.

SHARP CRYSTALS: Overly critical and judgmental.

CAVE: Being narrow-minded because you are fearful, insecure and thus defensive.

Your "Narrowness" Oracular Universe

ASTROLOGY

PLUTO: Stay silent, keep quiet; Stay within yourself (the underworld).

ALCHEMY

EARTH: Plunge into yourself for the questions and answers.

STALACTITES AND STALAGMITES: Deal with obstacles; Don't be paranoid of different values and beliefs.

TIME

CAVE: Have time alone; Night time.

GEOMANCY

CAVE: Be in your place, your refuge, your home.

SHAMANISM

MOLE: Go blindly with trust and faith; Don't look far.

AURA

BLACK: Keep your secret.

PSYCHOMETRY

SKIN: Feel your way through; Put the pressure on.

FULFILLMENT

Nine of Cups

Fulfillment is the *Hermit's* state of emotional satisfaction upon the completion of a task. Like the Hermit, get your work done and be happy. You have been given certain qualities and abilities. Turn these into outputs and celebrate. Manifest your potential and reward yourself. Enjoy the deep and quiet inner contentment that comes with attaining your smallest goals and highest dreams.

Be fulfilled during the process of realizing your purpose, which is to produce your talents for the service for others. Take pleasure in doing your work well. Appreciate the energy, time, and discipline you have devoted to do the job. Smile as you perform your tasks. Take a moment to acknowledge your skill. Toast your creativity.

Your "Fulfillment" Qualities

EVOLVED:

GRAPES: Know your natural wealth of talent.

WINE AND PEARLS: Manifest your talents; Produce with your gifts.

GRAPES INTO WINE: Know your purpose, your work.

FRUIT DRINKS: Drink from your passion and be rewarded; Follow your passions.

FULL CUPS: Happiness, joy, and contentment come with completing your work.

MANY FULL CUPS: Know that attainments bring a feeling of emotional luxury and richness.

OPEN SHELL AND CUP POURING WINE: Emotionally express your achievements.

SPIRITS: Feel exuberant and high in fulfilling your visions and dreams; Feel the spirit of life as you create with your talents.

UNEVOLVED:

MANY FULL CUPS OF WINE: Overindulgent and up-tight in your work to the point that you need alcohol for release; Overindulgent in alcohol and hedonism for fulfillment.

Your "Fulfillment" Oracular Universe

ASTROLOGY

SATURN: Have a Saturnalian celebration of hard work and discipline that has paid off.

ALCHEMY

WATER: Your ability to emotionally fulfill yourself gives you the inner strength to carry on and carry through.

GRAPES INTO WINE: Manifest your magic.

GLASS: The amorphous composition of glass represents a flexible and versatile nature that can find fulfillment easily everywhere.

TIME

CELEBRATION: Harvest time is celebration time; Completion time.

GEOMANCY

CELEBRATION: Find a showroom or a banquet hall to celebrate.

SHAMANISM

OYSTER: Self-realization through the manifestation of your potential (sand into pearls) is an aphrodisiac in the sense of lust for the creative life.

GRAPE: Be fruitful and abundant.

AURA

GOLD: Your are content from striving for your pinnacle of perfection—the outcome of transforming raw talent into production.

PSYCHOMETRY

WINE GLASS: Your contribution fulfills you.

HARVEST

Nine of Worlds

Harvest is the fruition of the *Hermit's* hard work. Like the Hermit, recognize that situations are ripe. Things have come to a crowning culmination. It is most fruitful to continue what has been started through to its absolute completion. Go the last mile. Do it right all the way to the end. Do not get impatient for the harvest. This is your opportunity to fully bear your inner riches to the world. You are in your full power and maturity. It is an extraordinary time to materialize, manifest, and realize your moon dreams. You have much to offer. Get on with it. Do not waste a moment! This is an optimum period for successful productivity. Do not let your efforts go to waste. Finish up and clean up!

Understand that your successes are preparations for the next go-around. Your harvest gives you the wherewithal to get through the transition to your next goal and to successfully start again. Use the abundance you have created to set up the next harvest.

Your "Harvest" Qualities

EVOLVED:

HARVEST: Reap what has been sown and nurtured; Harvest the fruits of your labor; Get it done.

RIPE FRUIT, CORN, WHEAT: Get everything primed and in top shape for the final step.

WHEAT: Move from pregnancy to birth to maturity.

SQUIRREL EATING: Take good care of yourself by your nutrition — "you are what you eat."

FULL MOON: Know that this is a vitally important completion task for you because it represents the fulfillment of your karma and your dreams.

BASKETS: Tie up loose ends; Resolve the unresolved; Finish up the unfinished.

FALLING FRUIT: Undone and incomplete affairs result in fallen fruit that putrifies and stagnates.

MOON CYCLE: Harvests and completions give you sustenance for the next cycle.

UNEVOLVED:

Wasted work; Saturation.

Your "Harvest" Oracular Universe

ASTROLOGY

VIRGO: Produce and achieve through planning, organization, discipline, and work.

FULL MOON: End the cycle.

ALCHEMY

EARTH: Make your success tangible, material, unquestionable, obvious, and measurable.

TIME

FALL: Your time is closing time; Fall; Virgo; 5 PM.

GEOMANCY

MATERIAL HARVEST: Look for harvests in the physical material world, such as the garden, home, business, bank account, relationships, body.

SHAMANISM

SQUIRREL: "Squirrel away" some of your harvest to be prudent; Insure; Prepare for the future by taking care of the present.

GRAPES, WHEAT, CORN, PUMPKIN, BERRY, NUT: Your seeds of potential are being manifested into reality.

AURA

GOLD: Think rich.

PSYCHOMETRY

HARVESTER: Use help for getting all the work done.

INTEGRITY

Nine of Wands

Integrity is the *Hermit's* spirit of unbending self-determination. Like the Hermit, be true to yourself. This means knowing yourself and valuing yourself. Have the backbone to walk your own path. Have the courage to stand alone. Defend your spirit (the inner light) without self-compromise. Be honest. Integrity is the path of the spiritual warrior. Have the vision, aspiration, and strength to climb to the top of your mountain. Follow the high road of the higher self.

You are integral, for your spirit is whole. You possess everything within yourself to fulfill your highest destiny. Protect the temple of your mind, heart, and body that preserves your spirit light. Keep fit mentally, emotionally, and physically, and your spirit light will naturally guide you.

Your "Integrity" Qualities

EVOLVED:

TEMPLE (CHURCH, MOSQUE): Sanctify your inner light; Honor your spirit; Respect yourself; Protect your inner spirit.

PATH: Follow your own path; Assume self-responsibility.

MOUNTAIN: Perform your karmic obligations (go with your spirit).

SPINAL CHORD: Have the backbone to stand up for yourself; Courage.

SOLITARY FIGURES: Be unafraid to stand alone; Be self-sufficient.

LIGHT: The light of the spirit is your guide; Express your truth.

FIGURE WALKING AWAY: Turn away from what is not right for you.

FACELESS STONE FIGURE: Be impenetrable to undesirable outside forces.

SPIRES: Aspire to higher consciousness; Grow up.

UNEVOLVED:

CHURCH: Dogmatic rigidity and ideology; Giving away your self-responsibility; Sanctimonious (holier than thou); Empty rituals; Following the flock.

Your "Integrity" Oracular Universe

ASTROLOGY

BACKBONE (LIBRA): Be just to your higher self.

ALCHEMY

AIR: Follow the lofty ideal and not the worldly expedient.

TURQUOISE: Defend your virtues.

TIME

Look for your time; Birthday; Time of resolution and decision.

GEOMANCY

TEMPLE, MOUNTAIN: Find your place of worship, meditation; Power spot.

SHAMANISM

BIRD: Listen to the angels that guide you; Trust your intuition.

PSYCHOMETRY

SPIRE: Act on your inspiration.

PRAYER STICK: Honor the great powers, and live in accordance with their higher designs.

DELUSION

Ten of Crystals

Delusion is the mind of *Fortune.* Like the Fortune mentality, expand your thinking. Be inventive. Use your imagination. Fortunes are built on dreams. Realize that your mind-boggling ideas will be considered delusions by many. Your imagination may give you mirages, false suns, or diamonds in the sky. But you won't know until you pursue the dream vision. Be a dreamer; follow the dream.

The Ten of Crystals, Delusion, is really a delusion in itself. It is a false title. This card means vision. Every vision, however, is an illusion until manifested on the physical level of reality.

Even if we materialize our dream, is it real? Is not everything an interpretation of the mind? Maybe it is all a mind game, all a delusion. But is not an illusion as real as anything else? Do not get caught up in the endless machinations of the mind. Allow your thoughts to be, and be entertained by them. But follow the illusion/vision of your choice—what your heart wants to do, where your passion lies. The mind will give you plenty of answers, all of them true and all of them false.

Your "Delusion" Qualities

EVOLVED:

DIAMONDS IN THE SKY: Use your imagination; Be farsighted; Tell a story; Weave a dream; Go on a vision quest; Think optimistically.

UNEVOLVED:

DIAMONDS IN THE SKY, FALSE SUNS, MIRAGES: Seeing only that which you want to see.

DIAMONDS IN THE SKY: False expectations; Delusions of grandeur; Messianic thinking; Pipe dreams; Hallucinations; Quixotic.

PYRITE: Fear of ruin—that all will come tumbling down and fall apart; Insecurity.

Your "Delusion" Oracular Universe

ASTROLOGY

ASTRAL LIGHT PHENOMENA: Look for a revelation, an inspiration, a flash.

ALCHEMY

AIR: An idea in the air is in the air for anyone; Get moving on your great ideas before someone else picks up on them; "Out there"; Space cadet.

PYRITE: Nothing is as it seems; You can be fooled by appearances.

DIAMONDS: Be desirous of beauty and riches.

TIME

Look at the past or future; Not now.

GEOMANCY

Look there; Not here.

SHAMANISM

RAVEN: You are an illusionist; Shape-shifter.

AURA

DIAMOND LIGHT: The color of reality changes depending on your point of view.

PSYCHOMETRY

LSD ("LUCY IN THE SKY WITH DIAMONDS"): Alter your mind.

PASSION

Ten of Cups

Passion is the heartthrob of *Fortune*. Your fortune is where your passion is. Listen to your passions, for they will reveal your genius and bring you success. Passionate living is the key to living fully and richly.

Follow the beat of your heart. Abandon your reservations. Don't think. Be spontaneous. Take the risk. You want it so bad that you can taste it, so taste it. Let your groin be your guide. Do it! Act! Live! Love! Enjoy! Who cares what others think. Be yourself. Want it all now. Go for it! Courage!

Your "Passion" Qualities

EVOLVED:

FLOWERING: Let your feelings come out through your way of living; Be a risk taker.

RED FLOWER BLOSSOMS: Be turned on, excited, thrilled, stimulated; Live your passion.

RED HOT SUN: Go with your burning energy.

WILD FLOWERS: Live with abandon.

SENSUAL AND AROMATIC FLOWERS: Live sensually and sexually.

LION: Live with confidence and courage.

LION'S TONGUE: Follow your desire and lust.

UNEVOLVED:

FIRE LION: Devouring; Consuming; Burn others out; Burn yourself out.

Your "Passion" Oracular Universe

ASTROLOGY

LEO: Dare to be colorful and outrageous.

ALCHEMY

FIRE: Your passion is energy—expansive and compelling.

GOLD: Be passionately driven to realize your highest dreams.

TIME

FLOWERS: Feel youthful and spring-like.

GEOMANCY

HEAT: Be in the heat of the night; In the heat of the day; In the heat of the action.

SHAMANISM

LION: Be selfish; Go get what you want.

WILD FLOWERS: Create through passion.

AURA

RED: Feel your lower chakra stimulation.

PSYCHOMETRY

DRINKING CHALICE: Fill yourself up; Be intoxicated with life.

REWARD

Ten of Worlds

Reward is *Fortune's* way of being successful in the material world. Reward means to know that you are a manifester of your visions and passions. You are "making it," and you deserve it. Take risks, expand, and think optimistically and abundantly. Make an opportunity out of every situation. Create ways of converting opportunities into outcomes of income. Concentrate on your material needs and desires. Do not be afraid to spend. The more you spend, the more you will make. Spending means taking the responsibility to earn.

Your income reward is the energy that fuels the next go around of your wheel of fortune. Do not stop now. Keep moving. Create, create, create. Abundance is a flow of income and output. Keep turning it over.

Your "Reward" Qualities

EVOLVED:

ABUNDANCE: Think prosperity; See yourself as rich; Partake in the physical luxuries of life; Celebrate your success.

JUPITER WHEEL OF FORTUNE: Convert; Adapt; Be opportunistic; LIfe has turned favorable for you; Strike it rich; Find the pot of gold at the end of the rainbow; Feel lucky; Risk.

SHOPPING BASKET: Life is a cornucopia; Treat yourself; Buy.

COINS: Financial success is yours; Money is the liquidity to move your wheel of fortune onward.

ORB OF THE CZAR: Professional achievement and advancement is yours; Esteem and value yourself.

UNEVOLVED:

SHOPPING BASKET: So trapped by material luxury and seduced by material comfort that you become security conscious and lose the "fortune mentality" of continuous growth.

Your "Reward" Oracular Universe

ASTROLOGY

JUPITER: Accumulate and consume.

ALCHEMY

EARTH: Manifest; Materialize.

TIME

FULL SHOPPING BASKET: You are rewarded in your pay period; Bonus time; Contract renewal; Promotion; Sale.

GEOMANCY

MARKET BASKET: Market place is where you find reward.

SHAMANISM

ANIMAL: Be acquisitive and inquisitive.

GOLDEN POPPY: Have fun; Spread the wealth (seeds) around.

AURA

GOLD: Harvest; Complete; Fulfill.

PSYCHOMETRY

MONEY: You have the means for purchasing your material needs and
    wants.

SHOPPING BASKET: Collect and acquire.

GROWTH

Ten of Wands

Growth is the spirit of *Fortune.* Fortune is attained by reaching for it. In the reaching, you grow. You are here to reach your fortune and thus to grow. Young or old, you are growing—for life experience is the stuff of which you grow. Now, however, is the time for accelerated growth through conscious growth. Know that you grow by the Fortune way of aspiring higher, stretching your limits, and extending yourself. Confront your fears of the heights of success because you have nowhere to go but up, to grow. So get on with it. Grow up!

Your growth is growth in consciousness. Perception, like light, is ever-expanding. Experience the unfamiliar and grow in your understanding. You will see with greater clarity your subconscious fears, your intuitive wisdom, and your personal power. Self-knowledge gives you self-confidence, purpose, and direction. Higher consciousness through growth is the key to attainment of your destiny and fortune.

Your "Growth" Qualities

EVOLVED:

REDWOOD TREE GROWING UPWARD: Aspire to grow.

OLD HAND REACHING: Grow through life experience; Reach.

BABY'S HAND REACHING: Grow through your curiosity; Stretch.

REDWOOD TREE GROWING TO THE SKYLIGHT: Grow in your understanding of the intuitive superconscious; Enlightenment through growth.

REDWOOD TREE GROWTH RINGS: Grow through awareness of your personal subconscious, your past.

REDWOOD TREE ROOTS GROWING DOWNWARD INTO EARTH: Grow through awareness of the collective or universal unconscious.

REDWOOD TREE GROWING TALL: Grow through awareness of the worlds in which you live.

REDWOOD TREE GROWING OUT: Grow through greater emotional self-expression.

REDWOOD TREE GROWING BIG: Grow through material success and abundance.

UNEVOLVED:

TREE FOSSIL: Forgetting to grow; Giving up; Unwilling to risk and reach.

Your "Growth" Oracular Universe

ASTROLOGY

STAR: Reach for your star; Become the star that you are.

ALCHEMY

FIRE, AIR, WATER, EARTH: Integrated growth; Growth of mind, heart, and body through growth in consciousness.

PETRIFIED WOOD: All the secrets of the past are contained in your cellular body.

TIME

ALL SEASONS: Contract in the Fall and Winter; Expand in the Spring and Summer; Your growth is cyclical like the seasons.

GEOMANCY

ANYWHERE: Learn to be at home anywhere; Be versatile and adaptable.

SHAMANISM
MALE: Grow majestic and powerful.
FEMALE: Grow flexible and beautiful.
TREE: Learn how to regenerate.
WHITE ROSE: You only blossom by going through changes.

AURA
WHITE: Grow by experiencing all your dimensions (all your colors).

PSYCHOMETRY
LADDER: Climb and keep climbing.

CHIROGNOMY
GNARLED OLD HAND: Growth is gained through the life experience of
    reaching higher.

CHAPTER SEVEN

The Inner Family

The Family cards are composed of Child, Man, Woman, and Sage for each Minor Arcana suit of cards. These family members represent our own inner family, the child, man, woman, and sage within ourselves.

In the traditional medieval tarot, these cards are called the "Royalty" or "Court" cards. The *Voyager* Child Cards are equivalent to the Page, Princess, or Prince in the medieval decks. The Child Cards are androgenous, for they are symbolized by boys and girls. The *Voyager* Man Cards can be likened to the Knight or King cards. The Voyager Woman cards are similar to the traditional tarot's Queens. The *Voyager* Sage Cards have no direct equals. The Sages represent a major evolution of the medieval tarot. The Sages honor the elder, or the grandmother/grandfather within us.

The following table illustrates the relationship of the Family card to the Minor Arcana suit and the human type for each.

Family Card	Crystals	Cups	Worlds	Wands
Child	Learner	Feeler	Player	Seeker
Man	Inventor	Surfer	Achiever	Actor
Woman	Guardian	Rejoicer	Preserver	Sensor
Sage	Knower	Regenerator	Master	Seer

Family cards are the personification of our human archetypalness, symbolized by the Major Arcana cards. Family cards represent the actual living out in the world of their correspondent Major Archetype card. For example, the Man of Crystals (Inventor) is like the Magician and Fortune Major Archetypes. He seizes an idea and spins it around like Fortune. He manifests this idea into a material reality. This tangible result has, like the Magician's power, the ability to change and transform situations and people. The correspondences are as follows.

FOOL-CHILD: CHILD OF CRYSTALS, CUPS, WORLDS, AND WANDS

CRYSTALS

MAGICIAN/FORTUNE: MAN OF CRYSTALS—INVENTOR
PRIESTESS/BALANCE: WOMAN OF CRYSTALS—GUARDIAN
STAR: SAGE OF CRYSTALS—KNOWER

CUPS

CHARIOT: MAN OF CUPS—SURFER
EMPRESS/MOON/STAR: WOMAN OF CUPS—REJOICER
MOON: SAGE OF CUPS—REGENERATOR

WORLDS

EMPEROR/FORTUNE: MAN OF WORLDS—ACHIEVER
EMPRESS: WOMAN OF WORLDS—PRESERVER
SUN/HIEROPHANT: SAGE OF WORLDS—MASTER

WANDS

MAGICIAN: MAN OF WANDS—ACTOR
PRIESTESS/STRENGTH: WOMAN OF WANDS—SENSOR
TIME-SPACE/HERMIT: SAGE OF WANDS—SEER

Family cards represent mastery over the Minor Arcana qualities of their respective suit, for they are like traditional tarot's high Royalty cards. The Family cards manifest the highest qualities of the Crystals,

Cups, Worlds, and Wands cards, and/or have mastered (overcome) the negative qualities depicted in these suits. For example refer to the following.

CHILD OF CRYSTALS: Mastery of NARROWNESS (9) and DULLNESS (7)
MAN OF CRYSTALS: Mastery of CREATIVITY (3) and CONFUSION (6)
WOMAN OF CRYSTALS: Mastery of EQUANIMITY (2) and NEGATIVITY (5)
SAGE OF CRYSTALS: Mastery of SYNTHESIS (8) and DELUSION (10)

CHILD OF CUPS: Mastery of ANGER (4) and SORROW (6)
MAN OF CUPS: Mastery of FEAR (7) and PASSION (10)
WOMAN OF CUPS: Mastery of EQUILIBRIUM (2) and LOVE (3)
SAGE OF CUPS: Mastery of STAGNATION (8) and FULFILLMENT (9)

CHILD OF WORLDS: Mastery of COMMENCEMENT (4) and SETBACK (5)
MAN OF WORLDS: Mastery of SYNERGY (6) and REWARD (10)
WOMAN OF WORLDS: Mastery of REFLECTION (2) and NURTURING (3)
SAGE OF WORLDS: Mastery of CHANGE (8) and HARVEST (9)

CHILD OF WANDS: Mastery of TRUST (6) and GROWTH (10)
MAN OF WANDS: Mastery of ASPIRATION (4) and OPPRESSION (5)
WOMAN OF WANDS: Mastery of PURITY (2) and COURAGE (7)
SAGE OF WANDS: Mastery of COMPASSION (3) and INTEGRITY (9)

NOTE: *Aces and Sages are equivalent in their mastery of Minor Arcana qualities. Both represent the highest aspects of their suits.*

As manifesters, the Family cards symbolize materialization of goals and objectives. They show the sequence of consciousness and events we experience in order to materialize our goals on the worldly, physical level of reality. There are four steps:

CHILD EXPLORER > MAN PRODUCER > WOMAN CONSERVER > SAGE ATTAINER

The first step of the manifestation cycle is *exploration* of possibilities. This is symbolized by the Child Cards, as they are all seekers and learners. The second stage of material manifestation is *production*, which is what we do with our discoveries and ideas. This is represented by the producers in the Family, the Man Cards. *Conservation* is the third sequence of the manifestation cycle. Represented by the Woman Cards, this means the maintenance, nurturing, and preservation of the health and growth of our new output. The Sage Card level of manifestation is *attainment*. This is the stage where everything is running smoothly. Exploration, production, and conservation continue. Attainment also means the teaching and sharing of experience and wisdom. The Sages pass on the legacy and tradition of successful manifestation. They sow the seeds for a new cycle of manifestation. The Sages are the true masters, the highest cards in the Family.

The Family cards not only represent our own inner family, they also symbolize other people in our lives. In a reading of the cards, the Family cards can be interpreted both ways: as ourself or as others. It generally follows that the family type we exhibit internally is also who we attract (our magnetism) in terms of other people. Others in our life mirror ourself. We draw to us mirror projections of ourself. In a childlike mood, for example, we find other children to play with. It is also true, however, that we pull in our opposite. A man, for example, attracts a woman to mirror his own feminine side.

In truth, we attract those who characterize what is lacking in ourselves, be they likenesses, opposites, or complements. Looking at ourselves in the mirror of our mind, we see, either consciously or subconsciously, what personality quality we must realize to become whole or complete. For example, we may need to nurture our own inner precious child and so may attract a parental figure who mirrors a man or woman adult nurturer.

The truly whole person fully manifests all members of the inner family equally. This means attracting all kinds of people equally. The whole individual is an inner community of family members and a member of a community composed of all other types.

CHILD

The Child Cards in the *Voyager* Tarot Deck are the physical manifestations of the Major Archetypal Fool-Child. *Voyager* Children are like the Fool-Child. They take leaps into the unknown to explore all of life. Like the number Zero, the Fool-Child's number, the Child Cards represent a state of openness and beginningness. They are like Zero, unpredictable as to how they follow the mysterious workings of their curiosity.

The Child is the explorer within us all. The Child of Crystals—Learner—explores new ideas and their application. The Child of Cups—Feeler—explores the world of feelings and emotions. The Child of Worlds—Player—explores new modes of playful expression and new worldly roles and functions. The Child of Wands—Seeker—explores the meaning of life, asking "Who am I?"

The wide-eyed Children are looking: The Learner is looking for knowledge, the Feeler is looking for expression, the Player is looking for fun, and the Seeker is looking for enlightenment.

LEARNER

Child of Crystals

The Child of Crystals—Learner—represents your curious mind. The curious mind is healthy. Expand your mind and you exercise it. Like the child, be open, inquisitive, and receptive. The world is full of wonders and new discoveries. Check them out. Look into things. Research.

See with a fresh point of view. Do not stay fixed on old knowledge, for it may block new understanding. Learning is a perpetual process of new insight. Every moment and every experience is new. Learn from everything. See with the look of amazement.

Keep your mind young. Acquire a new skill to keep your mind sharp and strong. Explore the powers of your mind. Examine how your beliefs and attitudes create your reality. A positive mind is an alert mind. Use all the different faculties of the mind such as imagination, intuition, reason, memory, vision.

Find shortcuts and creative solutions. Investigate the possibilities. Trust your own intelligence. Give your mind a chance. With openness and information, you can find a way to attain your goals and dreams.

Your "Learner" Qualities

EVOLVED:

WIDE-EYED CHILDREN: Follow your curiosity; Look and see; Look with
   wonder at the world; Investigate; Look at the feasibility; Explore
   the possibilities.

CRYSTAL CAVE: Explore new ideas and new beliefs; Learn the powers
   and pitfalls of the mind.

"CRACK IN THE COSMIC EGG": Seek new realizations and insights; Break
   through old conditioning, old values, and beliefs; Your learning
   never stops.

CHILD HOLDING DOLL: Let go of obsolete beliefs that have become your
   security blankets.

MYSTERY SHAPES: Imagine; Fantasize.

UNEVOLVED:

Limited ways of learning; Look at world through the
   narrow lens of old learning; Not adapting.

Your "Learner" Oracular Universe

ASTROLOGY

URANUS: Be open to a revolutionary breakthrough in your perception.

ALCHEMY

AIR MEETS EARTH: Break open the density of your ignorance (earth
   matter) through new awareness (air); Do something new; Look in a
   different way.

TIME

CRACK: Look to the future; A new dawning.

GEOMANCY

CRYSTAL CAVE: Be in the mind; Wherever there is new mental stimulation such as books, new places, interesting people, teachers.

SHAMANISM

MOLLUSK (BEHIND THE BOY): You evolve and grow through the expansion
   of your mind.

SEED: Conceive; Conceptualize.

AURA

WHITE: Look with innocence.

PSYCHOMETRY

GLOBE: Get to know yourself—who you are and where you come from; See the big picture and how things are connected.

FEELER

Child of Cups

The Child of Cups—Feeler—represents your state of emotional sensitivity. Like a child, be open to all your feelings. Feel everything. Do not censor any feelings. Emote spontaneously without premeditative thought or judgment. Discover your way of feeling. Be honest in your feelings.

Let your feelings out, let them flow, for you are a natural parade of feelings. One feeling is followed by another and another. Allow yourself to be a continuous succession of emotions. Your feelings, like water, are in constant motion, sometimes deep, then shallow, up and down, stormy and bubbly, calm and playful. You become more alive and vital through your show of feelings.

Through your continuous expression of feelings, you purify yourself emotionally. Get rid of unwanted feelings by expressing them. Feel the ecstatic renewal of your heart and spirit by showing your highest and most sublime emotions.

Your "Feeler" Qualities

EVOLVED:

MOODS ON FACES: Express your complete range of emotions; No masking of any emotion (authentic feelings).

FLOWERS: Accurately feel out situations through your feelings; Your emotions are revealers.

PARADE OF DIFFERENT FACES AND FEELINGS: Allow your feelings to flow by quickly; Process emotions out through their expression; Self-regenerate through emoting.

DIVER WITH BOTTLE: Discover your feelings; Find out how you bottle up your feelings.

UNEVOLVED:

Repress feelings; Unwilling to be emotionally vulnerable.

Your "Feeler" Oracular Universe

ASTROLOGY

NEPTUNE: Reveal your hidden feelings.

ALCHEMY

FIERY ASPECT OF WATER: Have the courage to let out your feelings, particularly your ill temper, with passion and gusto; Let them out and get them out.

SAND: Allow yourself to be soft, receptive, shifting, yin.

TIME

PARADE OF FEELINGS: It is an emotionally charged time that is swift and fleeting.

GEOMANCY

RAINBOW: Look for cloudbursts or sunbursts; Places subject to great changes in mood.

SHAMANISM

FISH: Feel your raw emotions of instinctual needs and drives.

FLOWER: Externalize your inner-felt emotions.

AURA

REDS: Show your excitement, passion, and anger; Be animate.
BLUES: Show your calmness, peacefulness, and despondency.

PSYCHOMETRY

BOTTLE: Your heart container of water or emotional abundance can be either for pouring out feelings or for containing them.

PLAYER

Child of Worlds

The Child of Worlds—Player—represents your own inner child's playfulness. Play at life. Make your life fun—a game, a dream, a play, a song, a sport, a discovery. Lighten up! Be a kid!

The world is a playground to play out your fantasies. All the world is a stage. Create plays with your imagination. Act out your plays. Do what you loved to do as a child and you will find your genius, your passion, and your success. Your happiness comes by recreating the happiest activities of your childhood.

Like the child, you are an apprentice. Learn how to live and how to practice your art by playing at it. Take the pressure off yourself. You are only an initiate going through a rite of passage. Enjoy the journey of life because the journey *is* life. Be a perpetual beginner. As a beginner, you can only do your best. Enjoy the process—the play of life.

Your "Player" Qualities

EVOLVED:

DISNEYLAND, FLYING SAUCERS, DREAM BUBBLES, BOOKS, PUDDLES: Create with your fantasy, imagination, and daydreams.

SWINGING, BALLOONING: Soar with what excites you.

PLAYING: Play; Play at your work; Take a vacation.

ART: Recreate yourself through recreation.

COMPANIONS: Play with your friends and buddies.

YOUNG MATADOR: Be an apprentice, a greenhorn, a rookie.

ABORIGINE AND MASAI YOUNG WOMAN: Your life is a continual rite of initiation.

READING AND INVESTIGATING: Go to "school"; Learn.

UNEVOLVED:

BUBBLES IN HAND: Always in a nonproductive fantasy world.

Your "Player" Oracular Universe

ASTROLOGY

MARS: Energize and initiate; "Let's go."

ALCHEMY

FIRE AND AIR: Be ready to move; You are a bubble in the wind (taken where led).

MUD: Be a creative builder; Slop around; Be natural with no sense of decorum.

TIME

SPRING: Spring forth; Leap forward; Go in spurts; Youthful period.

GEOMANCY

PLAYGROUNDS, WOODS, AND SECRET PLACES: Find places with no bosses or authority figures; Free spots.

SHAMANISM

SPARRING CALVES: Establish strength and self-confidence through competitive play with others.

BABY BIRD: Life is vulnerable and fragile (the bubble can burst), so enjoy it now.

AURA

HOT COLORS: Seek the exciting action.

PSYCHOMETRY

TOYS: Make believe.
BALL: Life is a ball.

SEEKER

Child of Wands

The Child of Wands—Seeker—represents the drive of your spirit to know yourself. Life is a path of seeking self-discovery. To seek your truth is to see. Try to see it all. Look at everything because you are everything. Find the eternal truths by looking at the world about you, and find yourself in the process. Use your physical senses to sense the truth. Use the great teachings to ponder and learn the truth. Use your meditative introspection to know the truth.

    Like the child hunter, be diligent and perserving in your pursuit of truth. Never stop looking. You must be a warrior—full of courage to hunt down the truth amidst the dark shadow-demons. Trust yourself and your inner sense, for the path to truth can only be your individual path. Trust the strength of the "path to enlightenment" to overcome all dark forces.

Your "Seeker" Qualities

EVOLVED:

WOLF AND ARROW: Hunt down the truth.

MEDITATOR: Seek to know "Who am I?" "Why am I here?"

JOURNEYER: Seek to know origins; "Where have I come from?" "Where am I going?"

JOURNEYER-MEDITATOR: Your life is a meditation, a continuous voyage of self-exploration through which truth is gained.

JOURNEYER-EXPLORER: Discover your inner home—who you are wherever you are; Seek a state of inner security through self-knowledge.

MONKS: Seek a mental knowledge of "enlightenment."

ANIMALS: Learn to trust your instincts in the pursuit of truth.

NO BAGGAGE: Travel light in order to travel far; Do not necessarily travel the path of truth, which is encumbered by too many preconceptions and conceptual baggage.

UNEVOLVED:

Afraid to explore the unknown; Lack of self-curiosity.

Your "Seeker" Oracular Universe

ASTROLOGY

EARTH: Know that you are at home at all times; Self-security.

ALCHEMY

FIRE AND EARTH: The inner light (truth) of the life spirit is revealed in the physical world.

IRON: You have already evolved a long way and are now on a path of enlightenment to create new materials that reflect your own progress.

TIME

DAWN: Seek new experiences and new knowledge.

NIGHT: Search within for truth.

GEOMANCY

FORESTS: Be prepared to accept the mysterious, the unexplainable.

SHAMANISM

WOLF: Seek your wild and untamed (unconditioned) self.

MOUSE: Go with a small ego, knowing that you are in the safe hands of the great spirit.

RABBIT: Be swift of mind and body.

DEER: Grow by leaps and bounds.

REDWOOD TREE: Grow up, climb up, look up, stretch up.

DANDELION SEEDS: Spread your seeds of light.

AURA

BLACK: Do not be afraid to question.

PSYCHOMETRY

STAFF: Watch out for beliefs and techniques that become crutches and prevent growth.

BOW AND ARROW: Be true to your insight.

MAN

The male members of the *Voyager* Family represent, of course, yang male energy. They signify action, expression, projection, going forth, manifesting, exhibiting, extroversion, assertion, drive, and ambition. They also represent change, revolution, invention, and progress.

The *Voyager* Man Cards are the human manifestations of various Major Arcana Archetypes. The Man of Crystals—Inventor—is the human projection of the Magician and the Fortune Archetypes. Both spin out revolutionary new ideas with quickness and cleverness. The Man of Cups—Surfer—is the human imprint of the Archetypal Charioteer. They move with courage and determination into new frontiers of personal expression. The Man of Worlds—Achiever—is the Archetypal manifestation of the Emperor and of Fortune. They are producers and empire-builders. The Man of Wands—Actor—represents the Archetypal Magician. Like the Magician, the Actor is adept at changing roles and personas.

The Man Cards represent the natural growth and evolution of the consciousness associated with the Child Cards. The Man of Crystals *invents* new concepts based on the knowledge *learned* by the Child of Crystals. The Man of Cups *surfs* or commands the *feelings* felt by the Child of Cups. The Man of Worlds *achieves* professional competence which was first *played* at by the Child of Worlds. The Man of Wands *acts* out a range of personas first discovered by the *seeking* Child of Wands.

INVENTOR

Man of Crystals

The Man of Crystals—Inventor—is *Fortune's* inventiveness. Vent your mind. Let new ideas in and vent them out. Brainstorm new thoughts without judgment or censorship. Spin ideas around. Synthesize old concepts into a new formulation. Be bold in your thinking and open in your curiosity. Each new moment creates an opportunity to fulfill ever-changing needs.

The true inventor is both a theoretician and empiricist, a revolutionary and a technician. Formulate your ideas into workable solutions. Make your theories practical. Apply your thinking. Make sure they work. Test them out. As an inventor, you are productive. Create and produce.

Your "Inventor" Qualities

EVOLVED:

CRYSTALS: See new points of view; Turn crystal of your mind around.

CRYSTAL EXPLOSION OF MANY CRYSTALS: Brainstorm; Gather in many ideas; Get information.

SKYLAB: Research; Check it out.

BOOKS, BUILDING, SKYLAB: Put your ideas into practical application; Be an idea entrepreneur.

CALIBRATION OVER MAN'S FACE: Test your ideas; Measure their worth.

UNEVOLVED:

Great ideas only spin around in the mind without putting them into practice and physical reality; Can't see your inventiveness.

Your "Inventor" Oracular Universe

ASTROLOGY

WORKING IN SPACE (SKYLAB): Chart the new frontiers of thought in different disciplines, and twist them together.

ALCHEMY

AIR AND LIGHT: Work in the invisible and abstract world of ideas; Pick ideas out of the air waves.

CRYSTALLIZATION: Make ideas into matter.

TIME

THOUGHTS: Lose yourself in thought; Be timeless.

GEOMANCY

IN THE MIND: Use a laboratory; Study; Drawing board; Computer console; Information places.

SHAMANISM

FEATHERS: Be sensitive to which way the wind is blowing.

PSYCHOMETRY

CRYSTAL: Your mind is your greatest natural resource; High frequency technology.

BOOKS: Read and write; Receive and create.

SURFER

Man of Cups

The Man of Cups—Surfer—represents the *Charioteer's* skillfull negotiation of the emotional roller coaster of life. Like the surfer, ride the highs and lows with equal balance. Watch that you do not go too high or too low. Maintain your emotional equilibrium. Make constant adjustments to go with the flow and yet retain control. Be flexible and opportunistic enough to take advantage of the emotional energies while maintaining your own center.

Have the courage to explore and express deep and different feelings. Be an emotional risk taker. Dare to ride scary feelings. In this state of openness and trust, you will experience the ecstasy of living.

Your "Surfer" Qualities

EVOLVED:

SURFER ON TOP OF WAVES: Maintain your emotional equilibrium; Surf through and beyond the storms of anger and waves of fear; Avoid the muddiness and stagnation of emotional low tides; Weigh and evaluate your feelings to stay on top of your emotions; Discriminate among emotional waves, knowing which to ride and which to let pass; Be flexible and adaptable.

FLOWERS: Express your emotions; Open up; Come out.

THRACIAN HORSE CUP: Like the the explorer Thracians, explore your unknown emotions.

SURFER: Be a thrill seeker and a high flyer, which comes with the courage of daring to feel.

UNEVOLVED:

SURFER: Fickle; Only feel what is pleasurable to feel.

Your "Surfer" Oracular Universe

ASTROLOGY

IRIS AND RAINBOW: Explore like a Sagittarius.

ALCHEMY

AIRY PART OF WATER: You are emotionally elusive; Unpredictable.

TIME

"SURF'S UP": Live in an upbeat tempo; High time.

GEOMANCY

SURFER: Be on the move; Here and there.

SHAMANISM

HORSE: Get into a rhythm; Find your balance.

AURA

RAINBOW LIGHT: Show your colors; Let your feelings be known.

PSYCHOMETRY

SURFBOARD: Use the available energy.

ACHIEVER

Man of Worlds

The Man of Worlds—Achiever—is the *Emperor's* drive to succeed at reaching his goals. Like the Achiever, set measurable and achievable goals. To attain your goals, aspire and be inspired. Have the courage to extend and push yourself. Take risks. Achievements come with manifesting and producing. Always build. Build off of each achievement. Look to increase and progress. Have a plan and a strategy. Utilize your resources. Establish a support team. Synergize. Work hard and work smart. Find new ways. Innovate. Look for shortcuts without compromising quality. Stay ahead of the game. Reward yourself with your successes, but never be satisfied. Keep running.

Your "Achiever" Qualities

EVOLVED:

WORKER BEE: Be all business; Be busy.
PRODUCTS: Produce; Manufacture; Make; Develop.
HOTEL, BRIDGE, COLISEUM: Think "big"; Be entrepreneurial; Plan.
JUPITER: Think "more and better."
ASTRONAUT: Extend the frontiers; Take risks.
RUNNER: Push the limits; Break records.
ROLLS ROYCE: Reward yourself.
CORPORATE TEAM: Use teamwork; Network; Synergize.
DRILLER: Exploit available resources.

UNEVOLVED:

Self-destructive ego; Punishes the body; Stressed out; Defacer of the land; Unprincipled competitiveness; Overly materialistic.

Your "Achiever" Oracular Universe

ASTROLOGY

SATURN: Exercise discipline.
JUPITER: Accumulate.

ALCHEMY

PLANE: Have great visions and ultimate goals; Air.
CAR: Bring your visions down to earth by attainable goals and reasonable time frames.
ENERGY SOURCES: Build upon your natural strengths.

TIME

NUMBER ONE: Be efficient ("Time is money"); Set up deadlines; Establish a timeline; Think down the road into the future.

GEOMANCY

PRODUCTS: Be at the office; In the production room.

SHAMANISM

BEE: Be diligent and persistent; Be professsional.

AURA

RED: Be assertive.

PSYCHOMETRY

PLANE, CAR, SPACE CAPSULE: Act swiftly; Use your impatience to get
    places.

BRIDGE: Span the world, span markets, span industries.

COLISEUM: Show and demonstrate your achievements; Sell.

NUCLEAR POWER PLANT: Transform and revolutionize.

ACTOR

Man of Wands

The Man of Wands—Actor—is the shaman that represents the free spirit of the *Magician*. You possess a thousand faces, capable of being anyone and doing anything. Do not limit yourself. Do it all. Be versatile and adaptable. Strive for greater mastery over your mind, heart, and body so that you can play out any role. Your perceptivity is lightning quick so act swiftly and spontaneously. Act now! Be able to change from moment to moment, but retain your inner sense of self.

You have the power to influence and transform. You can heal and reveal. In order to exercise your power and abilities, liberate your full spirit. In freeing your spirit—your total self and its many personas—you move beyond the narrow and small ego into a higher sense of universal self. As a channel for the great spirit, you become enlightened and an enlightener.

Your "Actor" Qualities

EVOLVED:

LIGHTNING BOLT WAND: Realize your universal nature and in so doing, transcend your personal ego; Recognize your true identity behind the masks and roles; Break through the concept of I, Me, and Mine.

MASK: Liberate; Be free to assume any identity; Be detached.

DEER, BIRD, BEAST: You are capable of assuming extra-human qualities; Tap into your genetic memory of past lives.

THE PLAY, DANCE, CEREMONY, COMBAT, RITUAL: Elicit different qualities and personas through the performance.

HORNS, FEATHERS, HAIR: You have fine perceptivity and sensory awareness.

ACTING AND MARTIAL ARTS: Use self-control, discipline, focus, concentration.

UNEVOLVED:

MASKS: Insecure; Afraid to reveal true self and real feelings; Psychological armor and defense mechanisms; Schizophrenia (lost amidst multiple personalities); Confused over self-identity and place; Frustrated over lack of achievement resulting from excessive changeability and fickleness (Jack of all trades, but master of none).

Your "Actor" Oracular Universe

ASTROLOGY

THUNDERBOLT: You have Jupiter- or Zeus-like mastery over earth roles and forms.

ALCHEMY

FIRE: You have the power of transmutation—able to break down and create new life.

SILVER: You can reflect anyone; "Fake it until you make it."

TIME

CEREMONY AND PLAY: It's time to perform; Showtime; Curtain call.

GEOMANCY

PLAY: Be on stage; In the light.

SHAMANISM

DEER: Defend and protect yourself by listening, disguising, and
disappearing.

FALCON: Hunt and seek the truth of your being.

BEAST: Acknowledge your mythical and mysterious origins and
qualities.

BAMBOO: Act upon the duality and androgeny of your yin malleability
and yang hardness; Use what works.

AURA

VIOLET AND INDIGO: High spectrum of color denotes your great
awareness; Meditate.

PSYCHOMETRY

MASK: Recognize that your personalities are illusion, appearance,
maya, and not reality; Try not to be typed, marked, measured,
defined; Survive through adaptability.

WOMAN

The *Voyager* Woman Cards symbolize our feminine energy. They represent great love and joy for life. As such, they seek to preserve, protect, conserve, and create life. They maintain the beautiful fabric of life through sharp attention, watchfulness, and guardianship. The Woman Cards enjoy the process of the present, which they nurture with great sensibility and *feeling*.

The Voyager female cards are natural counterparts to the Man Cards in the deck. The Woman of Crystals—Guardian—maintains the balance of mind that the Man of Crystals—Inventor—loses in his brilliant creativity. The Woman of Cups—Rejoicer—exalts in her deep, deep reverence for life, while the Man of Cups—Surfer quests for transient emotional highs. The Woman of Worlds—Preserver—maintains the quality of life while the Man of Worlds—Achiever—seeks to expand the quantity of life. The Woman of Wands—Sensor—knows what is behind the masks that we wear, whereas the Man of Wands—Actor —puts on all the masks.

The Woman Cards are the human expressions of their archetypal seeds, which are symbolized by the Major Arcana Archetypes. The Woman of Crystals is the *Priestess* incarnate: calm, cool, detached. She is also the humanization of the *Balance/Justice* Archetype: objective, balanced, centered. The Woman of Cups is the physical expression of the Moon: feeling, romantic, beautiful. She also represents the Star in her grace and life-giving emotional essence. The Woman of Worlds is the living epitome of the *Empress*, mother earth. The Woman of Wands is the fiery aspect of the *Priestess,* instinctive rather than intuitive, into the body rather than mind. She is an example of the *Strength* Archetype, a cat, full of awareness, curiosity, lust, and secrets.

GUARDIAN

Woman of Crystals

The Woman of Crystals—Guardian—represents the *Priestess'* independent state of mental reflection. Visualize, think, and plan about your own highest good. Keep your own counsel. Contemplate on what is right for you and what works for you. Focus on taking care of your own needs and aspirations. Be true to your point of view. Let nothing penetrate your concentration on the task at hand.

As the manifestation of *Balance*, the Guardian represents maintaining your balance of mind. Keep your cool by keeping your distance. Be detached and dispassionate. Hold to your course. Reflect before you act. Be at peace with yourself, accepting with equanimity whatever happens without losing your composure. Let anything negative be absorbed by the light of your positive and healthy mind. Look for the truth without being caught up in rhetoric and in projections of seeing what you want to see.

Your "Guardian" Qualities

EVOLVED:

DIAMOND: The hardness of the diamond signifies impenetrability, making the mind into the hardness of the diamond and so impenetrable by such mental negativities as confusion, delusion, narrowness, and defeatism.

CRYSTAL: Keep your clarity and your focus amidst doubt and distraction.

MEDITATIVE COUNTENANCE: Self-reflect; Introspect.

DIAMOND MIND: Be aware of the workings of your mind; Understand how you create problems through your mind.

CRYSTAL IN HAND: Maintain dominion over the mind; Use the mind as resource and tool.

COMPOSED AND CALM DEMEANOR: Keep your mental health by concentration and equanimity.

DIAMOND BRIGHTNESS AND SHARPNESS: Be sharp and clear when making decisions.

COOL BLUE: Stay noninvolved; Be dispassionate and mental.

MEDITATIVE: Meditate; Calculate.

"THIRD EYE" DIAMOND: Intuit; Visualize.

SELF-CONTAINMENT: Maintain your independence.

GUARDEDNESS: Be on guard against mental imbalance.

UNEVOLVED:

CHAINMAIL ON TOP OF HEAD: Too self-contained and protective; Do not allow for ecstatic states of altered consciousness; Hesitant to allow full expression to the crown chakra for fear of losing self-control.

Your "Guardian" Oracular Universe

ASTROLOGY

STAR: Show the way; Illuminate; Guide.

ALCHEMY

LIGHT: Examine and clarify in the light.

COOLING: Step back to reflect; Let issues stand, congeal, and reveal; Cool out.

TIME

DARK BLUE: Seek the night; Alone time.

GEOMANCY

DOWNWARD TURNED EYES: Find secret places; Personal and intimate places.

SHAMANISM

TRIANGLE: Be aggressive in your passivity.

AURA

TWILIGHT BLUE BLACK: Find mental clarity through lack of clutter, noise, and distraction; Privacy.

PSYCHOMETRY

CRYSTAL: Concentrate your energies.

CHIROGNOMY

CONICAL HAND: Use your sense of aesthetics (balance, proportion, line).

REJOICER

Woman of Cups

The Woman of Cups—Rejoicer—represents the *Empress* who feels and expresses the joy of life. Be in complete empathy with the great beauty and richness of being. Listen to these feelings and let them joyously bubble forth. Allow your love for the beauty of life to pour through. Express in feeling the freshness of the waterdrop, the magnificence of the sea, the tenderness of the flower, the grace of the fish, the mystery of the moon, and the exquisiteness of the shell. Heal and bring life to yourself and others through feeling fully and feeling deeply. Add to the beauty of life through the beauty of your heart.

Your "Rejoicer" Qualities

EVOLVED:

CONCH SHELL TO EAR: Listen to your feelings; Be in touch with your emotions.

OPEN FLOWER AND FACE: Fully express your feelings.

MOON AND OCEAN: Allow yourself to be deeply affected by emotions; Let yourself be influenced by emotional undercurrents, the surges and pulls of feelings; Live in harmony with your moon cycles.

HAPPY FACES: Express your beautiful feelings of joy, love, ecstasy, happiness.

SEA HORSE AND MOON: Be a romantic and a dreamer.

DAM, SHELL, AND MOON IN CUP: Contain your emotions so that you do not drown in them or drown others.

SPIDER WEBS: Be emotionally sensitive but not vulnerable; Protect yourself.

SHELL: Seek to be emotionally self-contained, not dependent upon others for fulfillment.

ECOLOGICAL COMMUNITY OF LIFE: Stay in union emotionally with all other sentient beings.

WATERS: Purify yourself of negative emotional states.

LOTUS: Know how to emotionally regenerate yourself (the lotus grows out of the mud).

UNEVOLVED:

SPIDER WEB: Overwhelming emotional influence that draws others into your emotional world without feeling for what they feel or want; Sticky and dominant emotional energy that is well-intended but lacks reflection and discrimination; insensitive.

Your "Rejoicer" Oracular Universe

ASTROLOGY

MOON: You are emotionally magnetic, attracting others to you through your genuine show of joyous feelings.

ALCHEMY

WATER: Accept and forgive; Cleanse through letting feelings out.

TIME

FULL MOON AND BLOSSOMING FLOWERS: Fulfill; Complete.

GEOMANCY

OCEAN AND REEFS: Find places of emotional regeneration and nurturing.

SHAMANISM

SEA HORSE: Acknowledge that you are rare, exotic, unfathomable, and mysterious.

SHELL: Be emotionally creative and regenerative by being protective.

LOTUS: Your emotions are like a flower, a projection of your soul.

AURA

WHITE: You are beautiful and joyous by nature and like nature.

PSYCHOMETRY

CUP: Be able to contain and pour out emotions; Be able to receive and give with openness.

PRESERVER

Woman of Worlds

The Woman of Worlds—Preserver—represents the procreative *Empress* mother. Protect and preserve by multiplying. Create. Give birth. Produce. Be conservative in your creativity in order to preserve the quality. Take your time and do it well. Creating is a labor of love. Work and enjoy the process of creating.

Once born, nurture and protect your "babies," whether they be projects, new activities, or actual children. Take responsibility for the growth of your creations. Maintain the health and integrity of your creations through slow growth and lots of tender loving care. Be realistic and practical in your expectations—one strand at a time.

Your "Preserver" Qualities

EVOLVED:

PREGNANCY: Create; Give birth.

MAKING WITH HANDS: Create with quality; Work with your hands; Keep the tradition.

WOMB: Protect and preserve; Nurture; Mother.

BIRD, NEST, EGG: Be a homemaker.

COOKING UTENSILS, FOODS: Enjoy the culinary arts.

WEAVINGS: Design; Make clothes; Use fashion.

VASE: Be a tool maker.

CLOTHES, FOOD, SHELTER, TOOLS: Build life support essentials.

CERAMICIST AND WEAVER: Enjoy the arts; Aesthetics.

DANCERS: Dance; Make music; Perform; Be in the theater.

DANCERS AND RAINBOW: Work is a dance; Bring joy, inspiration, beauty, and feeling to your professional and avocational pursuits.

EGGS, PREGNANCY: Purify the body, because it is under stress of carrying the load.

FOOD: Eat nutritionally.

DANCER STRETCHING: Nurture the body, its health, strength, and beauty.

UNEVOLVED:

HOME: Homebound; No curiosity; Dull; Slow; Heavy.

Your "Preserver" Oracular Universe

ASTROLOGY

EARTH: Be down to earth, earthy, practical; Take care of your environment and home.

ALCHEMY

EARTH: Manifest tangible physical products.

CALCIUM: Surround with protective hardening to insure the successful birth and growth of your creativity.

TIME

PREGNANCY: Be in progress; Grow; Gestate; Germinate.

GEOMANCY

WOMB: Be in your place of productivity (home, office, studio, etc.).

SHAMANISM

GULL: Build your nest (a suitable environment for productivity and growth).

APPLE: You are ripe, full, and fertile.

AURA

PINK AND BLUE: Use baby colors for enhancing nurturing through love (pink) and tranquility (blue).

PSYCHOMETRY

VASE, WEAVING, NEST: Create by weaving together; Provide; Support; Clothe; Beautify; Insure.

SENSOR

Woman of Wands

The Woman of Wands—Sensor—is the shamaness. She represents *Strength*, the fiery sensitivity and spirit of the *Priestess*. Like the Strength lioness, your body is finely honed to sense and detect. Let your physical senses alert and reveal. Allow your animal instincts to show you the way. As the Priestess, follow your natural extrasensory perception. Psyche out the situation. See through the disguised and unseen. Sense danger and feel opportunity.

Once the coast is clear, "take off your clothes and your concerns" and dance in the fire and passion of life. Exalt in the spirit. Having sensed that it is safe, move to the rhythms of nature. Feel the body electric. In the uninhibited, heightened, and altered emotional state, you radiate the light within. You can reveal and transform. You can heal and transmute. Let your spirit soar and be cleansed.

Your "Sensor" Qualities

EVOLVED:

WOMAN WITH HANDS ON BUTTONS PERFORMING PSYCHIC EXPERIMENTS: You are a psychic, medium, channel.

VIBRATIONS: Use your ESP.

HEADDRESS: Your hair and your aura are antenna for picking up vibrations; Keep your mind open to all possibilities; Be farsighted.

FIVE SENSES: Use your antenna of perception.

EYES: See in physical fact and in your mind's eye; Be clairvoyant.

EARS: Hear in physical fact and in your mind's ear; Be "clairaudient."

NOSE: Smell out the truth in physical fact and in your mind's nose.

HANDS: Feel out the truth in physical fact and in your mind's skin.

TONGUE: Taste the truth in physical fact and in your mind's taste.

SKIN, HAIR, NEURONS, FINGERS, FERNS, TEXTURES, WHISKERS: Your body is a sensorium; Your body registers and processes information through vibrations.

NAKED DANCER: Be sensual; Take off your clothes; Be naked and feel; Return to nature.

MANY LEVELS AND LAYERS: See into the many dimensions of yourself and others; Penetrate beyond the superficial and transparent reality into deeper subconscious phenomena.

HIDDEN FACES AND HANDS: See the subtleties, the obscure, the disguised.

FINGERNAILS: Strive for razor-sharp perception; Fingerpoint the essential; Diagnose; Use your insight.

BUDDHA'S GREEN AND GOLD HAND: Heal.

FINGERNAILS, CAT, SNAKE: Defend your position and integrity; Self-preserve.

OFFERING HAND: Counsel; Consult; Offer your observations.

AURIC PHOTOGRAPHS: Read auras.

PALMS: Read palms.

CELESTIAL HEADDRESS: Read the stars.

SYMBOLISM ON HEADDRESS: Read the signs and symbols; Read the tarot; Read dreams.

DANCER: Dance; Perform ceremonial ritual.

UNEVOLVED:

CAT: Overly possessive, territorial, jealous; Cat fights; Vicious; Vindictive; Controlling; Manipulative; Black magic.

Your "Sensor" Oracular Universe

ASTROLOGY

MOON: Be a receiver.

SUN: Be an enlightener, an awakener, a creator, and an empowerer.

ALCHEMY

FIRE: See with intensity; Burn out obstructions to your view.

SILVER: Look into the occult, the mysterious and magical.

TIME

LEVELS AND LAYERS: Be nontemporal; You can live in the past, present, and future simultaneously; Sunrise and sunset; Midnight and high noon; Times of energy transitions; You are able to bridge and weave past and future, conscious and subconscious.

GEOMANCY

MULTIPLE DIMENSIONS: Be nonspatial; Anywhere, here and there simultaneously; Unbound by the physical.

SHAMANISM

SNAKE: Know the ancient, the "water" past.

BIRD: Know the "air" future.

BLACK CAT: Know the dark side, the shadow, the negative, the night, the subconscious; Destroy superstition.

FEATHERS, GRASSES, AND FERNS: Feel your delicate sensitivities; Discern which way the wind is blowing; Feel the prevailing opinion and mood.

AURA

FLESH TONES: You have corporal intelligence, able to discern the degree of life and vitality; Diagnose health.

PSYCHOMETRY

HEADDRESS: Use tools and rituals for enhancing perception through the altered states of consciousness they help induce.

CHIROGNOMY

MANY DIFFERENT HANDS: You have some of the genius and magic of everyone.

SAGE

The Sages represent the "wise old souls" that we are. Androgynous, they symbolize the grandfather and grandmother within us. The Sages represent experience, know-how, and wisdom. It is the Sage within that we consult to answer our questions and dilemmas.

As the *attainers*, the Sages have asked the Child's questions, produced and conserved like the Man and Woman, and now repose in the fall-season of their life. They maintain, however, their childish curiosity, male dynamism, and female reverence for the quality of life. They are the embodiment of human perfection. Having attained the highest levels of human consciousness, they act as teachers and guides in the world.

The Sages are the human manifestations of the four natural elements. The Sage of Crystals is air, the Sage of Cups is water, the Sage of Worlds is earth, and the Sage of Wands is fire. They are at one with the world around them.

The Sages are the living representations of the highest Major Arcana Archetypes, which are symbolized by the "cosmos" cards. The Sage of Crystals—Knower—is the light of the *Star*. The Sage of Cups—Regenerator—is the regulator of our inner emotional waters like the *Moon*. The Sage of Worlds—Master—is the life-creating force of the powerful and productive *Sun*. The Sage of Wands—Seer—is *Time-Space*, infinite in consciousness. Together, they comprise the four cornerstones of our world, the *Universe*.

Having attained the heights and reached the end of the cycle, the Sages are close to a new beginning. Like the Universe Card, which leads back to zero, the Fool-Child, the Sage carries a new seed within. Hence, the Sages can be likened to the androgynous young child, forever youthful.

KNOWER

Sage of Crystals

The Sage of Crystals—Knower—represents the far sighted point of view of the *Star*. Like the distant stars, step away from your immediate view of reality to gain a broader perspective. Expand your narrow understanding into a cosmic awareness. Travel in your mind and/or in your body, go to the mountaintop, read a book. Do whatever it takes to get a different picture and a bigger picture of yourself and your situation. Overview. Find your time and location in the grand scheme of things. The greater your vision, the more you know yourself and your purpose.

Realize that your self-understanding is relative. See yourself from all different angles. Make intuitive leaps of connection between disciplines or ways of knowing yourself. See the synchronicity of all phenomena. Recognize the oneness of it all and yet see the diversity. The ability to shift about in your awareness gives you knowledge that reality is relative to the point of reference in your consciousness. The greater the perspective, the greater your consciousness. A "universal consciousness" allows you to be omnipresent and omnitalented.

Your "Knower" Qualities

EVOLVED:

FACE IN THE SKY: Be far sighted; Have big vision; See the larger picture; See trends as cycles; Gain a historical perspective.

CRYSTAL BALL: Futurize; See possible futures; A universe of possibilities is in your hand if you have universal consciousness; Think circularly.

EINSTEIN: Trust your intuitive insight; Be interdisciplinary and synthesize diverse information into a larger order; Wisdom and knowledge are gained from an expanding curiosity; Know how your point of view structures your reality (relativity); "Your imagination is more important than knowledge"—Einstein; Think big (cosmic thinking).

UNEVOLVED:

You don't see the connection between the cosmos and yourself; You forget to realize that you can see the outside world by knowing yourself, and that you can see yourself by knowing the outside world.

Your "Knower" Oracular Universe

ASTROLOGY

AQUARIUS: Bring forth your revolutionary ideas to share with human-kind for the benefit and evolution of all; Know that some will not be ready to understand you.

ALCHEMY

ETHERIC: See above and beyond the materialistic and physical; Think in abstract and in theory.

CRYSTAL: Investigate the nature of light and of light in matter.

TIME

EINSTEIN: Time is relative to your point of view; You can be in any time, past, present, and future.

GEOMANCY

EINSTEIN: Place is relative to your point of view; You can be anywhere.

AURA

VIOLET: Use the high frequencies of your mind; Crown chakra thinking.

PSYCHOMETRY

EYE-GLASSES: Alter your perception; See through a different lens.

CHIROGNOMY

WELL-SHAPED BALANCED HAND: You are all around; You are integrated
consciousness.

REGENERATOR

Sage of Cups

The Sage of Cups—Regenerator—represents the wellspring of your *Moon* emotional waters. Drink from the unending essence of your life spirit and find happiness. Generate new life vitality through joyousness. Find the fountain of perpetual youth through the joy of being. Laugh, smile, and bring pleasure to your life. Take care of your happiness, for it is the key to aliveness. Be responsible for your own happiness so that nothing can take away your vitality. Create happiness. Raise a toast to life. "Cheers." Be happy!

By regenerating yourself you regenerate others. Smile and bring a smile to the face of others. Heal another by your own emotional health. In joy, the world is recreated. In happiness there is growth.

Your "Regenerator" Qualities

EVOLVED:

SMILING FACES: Find joy, pleasure, fulfillment, happiness in being alive.

WATER CAVERN: You have an unending supply of emotional reserve in the life spirit.

FLOWERS: Know that in being alive you are beautiful, rich, youthful.

YOGI GARDENER WATERING THE DESERT: Be emotionally creative and regenerative (you can change a barren situation of no emotional vitality into a garden of delight and joy); Be emotionally self-sufficient (take care of yourself emotionally by tapping the well spring of life within the self); Be an emotional healer by your own happiness.

LAUGHTER: Laugh; See the humor of life; Laughter heals.

FLOWING WATERS: Purify unhealthy emotional states by watering yourself with love and compassionate care.

UNEVOLVED:

Waits passively for life to bring happiness instead of creating it.

Your "Regenerator" Oracular Universe

ASTROLOGY

EARTH (THE WATER PLANET): Make the earth blossom, create love, joy, and beauty on the planet through emotional vitality and happiness.

ALCHEMY

WATER: Live like water (feel, think, and behave like water); Drink lots of fluids.

NATURAL EARTH MINERALS: Fortify yourself by drinking the vitamins in the earth.

TIME

FLOWERING: It's time to come out, feel good, and look good; You are cured and restored.

GEOMANCY

WATER CAVERN: Find water spots; The wellspring of life within; Inner sources; Healing places.

SHAMANISM

DAISY: Wear bright colors and have fun.

AURA

RAINBOW (WATER LIGHT): Lighten up.

PSYCHOMETRY

WATERING VASE: Your heart and countenance are vehicles for expressing emotions that nourish others.

MASTER

Sage of Worlds

The Sage of Worlds—Master—represents the *Sun's* productive power. Like the Sage, you are a pro. With your know-how, master your craft. Trust your experience. Do your work befitting your mastery. Take pride in your workmanship. Know that your achievements and productivity are direct reflections of your character. Complete your work until you are satisfied to a turn. Enjoy your work as you enjoy yourself.

Become established—a force in your field of endeavor. Acknowledge your power and status. Dispense your knowledge to others. Teach, guide, advise. Contribute to the advancement of your field. Take responsibility for maintaining the quality of workmanship. Give back to the world what it has given you.

Your "Master" Qualities

EVOLVED:

FORGER AND TEA CEREMONY MASTER: Focus; Concentrate.

WHEELS: Know how the wheels of fortune turn; Know how the material world works; Complete, go the full cycle; End a cycle; Take responsibility for being a big wheel.

ASTROLAB: Know how to navigate through the worlds of lessons and opportunities.

BASKET WEAVER, FORGER, TEA MASTER: Be a master craftsman, expert, old pro; Treat your work as a sacred ritual and reflection of your spirit; Maintain discipline and good habits.

SMILING FACE: Be optimistic and keep a joyous attitude about your work.

CROWN: Acquire status; Use your power to lead; Honor your crowning achievements.

MOUNTAIN, BUCK, MOOSE: Do not fear being king of the mountain, on top, and established.

GOLD COINS: Create wealth; Create security.

FALL LEAVES: Harvest the seeds you have sown; Do not let anything go to waste; Recycle.

FACE LOOKING DOWN FROM ABOVE: Teach, counsel, and evaluate through the wisdom of your experience.

LEAVES ON GROUND: Leave a legacy; Be philanthropic.

WHEEL MOBILE: Tinker around; Fool around with your hobbies; Become a child again.

MEN IN BATHS: Use tender loving care for the body; Purify.

UNEVOLVED:

CROCHETY OLD MAN: Narrow minded; Set in ways; Parsimonious; Inflexible.

FURROWED BROW: Fearful; Worried.

Your "Master" Oracular Universe

ASTROLOGY

SETTING SUN: Be gentle; At ease.

ALCHEMY

EARTH: Productivity in the material world.
GRANITE: Establish a firm, solid, secure foundation.

TIME

FALL AND SUNSET: Have a finishing period; End of work day; End of a
cycle; Last phases.

GEOMANCY

LOOKING DOWN FROM ABOVE AND SITTING ON THE GROUND: You are above,
yet in; Detached, yet involved; In two worlds; Here and there.

SHAMANISM

ELK: You will find beauty and majesty through aging.
MAPLE TREE: Give to the world what you have to offer.

AURA

GOLD: Do the best you can do.

PSYCHOMETRY

WHEEL: Find your way or use in the world, and fill it with your tool
(natural skill).

SEER

Sage of Wands

The Sage of Wands—Seer—represents the light of *Time-Space*'s infinite radiance. Be like fire. Burn through to see the eternal truths. Live in the light of the spirit. Enlightened living comes from working with a "spiritual discipline"—any path or technique that helps you transcend the physical self and personal ego. Find and maintain your "practice." With this teacher, your eyes will be opened. Your illumination process will awaken great fire and energy within you. Come alive into the full passion of being and into the full heat of your personal power. Use your understanding to be fearless in the realization of your whole self. Apply the heat of your being to transform and heal. Radiate your light to reveal and counsel. Energize and inspire. Be the light!

Your "Seer" Qualities

EVOLVED:

SEERS: Master a spiritual art:
  Zen Calligrapher—Word mastery; Power of the written word.
  Tibetan Chanter—Voice mastery; Power of spoken word, sound.
  Sadhu—Meditation mastery; Power of silence, of stillness.
  Hawaiian Priestess—Vision-maker; Power of clairvoyance.
  Shaman—Medicine man; Healer; Power of the physical.
  Greek Orthodox Priest—Symbolist; Power of ritual and institution.
SADHU ON FIRE: Seek illumination to know the eternal light within you;
  Strive for self-realization through your "higher self"; Work on
  becoming fearless of death.
FIRE: Practice alchemy to transform yourself.
NAKED ABORIGINE SHAMAN: Be humble, trusting, and natural.

UNEVOLVED:

A visionary but lonely, destitute, misunderstood, and of no service
  to others; Unable to use wisdom in the world.

Your "Seer" Oracular Universe

ASTROLOGY

SUN: Be an awakener and previewer; Walk on the leading edge and
  vanguard.

ALCHEMY

FIRE: Create energy in yourself and in others; Live passionately.
GOLD: Seek the perfection of your spirit.

TIME

SUNSET: Accept that life leads to death.
SUNRISE: Understand that death leads to life.

GEOMANCY

PRIESTS: Seek a temple, church, place of worship; Find refuge;
  Inner sanctum.
FIRE: Power spot.

SHAMANISM

OWL: Seek to see into the dark where others cannot see.
HORUS FALCON: See into past, present, and future.

AURA

RED: Have the courage to be yourself.
BLACK: Do not fear the void, the other side, negation, death, egolessness.

PSYCHOMETRY

MATCHBOX: Control your inner fire (self-mastery); Be a firebrand and revolutionary.

Order Form for Works by James Wanless

Merrill-West Publishing
P.O. Box 1227
Carmel, CA 93921 (408)625-5792

Books

_____ Voyager Tarot Deck and Guidebook $35
_____ Voyager Tarot: Way of the Great Oracle $14.95
_____ New Age Tarot: Guide to the Thoth Deck $10.95
_____ Prophecy 1987 $6.95

Home Study Course

_____ StarTree $125 (A complete course for learning Tarot as a symbolic path of transformation. 516 pgs. "Reader of Tarot" Certification Degree $50).
_____ The Complete Voyager $125 (A complete series of ten classes on Tarot and the Voyager. 12 cassettes (17 hours) in a cassette portfolio).
_____ StarTree and The Complete Voyager $200

Audio Cassettes

_____ How To Read Tarot $35 (Four hour live workshop)
_____ The Marriage Dance: Tarot For Shamans and Lovers $19.95 (two hour live workshop)
_____ Mind's Eye Tarot $10 (60 min.)
_____ Voyager Journey to The Inner Universe $10 (60 min.)
_____ Yoga of Tarot $10 (60 min.)
_____ Heal Thy Self $10 (60 min.)
_____ Run to light $10 (60 min.)

Posters

_____ 1989 Year of the Hermit $12.95
_____ 1988 Year of Balance $12.95
_____ 1987 Year of the Chariot $12.95

Consultation

_____ One hour taped consultation in person or by mail $60

Free Catalog

_____ Magic and Mystery Guide to tools and toys of transformation.

Name _____

Address _____

Include 6% Sales Tax for California residents

Shipping Charges: Order up to $50......$2.75   Order over $50......$6.50

I understand that I may return any item for a full refund if not satisfied.